The Garland Library of War and Peace

The Garland Library of War and Peace

The United States and the World Court

by

Philip C. Jessup

with a foreword by

Elihu Root

together with related essays:

What's Wrong with International Law?
by
Wolfgang Friedmann

The Legal Process and International Law
by
Hans Kelsen

The Foreign Policy of a Free Democracy
and
The Fallacy of a "Preventive War"
by
Philip C. Jessup

with a new introduction
for the Garland Edition by
Philip C. Jessup

Garland Publishing, Inc., New York & London
1972

Library of Congress Cataloging in Publication Data

Jessup, Philip Caryl, 1897-
The United States and the World Court.

Reprint of works originally published in 1929, 1941, 1951, 1949, and 1935 respectively.
Includes bibliographical references.
1. Hague. Permanent Court of International Justice. 2. United States--Foreign relations. 3. International law. I. Friedmann, Wolfgang Gaston, 1907-1972. II. Kelsen, Hans, 1881- III. Title.
JX1971.5.J43 341.5'5 70-147750
ISBN 0-8240-0490-6

Printed in the United States of America

Introduction

When this brief book was published in 1929, Elihu Root wrote a foreword in which he voiced his optimistic conclusion that with the establishment and operation of the Permanent Court of International Justice at The Hague, "civilization has found a great new instrument for the maintenance of peace with justice." The sceptic and the realist and the revisionist may say that progress since 1929 has been slow; the spirit of Elihu Root would reply in words of his which have often been quoted: "Slow as measured by our lives perhaps, but not slow as measured by the lives of nations."

Actually those of us who worked ardently, though unsuccessfully, to persuade the Senate to approve American participation in the "World Court" did not envisage the overwhelming change which has come about. The United States took the lead in establishing the United Nations and having swallowed the whole whale of membership in the international organization, there was little worry about swallowing the minnow of participation in the International Court of Justice which is the "principal judicial organ" of the United Nations.

To be sure, the old isolationist trend is still sufficiently strong to emasculate our acceptance of the jurisdiction of the International Court by the Connally Amendment which permits us to refuse to submit to the Court whenever we please by an assertion that, in our opinion, the case involves a "domestic" question. Such reservations are reciprocal which means that if we try to sue another state in the Court at The Hague, that state can block the jurisdiction by throwing the Connally Amendment back in our face. The consequence of all this is that we have been laggard in supporting the old American tradition of settling international disputes by the decision of an international tribunal – a tradition which flourished in the nineteenth century as I have pointed out in the Jacob Blaustein Lectures, published in 1971 by the Columbia University Press with the title "The Price of International Justice."

We did litigate two cases in the UN Court – one with France concerning our treaty rights in Morocco and one with Switzerland which involved our sequestration during the war of an allegedly German company which Switzerland claimed was actually neutral Swiss. In the latter case we invoked the Connally Amendment but eventually we negotiated a settlement. In one other case we were a rather silent and uninterested party since our interests were really not involved and the case was thrown out on other jurisdictional grounds.

We have played our part in a number of cases which have been referred to the Court for advisory opinions. The most recent example is our vigorous argument before the Court at The Hague when it gave its opinion that South Africa has no right to continue in occupation of South West Africa, now known as Namibia. This was the first instance in which an advisory opinion had been requested by the Security Council; all the others have been asked for by the General Assembly. In the League of Nations, all the advisory opinions were requested by the Council and none by the League Assembly; it was the Senate's fear in the twenties that the Court might give an advisory opinion adversely affecting our interests which was the real point of opposition in the attempt to have the United States join the World Court at that time. This book gives the details of that controversy.

Our membership in the United Nations does make a great difference in another way. Even though a case or controversy does not go to the International Court of Justice, the United States may have to take a position in the Security Council or in the General Assembly of the United Nations and in a sense argue its case in one of those political forums. Recently, the General Assembly, by an overwhelming vote, condemned the United States for violating the Security Council's embargo on importations of chrome from Rhodesia. In the Security Council, the United States Representative had voted for the embargo but when the House of Representatives, responding to some lobbying interest, took the opposite view, the Administration failed to avail itself of a provision in the law which would have enabled us to comply with our international obligation. Unhappily, the White House, where foreign policy decisions are now generally made, has given many indications of its indifference to, or even contempt of, the United Nations. Small wonder that when, like a Johnny-come-lately, we try to secure action by the UN we find that we do not have the votes; the recent conflict over Bangladesh provided a prime example.

It is too much to ask of public opinion en masse *that it should always take a long-range view unless it is roused by its leaders in Washington. People don't readily see that peace-making and peace-keeping require constant, not occasional, efforts by a Great Power. The international organization has to be strengthened in little ways as well as in times of great crisis. We have, in Elihu Root's words, a great instrument for the maintenance of peace with justice. But it is like the conventional timepieces which have to be wound daily. If the instrument runs down, it is the fault, not of the instrument, but of the officials of government who should be using it.*

Judge Philip C. Jessup
Norfolk, Connecticut

THE UNITED STATES

AND THE

WORLD COURT

By PHILIP C. JESSUP

Assistant Professor of International Law
Columbia University

Foreword by
ELIHU ROOT

WORLD PEACE FOUNDATION PAMPHLETS

40 MT. VERNON STREET, BOSTON

VOL. XII 1929 NO. 4

{*PRICE 40 CENTS*}

World Peace Foundation

40 MT. VERNON STREET, BOSTON, MASSACHUSETTS

Founded in 1910 by Edwin Ginn

THE Foundation operates upon the policy that the actual facts concerning international relations and official international cooperation constitute the best possible arguments for lasting peace and improved international understanding. Its activities are, therefore, focused upon the task of making these facts available in clear and undistorted form.

FOREWORD

This book states intelligently and accurately the international proceedings following the resolution of January 27, 1926, by which the Senate consented upon certain conditions in the form of reservations, that the United States should adhere to the protocol or treaty, creating the Permanent Court of International Justice.

Professor Jessup is specially qualified to write such an account for he took part in much that was done and he understands the meaning and effect of the events which he describes. He shows how the principal States already supporting the Court have reached a willingness to accept all the Senate reservations in full, accompanied by a practical working agreement providing for the application of the reservations to concrete cases as they arise, in such a way as to avoid interference with current business in which the United States is not concerned. The book carefully confines itself to the explanation of facts without arguing about them.

To appreciate the full significance of the facts the reader must remember that all the apparently dry details are inevitable parts of a very great movement in human progress. Long before our time many sensible people began to think that as the private wars of former centuries had been in a great measure done away with by the establishment of Courts to decide personal controversies, just so public wars between civilized nations in an equal measure might be done away with by the establishment of International Courts to decide international controversies.

Very gradually, through many years, by an almost infinite number of small advances, that idea has established itself in the minds of men practically concerned in international affairs. The distinguished and universally acknowledged success of the Permanent Court of International Justice now sitting at the Hague proves that the idea was sound and that civilization has found a great new instrument for the maintenance of peace with justice. First was the dream and then the hope and then the practical policy and now is the test of the policy. America was long the foremost advocate of this great experiment. American idealism is for it. All the Presidents of the United States for more than thirty years, that is to say, all the men specially charged with the practical conduct of the foreign affairs of the United States, have been expressly and publicly for it. The House of Representatives, whose action would be required to appropriate our proportional contribution to the expense of the Court, has declared itself by formal resolution in favor of our adhesion. The Senate has advised and consented to adhesion upon five conditions designed to protect American interests. All the principal powers now in the Court are ready to accept all those conditions of the Senate.

Nothing remains but the question whether in the practical working arrangements proposed for giving effect to the Senate resolutions there is anything that so imperils the interests of the United States as to prevent the execution of a major public policy of the United States. To the study of that question this history should be a valuable contribution.

CONTENTS

Appendix II

THE UNITED STATES AND THE WORLD COURT

THE PROBLEM OF AMERICAN ACCESSION AND THE REVISION OF THE STATUTE

By PHILIP C. JESSUP

I. FROM SENATE RESERVATIONS TO ROOT PLAN

On January 27, 1926, some three years after President Harding had asked the Senate to advise and consent to the accession by the United States to the Protocol of Signature of the Permanent Court of International Justice, the Senate, by a vote of 77 to 16, adopted a resolution agreeing to that proposal, subject to five reservations and three additional qualifications. This Senatorial action followed a long period of discussion throughout the country and the indorsement of the World Court by two Presidents and by a large majority of the House of Representatives.[1]

One of the qualifications or conditions which the Senate included in its resolution was to the effect that the President, prior to signing the Protocol of Signature of the

[1] For the original submission to the Senate, the Resolution of the House of Representatives of March 3, 1925, and the Senate's resolution of January 27, 1926, see Hudson, *The World Court, 1922–1929*. Revised edition. World Peace Foundation, p. 158–168 (hereinafter cited simply as Hudson, *World Court*). See *infra*, p. 128 [768] for the Senate resolution.

Court, must secure the acceptance of the five reservations through an exchange of notes with the states already signatory to that Protocol. It might well be argued that this provision was an infringement upon the Executive's constitutional power to conduct the foreign relations of the United States, since it prescribed the method of conducting those relations. Nevertheless, Secretary of State Kellogg proceeded to write notes to all of the Signatory States and to the Secretary-General of the League of Nations, stating the terms of the five reservations. This action in itself served to emphasize the two different methods of conducting diplomatic affairs of general interest which are now followed in various parts of the world.[1]

Since the inauguration of the League of Nations, the Members have become accustomed to carrying on matters of common concern by joint conference, whereas the United States is still inclined to follow the ancient method of negotiation through foreign offices and diplomatic representatives. In line with their new, but already well-established practice, and because of their common interest in the matter, the Signatory States were not prepared to accept the Senate's reservations by a mere exchange of notes. On more technical grounds, it was also felt that, since the reservations would effectuate certain amendments in the Statute of the Court, and since this Statute was brought into being by a treaty which had been ratified by the various states, the more appropriate procedure would be to conclude an additional treaty by which the reservations could be given effect and the Statute amended accordingly. Thus, only five states sent unconditional acceptances of the reservations in reply to Secretary Kellogg's note.[2]

[1] This distinction was well pointed out by Elihu Root in his speech of acceptance of the Woodrow Wilson Memorial Award on December 28, 1926; see also *Committee of Jurists on the Statute of the Permanent Court of International Justice. Minutes of the Session held at Geneva, March 11–19, 1929*, p. 16 (C. 166. M. 66. 1929. V. 5). This document is hereinafter cited as *Minutes*.

[2] See Hudson, *op. cit.*, p. 185–186, for a table (taken from the *Fourth Annual Report of the Permanent Court of International Justice*, p. 126 (Series E, No. 4), indicating the replies from the various Governments.

At a meeting of the Council of the League of Nations, held at Geneva on March 18, 1926, Sir Austen Chamberlain (British Empire) suggested the points indicated above, and proposed that the Governments of the Signatory States and the Government of the United States should appoint delegates to attend a conference to be held in Geneva on September 1, 1926, for the purpose of discussing the whole question.[1] Sir Austen Chamberlain also indicated that certain parts of the Senate's reservations were not wholly clear, and that their correct interpretation required discussion with the United States.

The United States was duly invited on March 29, 1926, through a letter from the Secretary-General of the League, to attend the Conference of Signatories.[2] Secretary Kellogg, however, declined the invitation on the ground that he had no authority to vary the procedure laid down by the Senate, and on the further ground that the reservations were "plain and unequivocal." [3]

In spite of this position on the part of the United States, the Signatory States held their conference in Geneva during September, 1926. They were naturally hampered in their deliberations by the absence of an American representative, but they endeavored to ascertain the exact meaning of the reservations by reference to the debates in the Senate. Their conclusions were embodied in a Final Act and a Preliminary Draft of a Protocol. This Final Act and Draft of a Protocol were not communicated to the United States as such but, in accordance with the decision of the Conference, they formed the basis of replies sent by 24 different states in answering Mr. Kellogg's note of March 2, 1926. These replies, based on the conclusions of the conference, indicated that all of the reservations except the latter part of the fifth were acceptable to the other states, although with regard to some provisions it was suggested that the United States would find satis-

[1] See Hudson, *op. cit.*, p. 173, for pertinent text of extract from the Minutes of the Council.

[2] See *ibid.*, p. 172, for text of the invitation.

[3] See *ibid.*, p. 174, and *Minutes*, p. 98, for text of Mr. Kellogg's note.

faction for its desires in action already taken by the Court, and that formal acceptance of parts of the reservations would therefore be unnecessary.

The United States Government took no further official action until February 19, 1929, about two and a half years after it had been advised of the views of the other states. Nevertheless, certain interesting events occurred in the United States prior to that time. On December 7, 1926, Senator Trammell of Florida introduced in the Senate a resolution providing for the rescission of the Senate's resolution of January 27, 1926, on the ground that "a very large majority of the powers signatory to such protocol have not indicated their acceptance of it." This resolution was never even reported out of the Foreign Relations Committee, and on February 9, 1927, its sponsor's motion for consideration on the floor was tabled by a vote of 59 to 10.[1] On February 6, 1928, Senator Gillett introduced a resolution in accordance with which the Senate would respectfully suggest to the President "the advisability of a further exchange of views with the signatory states in order to establish whether the differences between the United States and the signatory states can be satisfactorily adjusted." An agreement was reached to take action on this resolution in the Foreign Relations Committee on December 5, 1928, but some 10 days before that date President Coolidge announced to a group of Senators breakfasting at the White House that he planned to resume negotiations in the Court matter. Senator Gillett accordingly announced that he would let the resolution lie over.[2] Secretary Kellogg's note of February 19, 1929, already referred to, seems to have been the outcome of this presidential declaration.

The Conference of Signatories in September, 1926, had

[1] Sen. Res. 282, 69th Cong., 2d sess., *Cong. Rec.*, Vol. 68, p. 37, 119, 3228, 3327; see Quincy Wright, "The Permanent Court of International Justice: the United States and the Court," *International Conciliation Pamphlet*, No. 232, September, 1927, p. 360 [40].

[2] Sen. Res. 139, 70th Cong., 1st sess. See The American Foundation, *The World Court*, fifth edition, April, 1929, p. 52.

suggested the desirability of a further exchange of views, and Mr. Kellogg's last letter stated that the Government of the United States felt that such an informal exchange of views as was contemplated would "lead to agreement upon some provision which in unobjectionable form would protect the rights and interests of the United States as an adherent to the Court Statute." [1]

Meanwhile certain other pertinent events had occurred. On September 20, 1928, the Assembly of the League adopted a resolution suggesting to the Council that it would be desirable to examine the Statute of the Court with a view to making such amendments as the experience of eight years of operation might indicate were desirable. The resolution pointed out that since a new election of the entire bench of the Court was to be held in September, 1930, in accordance with the Statute, the time was particularly appropriate for such an examination and possible revision. Acting upon this resolution, the Council, on December 13 and 14, 1928, decided to appoint a committee of experts to undertake the work in question. In addition to the other members of the committee, Elihu Root was invited to serve, and he accepted the invitation.[2] The committee members were selected as individual experts and not as governmental representatives, and the committee was accordingly of a character analogous to that which framed the original Statute of the Court in 1920; Mr. Root was also a member of that original committee.

Secretary Kellogg's note of February 19, 1929, was sent out while Mr. Root was en route to Geneva to attend the committee sessions. The note was transmitted to the Secretary-General of the League, as well as to the Signatory States. It thus came before the Council of the League at its meeting in Geneva on March 9, 1929. At that session the Council unanimously, and with a considerable show of friendliness toward the United States, adopted a resolution charging the Committee of Jurists to consider the whole

[1] See Hudson, *op. cit.*, p. 188, 190.

[2] For the Assembly and Council action, see the report of the Committee of Jurists, *infra*, p. 140 [780].

question of the accession of the United States to the Court, in addition to its primary function of considering the revision of the Statute.[1] The members of the Council, in stating their approval of the resolution, referred to the happy circumstance that Mr. Root had accepted the invitation to serve on this committee and that his cooperation might be expected to lead to a satisfactory solution of the outstanding difficulties regarding the accession of the United States to the Court.[2]

Before leaving the United States, Mr. Root had consulted Secretary Kellogg and certain members of the Senate. Although he was going to Geneva as a private citizen to attend a meeting of a committee which at that time was charged only with the task of amendments to the Statute and not with the consideration of American accession, it was quite natural, in view of his connection with the earlier history of the Court and his previous service as Secretary of State and as Senator, that the question of his own country's participation in the work of the Court should be prominent in his mind. He had already roughly formulated a plan for the solution of the existing difficulty and this plan he discussed with the official persons whom he saw in Washington. The plan seemed to them acceptable in principle, but no definitive text was in existence at that time to which they could give final approval. Mr. Root arrived in Geneva several days before the committee began its sessions, but while the Council of the League was meeting. In informal conversations with various statesmen who were serving as members of the Council, the question of American accession was discussed. By this time Mr. Root's plan had taken definite written form and the various persons consulted seemed to find it acceptable in principle.

Accordingly, when the committee met on March 11, the chairman immediately asked Mr. Root to submit to the

[1] See Hudson, *op. cit.*, p. 191, for the text of the Council's resolution, reprinting League of Nations, *Official Journal*, X, p. 564.

[2] *Official Journal*, X, p. 564.

committee the informal project which he had prepared.[1] This draft project immediately became the basis for discussion in the committee. It dealt only with the chief controversial point, namely, the second part of the fifth reservation. As a result of the discussion, four other members of the committee, M. Fromageot, Sir Cecil Hurst, M. Pilotti and M. Politis, submitted redrafts.[2] Other members of the committee made further oral suggestions. Mr. Root's original draft had been purely temporary in its form and was designed to explain the proposed arrangement without attempting to give it final form. Accordingly, to Mr. Root and to a majority of the other members of the committee, the redraft prepared by Sir Cecil Hurst appeared to be the most satisfactory basis for further discussion and it was accepted as such. The chairman appointed a subcommittee consisting of himself, Mr. Root, Sir Cecil Hurst and M. Politis, for the preliminary study of this draft. For this subcommittee, M. Politis reported a substantial agreement on the draft, subject to certain further modifications.[3] The matter was then discussed further in full committee and then referred to Sir Cecil Hurst and to Mr. Root for final redaction.[4] The committee then turned its attention to the other item on its agenda, that is, the revision of the Statute, and it was not until the 12th session, on the 18th of March, that the revised Root draft was again considered by the full committee.[5] After some discussion, the revised draft was unanimously adopted, together with the accompanying report of Sir Cecil Hurst. It should be noted, however, that the Draft Protocol which was thus finally accepted dealt with the

[1] The committee was composed of the following: Vittorio Scialoja, chairman; W. J. M. van Eysinga, vice-chairman; Henri Fromageot, Friedrich Gaus, Sir Cecil J. V. Hurst, Nobumi Ito, Massimo Pilotti, Nicolas Politis, Arnold Raestad, Elihu Root, Szymon Rundstein and Francisco J. Urrutia. The committee was also assisted by Stefan Osusky, chairman of the Supervisory Commission, and by Dionisio Anzilotti and Max Huber, the President and Vice-President of the Court.

[2] Root, *Minutes*, p. 9, and also Appendix, *infra*, p. 138 [778]; *Minutes*, Fromageot, p. 81; Hurst, p. 16; Pilotti, p. 10; Politis, p. 21.

[3] See *Minutes*, p. 22.

[4] *Loc. cit.*

[5] See *Minutes*, p. 76.

whole question of American accession and not solely with the latter part of the fifth reservation as did the original draft. This development was in accordance with Mr. Root's original plan, and followed upon his suggestion. The final Draft Protocol is based upon the Preliminary Draft of a Protocol which was incorporated in the Final Act of the Conference of Signatories of September, 1926.

According to the report of Sir Cecil Hurst, as adopted by the committee, this Draft Protocol was to be transmitted to the Council, which had appointed the committee. The report suggested to the Council that, if it approved the protocol, the text should be communicated to the Government of the United States by the Secretary-General of the League as a reply to Secretary Kellogg's note of February 19, 1929. It was further suggested that it should at the same time be communicated to all the Signatory States. Furthermore, since the proposal for the appointment of the committee originated in the Assembly, it was suggested that the Draft Protocol should also be communicated to that body for such action as might be deemed appropriate. Since the Draft Protocol would eventually take the form of a treaty requiring the ratification of the United States and of the various states which had already adhered to the Court, it was suggested that a further special conference might be called for the fall of 1929 in order that delegates of the various states might affix their signatures at that time.[1]

Similar action was taken with regard to the proposed amendments to the Statute.[2]

The reports on both subjects were transmitted to the Council and considered by it at its session in Madrid on June 11. M. Scialoja of Italy, who had presided over the Committee of Jurists, acted as rapporteur for the Council and submitted separate reports and draft resolutions on the subject of the accession of the United States and on the amendments to the Statute.

[1] See the Committee Report, p. 144 [784].

[2] These proposals will be considered in detail later, *infra*, p. 59 [699].

The report on the accession of the United States [1] merely follows that of Sir Cecil Hurst, pointing out that immediate transmission to the Governments of the United States and of the several Signatory States would afford them time for study of the question before the Assembly was called upon to pronounce upon the matter at its next session in September. The draft resolution accordingly provides that the Council adopts the report and Draft Protocol submitted by the Committee of Jurists and instructs the Secretary-General to communicate them to the United States in reply to Mr. Kellogg's note of February 19, 1929, and to the Signatory States. The resolution further instructs the Secretary-General to transmit these documents to the Assembly and to place the question on its agenda since the Assembly, like the Council, is "a body whose procedure in regard to the method of seeking advisory opinions from the Court would be affected by the adoption" of the proposed protocol. Since there has hitherto been some criticism in the United States of action by the League with reference to the Court, it seems desirable to call special attention to this sound reason for referring to the Assembly the protocol dealing with American accession.

M. Scialoja's report on amendments to the Statute also follows closely that of the Committee of Jurists, but suggests a somewhat different procedure. Sir Cecil Hurst's report on the accession of the United States had noted the possibility of the Council's convening a second conference of the Signatory States; the Committee of Jurists' report on amendments to the Statute had not included such a suggestion. Nevertheless, M. Scialoja recommended to the Council the calling of such a conference to consider the amendments to the Statute, but not to discuss the protocol for American accession. M. Scialoja felt that, though the Assembly had asked that proposals be submitted to it, the Council would be correctly interpreting the Assembly's wishes if it convoked a conference of the

[1] League of Nations Document, C. 275. 1929. V; Appendix, p. 146 [786].

states parties to the Statute to meet simultaneously with the Assembly. The two bodies might then consult together as necessary.

At the same time the Supervisory Commission might be asked to examine and report to the Assembly on the financial proposals contained in the committee's report. M. Osusky, chairman of the Supervisory Commission, had assisted the Committee of Jurists in an advisory capacity. It will be recalled that under Art. 32 of the Court Statute, it is the Assembly which, on the proposal of the Court, fixes the salaries, allowances and pensions of the judges. M. Scialoja's draft resolution contains provisions appropriate to the ends stated.

It may be noted that the Secretary-General was instructed to communicate the report of the Committee of Jurists to the Members of the League and to the states mentioned in the Annex to the Covenant — which includes the United States — but that the conference was to be only of "states parties to the Statute of the Permanent Court of International Justice." These resolutions were adopted by the Council at its session on June 12.[1]

On August 31, during its 56th session, the Council adopted a resolution inviting the Conference of Signatory States to consider the subject of the accession of the United States in addition to its consideration of the proposed Amendments to the Statute.[2] This action of the Council was subsequent to, and probably the result of, a communication from the American Government which will be described shortly. On September 3 the Council's resolution was considered by the First Committee of the Assembly, which reached the conclusion that this question should be considered by the conference before it was taken up by the Assembly. This procedure was unanimously adopted by the Assembly on the same day.[3]

The conference began its sessions on September 4 and

[1] League Doc. C. 274. 1929. V; Appendix, p. 122 [762].

[2] League Doc. A. 28. 1929. V. 14.

[3] *Verbatim Record of the Tenth Ordinary Session of the Assembly*, Third Plenary Meeting, September 3, p. 1.

appointed as Chairman Jonkheer van Eysinga of Holland, who had occupied a like position in the 1926 conference and who had served as vice-chairman of the Committee of Jurists in March, 1929. At its second meeting, on the afternoon of the same day, the conference unanimously adopted the draft protocol for the accession of the United States which had been prepared by the Committee of Jurists.[1] The draft protocol was accordingly referred by the conference to the Assembly, with the recommendation that it be referred to the First Committee;[2] this recommendation was followed by the Assembly. At the private first meeting of the conference, held in the morning, the Secretary-General of the League informed the delegates that he was reliably informed that the draft protocol was considered satisfactory by the Secretary of State of the United States, but that no official notice on the matter could yet be given out. At the public session in the afternoon, Sir Cecil Hurst, the British delegate to the conference, referred to "the very gratifying communication" made in the morning, which in his opinion made it clear that "the Government most interested in the question is prepared to accept the scheme as it is laid before this conference."[3] The official confirmation of this American approval was made by the Department of State on the same day. It was announced that on August 14 Hugh R. Wilson, American minister to Switzerland, had by instruction from Washington delivered an *aide mémoire* to the Secretary-General. This communication acknowledged the transmission of various documents relating to the draft protocol for American accession. It then proceeded with the statement "that after careful examination the Secretary of State considers that the said draft protocol would effectively meet the objections represented in the reservations of the United States and would constitute a satis-

[1] *Journal of the Tenth Assembly*, September 5, 1929, No. 4, p. 47; text of protocol in Appendix, p. 156 [796].

[2] *Report of First Committee*, League Doc. A. 49. 1929. V. 15; *infra*, p. 150 [790].

[3] New York *Times*, September 5, 1929, page 1.

factory basis for the adherence of the United States to the protocol and statute of the Permanent Court of International Justice, dated December 16, 1920, and that after the draft protocol has been accepted by the States Signatory to the Protocol of Signature and the Statute of the Permanent Court, he will request the President of the United States for the requisite authority to sign and will recommend that it be submitted to the Senate for its consent to ratification." [1]

The Protocol for American Accession was approved without any dissenting voice on September 14 by the Assembly, and was promptly signed by the following 49 states:

Australia, Austria, Belgium, Bolivia, Brazil, Bulgaria, Canada, Chile, China, Colombia, Cuba, Czechoslovakia, Denmark, Dominican Republic, Estonia, Finland, France, Germany, Great Britain, Greece, Guatemala, Haiti, Hungary, India, Irish Free State, Italy, Japan, Latvia, Liberia, Luxemburg, Netherlands, New Zealand, Nicaragua, Norway, Panama, Paraguay, Peru, Poland, Portugal, Rumania, Salvador, Serb-Croat-Slovene State, Siam, South Africa, Spain, Sweden, Switzerland, Uruguay, Venezuela.

The Acceptance of the Senate Reservations

Having noted the various events which have transpired since the Senate adopted its resolution on January 27, 1926, it may be convenient to consider *seriatim* and in detail the Senate reservations and the various steps which have been taken with regard to each one. This would seem to be particularly desirable, since the so-called Root Plan or Draft Protocol recommended by the Committee of Jurists opens with a statement that "the states signatories of the said protocol [of the Permanent Court of International Justice] accept the special conditions attached by the United States in the five reservations mentioned above

[1] Department of State, Press Release, September 5, 1929; *infra*, p. 148 [788].

[in the preamble], to its adherence to the said protocol upon the terms and conditions set out in the following articles." [1] The question in the United States, therefore, is whether the terms and conditions laid down by the Senate have been accepted by the states signatory to the Court Protocol.[2] It would seem that the answer to this question can be most easily ascertained by such a separate examination of the reservations.[3]

[1] Art. 1 of the Draft Protocol, *infra*, p. 156 [796].

[2] As noted *supra*, p. 11 [651], Secretary of State Stimson has already indicated his opinion that this question should be answered in the affirmative.

[3] This method has been followed by Professor Hudson, "The American Reservations and the Permanent Court of International Justice," 22 *American Journal of International Law* (1928), p. 1 *et seq.* (hereinafter cited as "Hudson, *American Reservations*.")

II. NEGOTIATIONS ON THE RESERVATIONS

First Reservation: "That such adherence shall not be taken to involve any legal relation on the part of the United States to the League of Nations or the assumption of any obligations by the United States under the treaty of Versailles."

It would seem to be a self-evident proposition that acceptance of one treaty — the protocol of the Statute of the Court — would not include acceptance of another treaty — the Covenant of the League (Art. 14 of which it fulfils) and other parts of the treaty of Versailles. Nevertheless, this reservation seems to have been designed to make assurance doubly sure, and to satisfy political exigencies.

When the Conference of Signatory States met in Geneva in 1926, this reservation was naturally the first item considered. Henri Rolin of Belgium, a very astute jurist, declared that this reservation "merely expressed the legal situation." The president of the conference, M. van Eysinga of the Netherlands, "thought that all the members of the conference would share this opinion. In these circumstances, the conference could but accept the first reservation." This proposal was unanimously adopted without further discussion.[1]

The final conclusions of the conference, as already noted, were embodied in a Final Act and a Preliminary Draft of a Protocol. As to the first reservation, the Final Act declared as follows:[2]

> It may be agreed that the adherence of the United States to the Protocol of December 16, 1920, and the Statute of the Perma-

[1] *Minutes of the Conference of States Signatories of the Protocol of Signature of the Statute of the Permanent Court of International Justice* (League of Nations Document, 1926. V. 26), p. 11, hereinafter cited as *Minutes of the Conference;* see also Hudson, *op. cit.*, p. 3.

[2] *Minutes of the Conference*, p. 77; Hudson, *World Court*, p. 178.

nent Court of International Justice annexed thereto shall not be taken to involve any legal relation on the part of the United States to the League of Nations or the assumption of any obligations by the United States under the treaty of peace of Versailles of June 28, 1919.

Since this is a general matter and involves no change in the Statute or operation of the Court, it was not necessary to include any reference to it in the Draft Protocol. Secretary Kellogg's note of February 19, 1929, notes that this reservation was accepted.[1]

In view of these facts, the Committee of Jurists which met in Geneva in March, 1929, did not discuss this reservation. The report which it adopted declares that

> No difficulty has at any time been felt with regard to the acceptance of the conditions laid down by the United States

in the first four reservations.[2] Nor is this reservation expressly mentioned in the Draft Protocol which the same committee adopted on the basis of Mr. Root's suggestions. It will be convenient here to pause to consider the situation under this protocol of an omission of such express acceptance.

In drafting the text which was eventually used in drawing up the protocol just referred to, Mr. Root had taken as a basis the Final Act and Preliminary Draft of a Protocol adopted by the 1926 Conference of Signatories. In those documents he found the acceptance of the first reservation but no express mention of it in the protocol itself. Accordingly it seemed useless to include it in the new protocol. But some phraseology had to be adopted to make clear the implicit acceptance of the reservation. This is accomplished by the language of the preamble and of Art. 1, which is as follows: [3]

[1] Hudson, *op. cit.*, p. 188.

[2] *Ibid.*, p. 196.

[3] *Ibid.*, p. 192; italics inserted.

> The states signatories of the Protocol of the Statute of the Permanent Court of International Justice, dated December 20, 1920, and the United States of America, through the undersigned duly authorized representatives, have mutually agreed upon the following provisions regarding the adherence of the United States of America to the said Protocol *subject to the five reservations formulated by the United States in the resolutions adopted by the Senate on January 27, 1926.*
>
> Art. 1. The states signatories of the said Protocol *accept the special conditions attached by the United States in the five reservations* mentioned above to its adherence to the said Protocol *upon the terms and conditions set out in the following articles.*

The Draft Protocol prepared by Mr. Root and adopted by the committee thus takes the complete acceptance of the five reservations as its basic point of departure. It is only where the protocol specifies "terms or conditions" that there is any variation in this acceptance. Since the protocol contains no "terms or conditions" relative to the first reservation, its acceptance is unconditional and absolute.

> **Second Reservation: "That the United States shall be permitted to participate through representatives designated for the purpose and upon an equality with the other states, Members, respectively, of the Council and Assembly of the League of Nations, in any and all proceedings of either the Council or the Assembly for the election of judges or deputy-judges of the Permanent Court of International Justice or for the filling of vacancies."**

In considering this reservation one should keep in mind that the judges and deputy-judges are elected from a list of nominees, by the Council and Assembly sitting simultaneously but independently. Art. 4 of the Court Statute provides that the "members of the Court shall be elected by the Assembly and by the Council" and Art. 10 provides that "those candidates who obtain an absolute majority of votes in the Assembly and in the Council shall be considered as elected."

When this reservation was discussed by the 1926 Conference of Signatories, the President pointed out that it might be said to constitute an amendment to the Statute. The Statute provides that candidates receiving a majority of votes of the Members of the Council and Assembly would be elected; under the second reservation it would be necessary to count also the vote of the United States. The conference, however, fully agreed that this claim of the United States was entirely reasonable and acceptable.[1] A suggestion was made that the desired object could be accomplished by the Council and Assembly inviting the United States to join them for the purposes of election, but this was not the prevailing view of the conference. The drafting committee appointed by the conference to formulate its results decided upon a simple acceptance of the second reservation and the Final Act accordingly contains the following paragraph:[2]

> It may be agreed that the United States may participate through representatives designated for the purpose and upon an equality with the other states, Members of the League of Nations, represented in the Council or in the Assembly, in any and all proceedings of either the Council or the Assembly for the election of judges or deputy-judges of the Permanent Court of International Justice, or for the filling of vacancies.

In incorporating this agreement into the protocol, however, it was thought best to specify that the vote of the United States should "be counted in determining the absolute majority of votes required by the Statute" in order that the above-mentioned amendment to the Statute might be clearly effected.[3] The protocol thus contains this express direction to the tellers who count the votes

[1] *Minutes of the Conference*, p. 11, 12, 46, 47.

[2] *Ibid.*, p. 77; Hudson, *op. cit.*, p. 178.

[3] *Minutes of the Conference*, p. 81; Hudson, *op. cit.*, p. 181; see also Hudson, *American Reservations*, p. 4.

instead of leaving it to them to make the necessary deduction from the general language. This extra measure of care may also be attributed to the fact that Europeans are always careful to note the difference between a "majority" (plurality) and an "absolute majority."

As in the case of the first reservation, Mr. Kellogg's letter of February 19, 1929, notes that the second reservation had also been accepted.

For the same reasons which influenced the Conference of Signatories, Mr. Root and the Committee of Jurists of which he was a member, included in the new protocol the same provision and in the same words. The fact that an amendment to the Statute was involved and that an explanatory sentence was added in the interests of clarification made it inappropriate to leave the acceptance of this reservation to be implied from the blanket acceptance clause. The "terms and conditions" in this case, however, are only such as seemed necessary to give effect to the Senate's intention. The final language in which the second reservation is accepted is therefore as follows:[1]

> Art. 2. The United States shall be permitted to participate, through representatives designated for the purpose and upon an equality with the signatory states, Members of the League of Nations, represented in the Council or in the Assembly, in any and all proceedings of either the Council or the Assembly for the election of Judges or Deputy Judges of the Permanent Court of International Justice, provided for in the Statute of the Court. The vote of the United States shall be counted in determining the absolute majority of votes required by the Statute.

Third Reservation: "That the United States will pay a fair share of the expenses of the Court as determined and appropriated from time to time by the Congress of the United States."

Art. 33 of the Court Statute provides that "the expenses of the Court shall be borne by the League of Nations, in

[1] Hudson, *World Court*, p. 192.

such manner as shall be decided by the Assembly upon the proposal of the Council." [1] The Senate did not wish to have the United States' share of the contributions fixed by the League bodies and therefore left the amount to be determined by Congress. This arrangement met with no objection from the Signatory States, who seemed to rely fully on the fairness of the United States to contribute a just proportion.[2] At the 1926 Conference of Signatories the president remarked "that this paragraph, which could hardly be called a reservation, since it consisted in an offer to participate in the expenses of the Court, gave rise to no objection." [3] This was unanimously agreed to without any discussion. The Final Act accordingly says: [4]

> It may be agreed that the United States pay a fair share of the expenses of the Court as determined and appropriated from time to time by the Congress of the United States.

Since this reservation involves no amendment to the Statute, no express reference was made to it in the 1926 Preliminary Draft of a Protocol or in the committee's Draft Protocol of March, 1929. Its specific acceptance, accordingly, like that of the first reservation, is implied from the general acceptance. In common with the first two reservations, this reservation also was mentioned in Mr. Kellogg's note of February 19, 1929, as having been accepted.

Fourth Reservation — First Part: "That the United States may at any time withdraw its adherence to the said Protocol . . ."

The Statute of the Court contains no provision for the withdrawal of any state which has signed the protocol of

[1] *Infra*, p. 96 [736].

[2] The American quota would probably be the same as that of Great Britain, which in 1927 amounted to approximately $42,000; see Hudson, *American Reservations*, p. 5. However, it is noted that the Inter-parliamentary Union in adopting the League basis for allocation of expenses to its own budget assigns the United States a larger quota than Great Britain.

[3] *Minutes of the Conference*, p. 12.

[4] *Ibid.*, p. 77; Hudson, *World Court*, p. 178.

December 16, 1920, or acceded to it. It was the belief of some persons that a right of denunciation or withdrawal was implicit in every international convention, but this view was not universally held.[1] Regardless of the legal aspects of the matter, the conference had no objection to granting this right of withdrawal to the United States. It was felt, however, that if this right should be exercised at some future time a somewhat anomalous situation would result. The part of the fourth reservation now under consideration was merely one of several conditions under which the United States proposed to accede. If the arrangement did not subsequently prove to be satisfactory to the United States that state could withdraw, but it would leave the other states with an instrument whose organization had been somewhat altered in order to meet the wishes of the American Government. The Signatory States had in mind especially the second part of the fourth reservation, which provides that the Statute can not be amended without the consent of the United States, and the fifth reservation which deals with advisory opinions. It was accordingly considered only fair that the Signatory States should likewise have a power of withdrawal — not of withdrawal from the Court, but from the acceptance of the special conditions of the United States. Differently stated, the Signatory States felt that if the United States was to be given the privilege of restoring the *status quo ante*, they themselves should be accorded a like privilege. The Drafting Committee of the conference in giving expression to this idea stated that it had "been anxious to invest the exercise of such a right [of withdrawal by the Signatory States] with the character of a collective decision taken by a sufficiently large majority to insure that it is inspired exclusively by objective considerations arising from the discovery of some serious practical difficulty."[2] The Final Act accordingly contains the following statement on this point:[3]

[1] *Minutes of the Conference*, p. 12–13, 15 *ff*.

[2] *Ibid*., p. 53; see also discussion of the Drafting Committee's report, *ibid*., p. 55 *ff*.

[3] *Ibid*., p. 77; Hudson, *op. cit*., p. 178–179.

> It may be agreed that the United States may at any time withdraw its adherence to the Protocol of December 16, 1920.
>
> In order to assure equality of treatment, it seems natural that the signatory states, acting together and by not less than a majority of two-thirds, should possess the corresponding right to withdraw their acceptance of the special conditions attached by the United States to its adherence to the said Protocol in the second part of the fourth reservation and in the fifth reservation. In this way the *status quo ante* could be re-established if it were found that the arrangement agreed upon was not yielding satisfactory results.
>
> It is to be hoped, nevertheless, that no such withdrawal will be made without an attempt by a previous exchange of views to solve any difficulties which may arise.

Although this provision was not considered as an amendment to the Statute,[1] the fact that it introduced a new element and established a method of procedure made it appropriate to include it in the protocol. The article in the protocol dealing with this matter is number 7, and reads as follows: [2]

> The United States may at any time notify the Secretary-General of the League of Nations that it withdraws its adherence to the Protocol of December 16, 1920. The Secretary-General shall immediately communicate this notification to all the other states signatories of the Protocol.
>
> In such case the present Protocol shall cease to be in force as from the receipt by the Secretary-General of the notification by the United States.
>
> On their part, each of the contracting states may at any time notify the Secretary-General of the League of Nations that it desires to withdraw its acceptance of the special conditions attached by the United States to its adherence to the Protocol of December 16, 1920, in the second part of its fourth reservation and in its fifth reservation. The Secretary-General shall immediately give communication of this notification to each of the states signatories of the present

[1] See Hudson, *American Reservations*, p. 5.

[2] *Minutes of the Conference*, p. 83; *infra*, p. 158 [798]. The text is Art. 8 of the Draft Protocol of the Committee of Jurists.

> Protocol. The present Protocol shall be considered as ceasing to be in force if and when, within one year from the receipt of the said notification, not less than two-thirds of the contracting states other than the United States shall have notified the Secretary-General of the League of Nations that they desire to withdraw the above-mentioned acceptance.

In his note of February 19, 1929, Mr. Kellogg included the fourth reservation among those which had been accepted. The Committee of Jurists in 1929 felt no need for discussing this reservation and in the Draft Protocol which it adopted the text of the 1926 draft is repeated *in ipsis verbis*.

It will be noted that the United States is thus accorded a privileged position in that it may effect its withdrawal by a simple notice to the Secretary-General of the League, with whom the ratifications of the Protocol of Signature are deposited. On the other hand, the other states must secure a two-thirds majority in order to bring about a similar result. It should be further pointed out that, even if the Signatory States had flatly accepted the first part of the fourth reservation, it would have been necessary subsequently to make some such arrangement as this in order to provide an appropriate method by which the withdrawal of the United States could be brought about. In concluding, therefore, the consideration of the first part of the fourth reservation it can be said that the "terms and conditions" on which this reservation is accepted can be stated as follows:

(1) The withdrawal of the United States is to be accomplished by the simple and logical method of notifying the Secretary-General of the League;

(2) The United States concedes to the other states the reciprocal right of withdrawal.

This second point seems eminently fair and one can not see how objection could be raised to it in the United States. On the other hand, it must be admitted that it does introduce a new element which might properly be referred to the Senate for its approval.

Fourth Reservation — Second Part: " . . . the Statute for the Permanent Court of International Justice adjoined to the Protocol shall not be amended without the consent of the United States."

The Statute of the Court itself contains no provision for its amendment, but it seems to be an established rule of international law that no multipartite treaty can be amended without the consent of all parties thereto. This was the point of view expressed by a number of the members of the 1926 Conference of Signatories.[1] The Drafting Committee was of the opinion that all could agree that, "the Statute having been approved in 1920 by a unanimous agreement of the signatory states," it could be "only susceptible of modification by another unanimous agreement." [2] The committee accordingly in the Final Act states that [3]

> It may be agreed that the Statute of the Permanent Court of International Justice annexed to the Protocol of December 16, 1920, shall not be amended without the consent of the United States,

but in the protocol it gave expression to the general rule just mentioned by providing that [4]

> Art. 2. No amendment of the Statute annexed to the Protocol of December 16, 1920, may be made without the consent of all the contracting states.

As already noted, Mr. Kellogg in his note of February 19, 1929, acknowledged that this reservation had been accepted. The Committee of Jurists in March, 1929, saw

[1] See, for example, the views of M. Dinichert, *Minutes of the Conference*, p. 15; of the President, *ibid.*; and of M. Rolin, *ibid.*, p. 18.

[2] *Ibid.*, p. 53.

[3] *Ibid.*, p. 77; Hudson, *World Court*, p. 179.

[4] *Minutes of the Conference*, p. 81; *infra*, p. 130 [770].

no reason to alter this conclusion, but in the interest of simplification a slightly different phraseology was adopted, so that the final acceptance of this second half of the fourth reservation reads as follows:[1]

> Art. 3. No amendment of the Statute of the Court may be made without the consent of all the contracting states.

While it is true that the "terms and conditions" on which this reservation is accepted consist in requesting that the United States again accord a reciprocal right to the other parties, it can scarcely be maintained that any new element is thus introduced, since the pre-existing rule of international law made the requirement of unanimity for such amendments implicit in the treaty.[2]

> **Fifth Reservation — First Part: "That the Court shall not render any advisory opinion except publicly, after due notice to all states adhering to the Court and to all interested states, and after public hearing or opportunity for hearing given to any state concerned. . . ."**

Both parts of the fifth reservation deal with advisory opinions, which have formed the center of vigorous discussion in the United States. So much has been written on this subject that it scarcely seems necessary at this time to review anew the entire controversy, but certain aspects of it may be brought to mind.[3]

The Statute of the Court itself does not provide for the rendering of advisory opinions, but its Art. 36 says that the Court has jurisdiction in "all matters specially provided for in treaties and conventions in force."[4] One of the con-

[1] *Infra*, p. 156 [796].

[2] See Hudson, *American Reservations*, p. 5–6, especially note 18, p. 6, and his reference to Professor Quincy Wright's article in 21 *American Journal of International Law*, p. 13.

[3] On advisory opinions in general, see Hudson, "The Advisory Opinions of the Permanent Court of International Justice," *International Conciliation*, November, 1925, No. 214.

[4] *Infra*, p. 96 [736].

ventions in force at the time was the Covenant of the League of Nations, Art. 14, which provides that "the Court may also give an advisory opinion upon any dispute or question referred to it by the Council or Assembly." Many persons in the United States feared that this phase of the Court's jurisdiction was incompatible with its functions as a judicial body, and they feared that the Court might deteriorate into a secret adviser of the League. The Court itself soon took steps which should have dispelled this fear. In the rules which it adopted on March 24, 1922, it provided in Art. 73 that when a request for an advisory opinion came to the Court the Registrar should immediately notify the Members of the League, the states mentioned in the Annex to the Covenant and any "international organizations which are likely to be able to furnish information on the question." Art. 74 of the rules further provided that advisory opinions should be printed and published.

On July 31, 1926, just about six months after the Senate passed its resolution containing the five reservations, the Court revised these rules in a way which brings their provisions into full accord with the first part of the fifth reservation.[1] The revision of Art. 73 requires notice to be given to a broader category of states which includes Members of the League, states "admitted to appear before the Court" and international organizations considered likely to be able to furnish information. The notice must now also contain a statement that the Court "will be prepared to receive, within a time-limit to be fixed by the President, written statements, or to hear, at a public sitting to be held for the purpose, oral statements relating to the question." There is further provision for comments by any of the parties notified upon the statements submitted by other parties.[2]

The previous provision in Art. 74 relating to the publication of advisory opinions is amplified by the require-

[1] The original rules are printed in Publications of the Court, Series D, No. 1, p. 66 *ff.*, and the revised rules in *ibid.*, p. 33 *ff.*, and in Hudson, *World Court*, p. 121 *ff.*

[2] Hudson, *op. cit.*, p. 137–138; *infra*, p. 102 [742].

ment that "advisory opinions shall be read in open Court, notice having been given to the Secretary-General of the League of Nations and to the representatives of states, of Members of the League and of international organizations immediately concerned." [1]

These new rules were indeed largely clarifications of the current practice of the tribunal, but they constitute the most complete possible arrangements for carrying into effect the first part of the fifth reservation.

This fact was naturally noted by the Conference of Signatories in 1926. The president at once pointed them out and stated that he assumed they would satisfy the desiderata named by the Senate.[2] With practically no discussion, the conference noted its acceptance of the first part of the fifth reservation. At a subsequent session of the committee, however, the president, with what has proved to be an accurate foresight, said that, while it was true that the rules met the desires of the United States regarding publicity, yet the United States might say "that the Court might alter its Rules any day." [3] The drafting committee had this suggestion in mind in preparing the Final Act, the appropriate paragraph of which is couched in the following terms: [4]

> In the matter of advisory opinions, and in the first place as regards the first part of the fifth reservation, the Government of the United States will, no doubt, have become aware, since the dispatch of its letters to the various Governments, of the provisions of Arts. 73 and 74 of the Rules of Court as amended by the Court on July 31, 1926 (Annex A). It is believed that these provisions are such as to give satisfaction to the United States, having been made by the Court in exercise of its powers under Art. 30 of the Statute. Moreover, the signatory states might study with the United States the possible incorporation of certain stipulations of principle on this subject in a protocol of execution

[1] Hudson, *op. cit.*, p. 138, and *infra*, p. 103 [743].

[2] *Minutes of the Conference*, p. 19.

[3] *Ibid.*, p. 46; see also other views expressed by the president on p. 50.

[4] *Ibid.*, p. 77; Hudson, *op. cit.*, p. 179.

such as is set forth hereafter (Annex B), notably as regards the rendering of advisory opinions in public.

Apparently the conference believed that it would be unnecessary to insert in the protocol detailed provisions on this point, and they accordingly contented themselves with the brief statement of Art. 3 that [1]

> The Court shall render advisory opinions in public session.

As the president of the 1926 conference had foreseen, the United States was not content with the provisions in the Rules of Court. Mr. Kellogg pointed out in his note of February 19, 1929, that the rules of the Court are "subject to change at any time," and that for this reason the provision in the protocol "did not furnish adequate protection to the United States." [2]

This was the situation which had to be met by Mr. Root and the Committee of Jurists in March, 1929. It was evident from the proceedings of the 1926 conference that there was no basic objection to the first part of the fifth reservation, and it could therefore be assumed that an agreement on phraseology could easily be reached. In his original draft proposal Mr. Root suggested the following language which would serve to cover the question of notice and at the same time to perpetuate the practical procedure laid down by the amended Art. 73 of the rules of the Court: [3]

> Whenever a request for an advisory opinion comes to the Court, the Registrar shall notify the United States thereof, among other states mentioned in the now existing Art. 73 of

[1] *Minutes of the Conference*, p. 83; *infra*, p. 130 [770]. The members of the conference do not seem to have considered at any length the point made by Professor Hudson that it would be an unsound principle to deprive the Court of its power to make rules governing its own procedure by incorporating stipulations on these points in the treaty itself. While agreeing with the principle advocated by Professor Hudson, it may be noted that the Statute already contains 26 articles (Arts. 39–64) regulating the Court's procedure. For these views of Professor Hudson, see his *American Reservations*, p. 7–9.

[2] Hudson, *World Court*, p. 190.

[3] *Minutes*, p. 9.

> the Rules of Court, stating a reasonable time-limit fixed by the President, within which a written statement by the United States concerning the request will be received.

In preparing the final draft of the protocol which was ultimately adopted by the Committee of Jurists the provision just quoted was retained in Art. 5, but in addition there was inserted the following Art. 4:[1]

> The Court shall render advisory opinions in public session after notice and opportunity for hearing substantially as provided in the now existing Arts. 73 and 74 of the Rules of Court.

It seems beyond question that these provisions constitute a complete acceptance of the first part of the fifth reservation. They have the distinct advantage over a simple statement of acceptance in that, by their reference to the existing Rules of Court, they make immediately available an exact procedure by which the reservation can be made practically useful.

The perpetuation of this provision in treaty form would be an excellent thing for the Court, preventing permanently any deviation from the essentially judicial nature of its conduct which it has hitherto so wisely and courageously followed. The Senate will have made a distinct contribution to the cause of international justice by accomplishing this result.

Fifth Reservation — Second Part: ". . . nor shall it [the Court], without the consent of the United States, entertain any request for an advisory opinion touching any dispute or question in which the United States has or claims an interest."

It is this reservation which has caused the greatest difficulty because its terms are open to several interpretations. Some of the possible interpretations would result

[1] *Minutes*, p. 132; *infra*, p. 156 [796].

in the conferring of powers the exercise of which, it was feared, might destroy the utility of advisory opinions as an instrument for the pacific settlement of international disputes. This view was expressed by Sir Austen Chamberlain in the meeting of the Council on March 18, 1926, at which it was decided to convoke the 1926 Conference of Signatories. The British foreign minister as his country's representative in the Council declared: [1]

> The terms of the fifth paragraph of the Senate resolution necessitate further examination before they could safely be accepted by the states which are parties to the Protocol of 1920. This paragraph is capable of bearing an interpretation which would hamper the work of the Council and prejudice the rights of Members of the League, but it is not clear that it was intended to bear any such meaning. The correct interpretation of this paragraph of the resolution should be the subject of discussion and agreement with the United States Government.

But since the United States did not accept the invitation to attend the conference, no discussion and consequently no agreement resulted. The members of the conference were forced to rely largely on the Senate debates and these afford conflicting points of view.

Before proceeding further, three types of advisory opinions may be suggested. The first is the type of secret confidential advice from the Court to the Council or Assembly which was regarded with particular repugnance in the United States Senate. It may safely be said that this type of advisory opinion does not exist and never has existed. The rules of the Court from the very first have made it impossible and under the protocol adopted by the Committee of Jurists this result is made certain and permanent. If the Council of the League desires this type of advice it must seek it from an *ad hoc* committee of jurists as has been done on several occasions.[2]

The second type of advisory opinions is that in which

[1] Hudson, *op. cit.*, p. 173.

[2] See the remarks of President Scialoja in the Committee of Jurists, *Minutes*, p. 12.

the Council [1] acts as a transmitting agency or letter box, although even in such cases it preserves its liberty of action.[2] This is the type exemplified in Advisory Opinions 1, 2, 3 and 13, concerning the functions and competence of the International Labor Organization. When a problem arises in that organization it requests the Council to seek from the Court an advisory opinion interpreting the treaty provisions under which the Labor Organization operates. The same situation exists with regard to other organizations.

The third type of advisory opinion is undoubtedly the most important and it is the one which is usually in mind when this device is referred to as a method of pacific settlement of international disputes. In a sense these advisory opinions are a form of international arbitration although, unlike arbitral awards, they do not bind the parties to a dispute. The situation described is evident from a consideration of the Fourth Advisory Opinion.[3] France adopted certain nationality decrees for Tunis and Morocco which Great Britain claimed unlawfully infringed upon the rights of British subjects in those protected areas by compelling them to serve in the French army. The British Government offered to arbitrate the question as to France's right to enforce such decrees. The French Government replied that nationality laws were of solely domestic concern and that arbitration was impossible. Great Britain accordingly appealed to the Council of the League. It was suggested that the Court should be asked to render an advisory opinion upon the question whether the matter in issue was solely a subject of domestic jurisdiction. Although the French Government had been unwilling to agree to arbitration, it was content to raise no objection in the Council against the reference of this question to the Court. The Court expressed the opinion that while, in

[1] Although both the Council and Assembly have the privilege of requesting advisory opinions, the latter body has not yet exercised that privilege and in general hereafter only the Council will be referred to.

[2] *Minutes*, p. 76.

[3] Publications of the Court, Series B, No. 4, summarized in Hudson, *op. cit.*, p. 60 *ff*.

general, nationality questions camė within the category of domestic questions, this was not the case when the matter was covered by an international treaty. As a result of this opinion, the two countries effected an amicable adjustment of their differences.[1]

In numerous other cases also, it has been found that, when national susceptibilities and political complications prevent a direct submission to an international judicial tribunal, the parties are willing that some legal point in the dispute should be submitted to the Court for an advisory opinion. It must be borne in mind that while the law's delays are the object of complaint in the private law field, internationally a delay is often the means of preventing war. This is the basic theory of the "Bryan peace treaties," which provide a "cooling-off" period. But the delay must be accomplished by some step toward solution since, if nothing is done, national feelings grow steadily more intense until the war-fever is fully aroused.

It was these factors which the statesmen at Geneva had in mind when considering the fifth reservation. There being no way of determining how or when the consent of the United States would be manifested for the requesting of an advisory opinion, it was feared that the American decision might be so long delayed as to destroy the utility of the function of such reference to the Court.[2]

From the point of view of the United States, a further classification of advisory opinions should be noted, since much stress was laid upon it in the subsequent discussions. An advisory opinion may relate to a dispute to which the United States is a party or it may relate to a dispute or question other than a dispute in which we are less directly interested.

The first grouping, stated in general terms, raises the question whether the Court can or will render an advisory opinion concerning a dispute between a Member of the League and a non-Member when the latter does not con-

[1] League of Nations, *Treaty Series*, XVIII, p. 306.
[2] Hudson, *American Reservations*, p. 9–18.

sent. This issue was raised before the Court and settled in 1923.[1]

In that year the Council, on the suggestion of Finland, requested the Court to render an opinion regarding the treaty of Dorpat of October 14, 1920, between Finland and Russia. This was the now famous "Eastern Carelia case." The question arose from an acute dispute between the two countries; Finland was a Member of the League, Russia was not. The Soviet Government sent a telegram to the Court in which it forcefully denied the Court's competence to consider the question and refused to take any part in the proceedings.

On July 23, 1923, the Court announced its conclusion that it could not render any opinion. The Court declared that it "is well established in international law that no state can, without its consent, be compelled to submit its disputes with other states either to mediation or to arbitration, or to any other kind of pacific settlement." The Court further pointed out that "answering the question would be substantially equivalent to deciding the dispute between the parties. The Court, being a court of justice, can not, even in giving advisory opinions, depart from the essential rules guiding their activity as a court." To state this result in terms of American interests, the Court has decided that it can not render any advisory opinion regarding an actual dispute between the United States and a Member of the League without the former's assent.

There is no such judicial precedent for a dispute or question to which the United States is not a party but in which it has an interest. In the nine·years of its existence the Court has rendered 16 advisory opinions, none of which has affected American interests. This is not proof that a question involving our interests will never be submitted to the Court, but it does indicate that the occasions, if they ever do arise, will not be frequent. The situation, however, which the Senate seems to have had in mind in framing the fifth reservation is one in which, for example, a dispute

[1] Advisory Opinion No. 5, Series B, No. 5, summarized in Hudson, *World Court*, p. 64–66.

arises between Great Britain and the Argentine Republic, wherein somehow the Court might be asked to define the Monroe doctrine. Or a dispute might arise between Australia and Japan regarding immigration laws and the Court be asked to give its opinion on the power of one state to exclude the nationals of another. In this connection, it should be noted that such an opinion could be rendered now at any time before the United States adheres to the Court Statute. In other words, this is not a situation which would arise from the fact of our participation. Nor is it true that such an opinion would have any more binding effect upon us if we were a participant. The advisory opinions of the Court, as their name implies, are merely advisory, and have no direct compelling legal force. Neither the Council of the League nor the states involved are compelled to act in accordance with the opinion. But the Court has achieved, through the very excellence of its work, a position of respect and authority, and its views have great influence throughout the world. This influence, however, resting on merit, is just as great with regard to a nonparticipating as to a signatory state. The signature of the protocol of December 16, 1920, and the acceptance of the Statute incidental thereto, imposes no new legal or moral obligation with regard to acquiescence in advisory opinions.[1]

To return to the discussion of this second part of the fifth reservation in the 1926 Conference of Signatories, it is found that one of the basic difficulties which pervaded this and subsequent discussions was a matter of the interpretation of the Covenant of the League. It was generally believed that by this stipulation the Senate sought to secure a veto power over requests for advisory opinions.[2] It was therefore pertinent to inquire whether such a power would place the United States in a privileged or in an equal position as against the Members of the League. The question resolved itself therefore into this: In adopting a motion to

[1] Hudson, *American Reservations*, p. 15.

[2] This point will be analyzed later; see *infra*, p. 57 [697].

request an advisory opinion from the Court, is it necessary to have a unanimous vote in the Council or Assembly, or does a majority vote suffice? If the former be true, then each state represented has a veto power and a like position could properly be claimed by the United States. This would not be so if the latter alternative is correct.

The pertinent article of the Covenant is number 5, which provides that except for "matters of procedure" — which includes the appointment of "committees" to investigate particular matters — "decisions at any meeting of the Assembly or of the Council shall require the agreement of all the Members of the League represented at the meeting." It has not yet been decided whether the requesting of an advisory opinion is a procedural matter. As Professor Hudson has well said, "The question is one of politics as well as law, and the last word does not belong to the lawyers." [1] The truth of this statement will be more apparent in a subsequent discussion.

In the discussions of the 1926 Conference of Signatories, great weight was attached to a declaration made in the Senate by Senator Walsh of Montana. Senator Walsh maintained that the Council must proceed by unanimity in requesting an advisory opinion and that therefore the United States was seeking merely a position of equality.[2] From this position the conclusion was logically reached that some formula which would assure the United States a position of equality would be satisfactory to that Government.

It was recognized, however, that the difficulty might be avoided if the question of unanimity could be definitely settled and several members of the conference were in favor of asking the Council to request the Court to give an advisory opinion on the matter.[3] This view did not prevail.

The conference constantly bore in mind the distinction

[1] Hudson, *American Reservations*, p. 12; *ibid.*, note 27, for collection of citations to views of writers on the subject.

[2] *Minutes of the Conference*, p. 22, speech of M. Rolin.

[3] See remarks of M. Rolin, M. Pilotti and M. Dinichert, *ibid.*, p. 23, 26 and 39.

between disputes to which the United States was a party and other disputes or questions. With regard to the former category the conference seemed to feel that the American Government was justified in insisting that its consent must be first secured. But the conference believed that this desire had already been gratified by the jurisprudence of the Court itself in the Eastern Carelia case. So far as the second category of cases was concerned, the conference felt that the according of a position of equality with the states represented in the Council and Assembly would be fair and probably satisfactory to the United States.[1]

There was, however, the further procedural difficulty of determining how and when the consent of the United States would be made known. Was this a matter which would have to be referred to the Senate, which might not be in session when the question arose; or did it fall within the powers of the Executive? Would the United States designate some one to sit with the Council or Assembly for this purpose, or would negotiations have to be carried on with Washington? Would the Council know the views of the United States before reaching its decision or would these views be made known only to the Court after it had received the request? [2] In view of the above-mentioned importance of the time element in some cases, it is obvious that these questions could not be overlooked. On the other hand, it seemed fruitless to discuss them without the presence of a representative of the United States.

There was some discussion also of the wording of the reservation — "has or claims an interest" — [3] but, in view of the formula finally adopted, the definitive interpretation of this phrase was unnecessary.

These various points are made clear in the Final Act.[4] As regards disputes to which the United States is a party, the Eastern Carelia case is referred to as meeting the desire of the United States. As regards other disputes

[1] See report of Drafting Committee, *Minutes of the Conference*, p. 53–54.

[2] See remarks of Sir George Foster, *ibid.*, p. 28–30.

[3] *Ibid.*, p. 25, 32, 37, 38 and 44.

[4] *Ibid.*, p. 79; Hudson, *World Court*, p. 179–180.

or questions in which the United States claims an interest, it is agreed that a position of equality with states represented on the Council or Assembly should be accorded and it is noted that the conference understands that this is the object of the United States. Attention is then drawn to the uncertainty attending the question of unanimity. The last two paragraphs of the Final Act are clear descriptions of the whole situation regarding advisory opinions and should be read in full: [1]

> Great importance is attached by the Members of the League of Nations to the value of the advisory opinions which the Court may give as provided for in the Covenant. The conference is confident that the Government of the United States entertains no desire to diminish the value of such opinions in connection with the functioning of the League of Nations. Yet the terms employed in the fifth reservation are of such a nature as to lend themselves to a possible interpretation which might have that effect. The Members of the League of Nations would exercise their rights in the Council and in the Assembly with full knowledge of the details of the situation which has necessitated a request for an advisory opinion, as well as with full appreciation of the responsibilities which a failure to reach a solution would involve for them under the Covenant of the League of Nations. A state which is exempt from the obligations and responsibilities of the Covenant would occupy a different position. It is for this reason that the procedure to be followed by a non-Member state in connection with requests for advisory opinions is a matter of importance and in consequence it is desirable that the manner in which the consent provided for in the second part of the fifth reservation will be given should form the object of a supplementary agreement which would insure that the peaceful settlement of future differences between Members of the League of Nations would not be made more difficult.
>
> The conference ventures to anticipate that the above conclusions will meet with acceptance by the United States. It observes that the application of some of the reservations of the United States would involve the conclusion of an appropriate agreement between the United States and the other states signatories of the Protocol of December 16, 1920, as was indeed

[1] *Minutes of the Conference*, p. 79; Hudson, *op. cit.*, p. 180.

envisaged by the Secretary of State of the United States in his reply to the Secretary-General of the League of Nations dated April 17, 1926. To this end, it is desirable that the states signatories of the Protocol of December 16, 1920, should conclude with the United States a protocol of execution which, subject to such further exchange of views as the Government of the United States may think useful, might be in the form set out below.

In drafting a text for incorporating these conclusions in the Preliminary Draft of a Protocol, both classes of disputes or questions would seem to be covered, though no attempt was made to perpetuate the doctrine of the Eastern Carelia case in treaty form. It seemed clear, however, from the words of the Final Act that the Signatory States were fully in accord as to the soundness of that doctrine.[1] The text in question is contained in Art. 4 of the protocol and is as follows:[2]

The manner in which the consent provided for in the second part of the fifth reservation is to be given, will be the subject of an understanding to be reached by the Government of the United States with the Council of the League of Nations.

The states signatories of the Protocol of December 16, 1920, will be informed as soon as the understanding contemplated by the preceding paragraph has been reached.

Should the United States offer objection to an advisory opinion being given by the Court, at the request of the Council or the Assembly, concerning a dispute to which the United States is not a party or concerning a question other than a dispute between states, the Court will attribute to such objection the same force and effect as attaches to a vote against asking for the opinion given by a Member of the League of Nations either in the Assembly or in the Council.

[1] In view of this fact and of subsequent developments, it is no longer necessary to debate the supposed disagreement with the doctrine expressed by the Council, nor the action of the Court in the subsequent Mosul case, which has improperly been claimed by some persons to be contrary to the Carelia case. For the Council's action on the Carelia case, see *Official Journal*, November, 1923, p. 1335–1337. For discussion of the Mosul case, see Hudson, "The Fourth Year of the Permanent Court of International Justice", *International Conciliation*, April, 1926, No. 219, p. 1, 19 *ff.*

[2] *Minutes of the Conference*, p. 83; *infra*, p. 130 [770]. For detailed discussion of the Conference debates, see Quincy Wright, "The United States and the Court," *International Conciliation*, September, 1927, No. 232, p. 339 *ff.*, and the same writer in 21 *American Journal of International Law*, p. 9 *ff.*

The Final Act and the Preliminary Draft of a Protocol thus contemplated some further negotiations on the formulas to be adopted. In his note of February 19, 1929, Mr. Kellogg recognized this fact. He pointed out that it was the second part of the fifth reservation which "raised the only question on which there is any substantial difference of opinion." Alluding no doubt to that part of the Final Act quoted above which deals with the importance attached by the Members of the League to advisory opinions, Mr. Kellogg wrote in friendly and sympathetic terms.[1] "The Government of the United States," he declared, "desires to avoid in so far as may be possible, any proposal which would interfere with or embarrass the work of the Council of the League of Nations, doubtless often perplexing and difficult, and it would be glad if it could dispose of the subject by a simple acceptance of the suggestions" of the Conference of Signatories. Nevertheless, certain "elements of uncertainty" in these suggestions seemed to him not to preclude agreement, but to "require further discussion." He noted that the "powers of the Council and its modes of procedure depend upon the Covenant of the League of Nations, which may be amended at any time. The ruling of the Court in the Eastern Carelia case" was also, he pointed out, "subject to change at any time." "For these reasons," he concluded, "without further inquiry into the practicability of the suggestions, it appears that the Protocol submitted by the 24 Governments in relation to the fifth reservation of the United States would not furnish adequate protection to the United States." But again Mr. Kellogg fortunately took pains to indicate that the situation was not hopeless, but that the door was wide open for further negotiation. In this spirit he declared:

> Possibly the interest of the United States thus attempted to be safeguarded may be fully protected in some other way or by some other formula. The Government of the United States feels that such an informal exchange of views as is contemplated by the 24

[1] Hudson, *World Court*, p. 189.

Governments, should, as herein suggested, lead to agreement upon some provision which in unobjectionable form would protect the rights and interests of the United States as an adherent to the Court Statute, and this expectation is strongly supported by the fact that there seems to be but little difference regarding the substance of these rights and interests.

So it was that when the Committee of Jurists met in Geneva a few weeks later, the problem had been crystallized into one of finding a formula which would meet the views of the Signatory States and at the same time fully safeguard the interests of the United States. The framing of such a formula is Mr. Root's most recent contribution to the Court in the creation of which he was so largely instrumental.

In the period of a little more than two years which elapsed between the end of the 1926 Conference of Signatories and the dispatch of Mr. Kellogg's letter, much discussion had ensued as to the meaning of the words "claim" and "interest" in the fifth reservation. Numerous solutions had been suggested.[1] Mr. Root followed other lines of approach which he explained to the Committee of Jurists.[2] Two great difficulties had been experienced in the past, the one in defining "interest," the other in solving the question of the necessity of unanimity in the Council. Mr. Root avoided both these difficulties. He noted that it was practically impossible to find an abstract formula of general application which would apply satisfactorily to so multiform a conception as "interest." The United States has an "interest" in every rule of international law and in the prosperity of every country which is a customer for its products. But these, apparently, were not the "interests" which the Senate wished to safeguard. Moreover, it was apparent that a definition in terms of "legal interest" would be inade-

[1] See, for example, Esther Everett Lape, "A Way Out of the Court Deadlock," *Atlantic Monthly*, October, 1927, p. 517; Raul Fernandes, "The United States and the Permanent Court of International Justice," originally published in 34 *Revue Général de Droit International Public*, p. 561, translated into English and republished by the American Foundation. See views of Professor Hudson on these suggestions and his own profound solution in *American Reservations*, p. 13–21.

[2] *Minutes*, p. 11, 13, 15.

quate, since it would exclude such matters of policy as the Monroe doctrine. Mr. Root accordingly endeavored to shift the discussion from the abstract to the concrete and directed his plan toward a procedure for dealing with individual concrete cases as they arose. Following the position indicated by Mr. Kellogg in his note of February 19, 1929, he asserted that "there was no intention on the part of the United States to hamper the procedure of requesting advisory opinions upon unreal and unsubstantial grounds."[1] His design was to afford to the United States guaranties of protection which would be definite and permanent and at the same time to give assurance to the states Members of the League that there would be no undue interference with the use of advisory opinions.

For the accomplishment of these aims Mr. Root took two points of departure. The first was the acceptance of the five reservations and the second was the Final Act and Preliminary Draft of a Protocol adopted by the conference of 1926. It was possible for him to do this because, as Mr. Kellogg had said, there was "little difference regarding the substance" of the rights and interests of the United States. The difficulty was therefore in reality a procedural one, and the "Root Plan" is a procedural device. One aspect of this procedural difficulty was the uncertainty as to how the consent of the United States should be made known. In a great majority of actual cases, the emphasis in the fifth reservation would be on the words "the consent of the United States" and not on the statement that the Court shall not "entertain any request for an advisory opinion." The Root plan is also a device for manifesting that consent.

Although Mr. Root's draft avoided the necessity for settling the vexed question of unanimity,[2] this topic did not escape the attention of the Committee of Jurists. At the meeting of the Assembly in September, 1928, an attempt had been made to reach a solution of this question, but the move had been sidetracked by the adoption of an innocuous

[1] *Minutes*, p. 13.

[2] See the appreciation of this fact by Mr. van Eysinga, *ibid.*, p. 13, and by M. Politis p. 14; see also Mr. Root's own statement, p. 15.

resolution suggesting that the Council consider the matter at an appropriate time.[1] The discussion in the committee clearly brought out the political complications of the issue to which allusion has been made above. For the large states, the rule of unanimity would seem to be preferable because, as Members of the League, they are deemed to have consented in advance to the rendering of advisory opinions in disputes to which they are parties,[2] and accordingly they wish to be able to control requests for such opinions. Such control would be theirs only if the unanimity rule applies.[3] In this respect their position is not as free as that of the United States as a non-Member of the League. On the other hand, the small states have constantly been eager to increase the scope of the Court's activity, since they see in that tribunal a possible safeguard for rights which they are not powerful enough to enforce in other ways. Thus, too, they would welcome the adoption of a rule that advisory opinions could be requested from the Court by a majority vote.[4] Forty-two states, including the British Empire, France, Germany and Italy, have signed the so-called "optional clause," providing for the compulsory jurisdiction of the Court.[5]

[1] *Records of the Ninth Assembly. Plenary Meetings*, p. 73, 138 (*Official Journal*, Spec. Sup. No. 64).

[2] In the Eastern Carelia case, the Court seems to have taken this view. After declaring that under international law no state could be compelled to submit its disputes to any form of pacific settlement without its consent, it noted that this consent "can be given once and for all in the form of an obligation freely undertaken" or in a special case by consent *ad hoc*. "The first alternative," the Court says, "applies to the Members of the League who, having accepted the Covenant, are under the obligation resulting from the provisions of this pact dealing with the pacific settlement of international disputes. As concerns states not Members of the League, the situation is quite different; they are not bound by the Covenant." Series B, No. 5, p. 27.

[3] There is also, of course, the possibility of a rule of "qualified unanimity," requiring the affirmative vote of all states except the actual parties to the dispute; see Hudson, *American Reservations*, p. 11, especially note 28.

[4] The writer should not be understood as asserting that the above views are held by all the large and small states respectively. An attempt has been made merely to point out lines of general interest of each group.

[5] See *infra*, p. 82 [722]. The 1929 session of the League Assembly witnessed the signature of 15 of the total number of states, including those of the British Empire, Italy and France. This general acceptance of the compulsory jurisdiction of the Court by the great states may alter materially the situation described in the text. The states which signed the optional clause at Geneva in September 1929 are: Australia, Canada, Czechoslovakia, France, Great Britain, Greece, India, Irish Free State, Italy, Latvia, New Zealand, Nicaragua, Peru, Siam and South Africa.

This antithesis may be traced in the committee discussions. The chairman, M. Scialoja of Italy, while asserting that his personal view had always been that technically a majority vote would suffice, pointed out that, because no decision on the question could be reached, "in practice advisory opinions were not asked for" on recent occasions, the Council consulting instead groups of jurists.[1] Anticipating that complications would arise under the procedure suggested by Mr. Root, he believed that the ultimate effect "would be a tendency to abolish the whole system of advisory opinions. Personally, he would not greatly regret their disappearance." [2] He favored a solution of the difficulty by deciding upon the unanimity rule.

A different point of view was expressed by M. Raestad, former foreign minister of Norway, in a powerful statement which he made at the twelfth session of the committee.[3] M. Raestad said that the group of nations to which his own country, Norway, belonged, attached the greatest importance to the adhesion of the United States to the Court. But at the same time these nations considered the maintenance of the system of advisory opinions as of equal importance. If the adhesion of the United States could not be secured without endangering this system, Norway and the other countries would be placed in an extremely difficult situation.[4] M. Raestad was glad to note, however, that these countries were not actually placed in such a dilemma since the issue was avoided under Mr. Root's plan.

Sir Cecil Hurst's report on the question of the accession of the United States alludes to these matters. He notes that the committee's task would have been simplified if it had felt able to recommend abandoning the whole system of advisory opinions. "The committee, however, is of opinion that it can not recommend any such drastic solution. The system of asking the Court for an advisory

[1] *Minutes*, p. 11.

[2] *Ibid.*, p. 15.

[3] *Ibid.*, p. 76–77.

[4] It may be pertinent to recall here that the accession of the United States can be accomplished only by the unanimous consent of the present Signatory States.

opinion has proved to be of substantial utility in securing a solution of questions which could not conveniently be submitted to the Court in any other form. It has also on occasions enabled parties to a dispute to ask for the submission of their difference to the Court in the form of a request for an advisory opinion when they were for various reasons unwilling to submit it in the form of international litigation." [1]

The report continues: [2]

> The committee has also felt obliged to reject another method by which satisfaction might without difficulty be given to the conditions laid down by the United States. It is that of recommending the adoption of a rule that in all cases a decision on the part of the Council or of the Assembly to ask for an advisory opinion from the Court must be unanimous.
>
> As is pointed out in the Final Act of the Special Conference of 1926, it was not then possible to say with certainty whether a decision by a majority was not sufficient. It is equally impossible to-day. All that is possible is to guarantee to the United States a position of equality in this matter with the States which are represented in the Council or the Assembly of the League.

The method by which the Root Plan avoids this pitfall will be described shortly. Meanwhile we may return to a consideration of its general scope and special provisions.

It has already been noted that the Root Plan was based on the Final Act and Preliminary Draft of a Protocol formulated by the 1926 Conference of Signatories. The plan retained the distinction between disputes to which the United States is a party and disputes in which the United States merely has an interest. But Mr. Kellogg had pointed out that the United States could not be satisfied with the conference's reference to the jurisprudence of the Court, since the precedent of the Eastern Carelia case could be reversed at any time. The conference had in reality agreed that no opinion should be rendered without the consent of the United States in any dispute to which

[1] *Infra*, p. 141 [781].

[2] *Infra*, p. 142 [782].

the United States might be a party. But the form in which this agreement was expressed was unsatisfactory. In Mr. Root's original plan the first paragraph stated this point flatly.[1] But his second paragraph laid a like prohibition on the rendering of an advisory opinion without the consent of the United States touching any other dispute or question in which the United States claims an interest. Thus the whole field is covered.

The original Root Plan then has three paragraphs whose purpose is described in the third paragraph of the plan. "The manner in which shall be made known whether the United States claims an interest and gives or withholds its consent shall be as follows:—" There are three possible steps or stages in the procedure: first, exchange of views with the Council or Assembly; second, notice from the Court with opportunity for hearing; third, stay of Court proceedings and further exchange of views with the Council or Assembly.

It will be seen that the fundamental point in Mr. Root's scheme is this exchange of views with the League organs which propose requests for advisory opinions. Since there has been some objection in the United States to dealing with the League in matters relating to the Court, certain observations on this point may be in order. The Preliminary Draft of a Protocol adopted by the 1926 Conference of Signatories had, in its Art. 4, suggested that an understanding be reached between the Government of the United States and the Council of the League as to the manner in which the consent of the United States should be given. Thus, in effect, the Signatory States constituted the Council their agent to make this arrangement. All the Signatory States at that Conference were also Members of the League. Indeed, Brazil, which has withdrawn from the League, is at present the only non-Member state which is a party to the Court treaty. It was thus quite natural for these states to select as agent the body which may be called the executive committee of the League of Nations.

[1] The text of the original plan is in *Minutes*, p. 9, and Appendix, p. 138 [778].

There would appear to be no reason for our refusing to deal with any agent which they chose to designate. There are numerous precedents for like action in the past. When, in 1911, the United States wished to become a member of the Permanent International Council for the Exploration of the Sea at Copenhagen,[1] it could not deal directly with the Council, but had to negotiate through the Danish Government, which acts as its agent in all diplomatic affairs.[2] Similarly, the Commission Internationale pour l'Exploration Scientifique de la Mer Méditerranée conducted its diplomatic negotiations through the Prince of Monaco.[3] The two Hague Peace Conferences of 1899 and 1907 had no formal permanent organization, so that difficulty was experienced when it was desired to convene a third conference. On January 31, 1914, Secretary of State Bryan sent out a circular instruction to our diplomatic officers regarding such further conference and he pointed out the need of an agency through which the various Governments might operate.[4] He suggested the formation of an "international preparatory committee" and thought that the Administrative Council of the Permanent Court of Arbitration at The Hague might well be used in this capacity. This council, not wholly dissimilar in composition to the Council of the League, is composed of the Netherlands minister for foreign affairs and the diplomatic representatives of the contracting states accredited to The Hague. Secretary Bryan's further statement in this connection is rather apt to the situation regarding the need for an agent such as the Council of the League, for handling the negotiations of the states parties to the Court treaty with the United States. "To this Council," — that is, the Administrative Council

[1] This Council is the most important international organization for the study and protection of deep-sea fisheries. It has been in existence for 27 years and has now a membership of 14 countries. The United States has not continued its participation since the war, due to the fact that such marine problems of particular interest to the United States are now handled by a separate organization on this side of the Atlantic.

[2] *Rapports et Procès-Verbaux* of the Council, Vol. XV, p. 12 and 42, and Vol. IL, p. 112.

[3] See *Bulletin de l'Institut Océanographique*, No. 167.

[4] United States, *For. Rel.*, 1914, p. 4.

of the Permanent Court of Arbitration, — he said, "the task of preparation for the conference may readily and appropriately be committed. The place at which the council sits leaves nothing to be desired from the point of view of convenience, while the intrusting of the work to a competent body already in existence would result in an appreciable saving both in time and expense."

With a similar purpose, the Second International Opium Conference of 1913, at which the United States was represented, designated the Dutch Government as the general agent for handling affairs under the convention adopted. As ratifications of the Court treaty are deposited with the Secretary-General of the League as agent, so ratifications of this opium treaty were deposited with the Dutch Government. With this Government as agent, we negotiated also for arranging a third conference.[1]

Adopting a slightly different method, but with the same purpose in view, the convention for the protection of industrial property, which was ratified by the United States on June 20, 1912, continued the organization of the prior conventions of 1883 and 1900, whereby a Union for the Protection of Industrial Property was set up with a central bureau at Bern. For this bureau the Swiss Government acts as agent for the exchange of information, the preparation of further conferences and the like.[2] Similar examples of this kind could be multiplied, but it will suffice to note that the slavery convention of 1926, to the ratification of which the Senate consented on February 25, 1929, makes the Secretary-General of the League the agent for the exchange of information, the deposit of ratifications and the like.[3]

As Mr. Hughes has said, "there is no more difficulty in dealing with the organization of the League in this way for the purpose of protecting our interests or furthering our policies than there would be in dealing with the British

[1] United States, *For. Rel.*, 1912, p. 217–219; 1914, p. 924–926.

[2] *Ibid.*, 1913, p. 1363.

[3] United States, *Treaty Series*, No. 778.

Empire."[1] At the present time we have exchanged ministers with Canada and the Irish Free State, thus recognizing their independent status and dealing with them direct. But for dealings with the other Dominions of equal status, such as Australia and New Zealand, we still use the agency of the British Foreign Office.

Now in the negotiations of the United States relative to the Permanent Court of International Justice, it is possible to write 50 or more notes to the several participating Governments. But it has been seen that these Governments prefer to meet together to discuss these matters. It would also be conceivable that for the purpose of manifesting our consent to the rendering of an advisory opinion, one might suggest separate notice to each interested state. But such an awkward and tedious process could not possibly be accepted by the other states and it would scarcely recommend itself, on the grounds of efficiency, to the United States. In the above-quoted words of Mr. Bryan, negotiation with some agent of the many states involved "would result in an appreciable saving both in time and expense."

So Mr. Root, following these ideas and precedents, suggested in his plan direct dealing with the Council or Assembly of the League, in which requests for advisory opinions originate.

In the original Root Plan, however, it is merely provided in the first instance that, "whenever in contemplation of a request for an advisory opinion it seems to them desirable, the Council or Assembly may invite an exchange of views with the United States and such exchange of views shall proceed with all convenient speed."

The second step in the plan is based on the existing Rules of Court and provides that

> Whenever a request for an advisory opinion comes to the Court, the Registrar shall notify the United States thereof among other states mentioned in the now existing Art. 73 of

[1] Speech of Charles Evans Hughes at New York Republican State Convention, April 15, 1924.

the Rules of Court stating a reasonable time-limit fixed by the President [of the Court] within which a written statement by the United States concerning the request will be received.

If in response to this notice the United States advises the Court that the request "touches a dispute or question in which the United States has an interest and that the United States has not consented to the submission of the question," then all proceedings in the Court are stayed until such an exchange of views as previously described takes place. The final paragraph of the plan is descriptive of what may happen in the exchange of views and should be read in full:

If after such an exchange of views either while a question is in contemplation or after a question has gone to the Court, it shall appear (1) that no agreement can be reached as to whether the question does touch an interest of the United States within the true meaning of the second paragraph of this article; and (2) that the submission of the question is still insisted upon after attributing to the objections of the United States the same force and effect as attaches to a vote against asking for the opinion given by a Member of the League of Nations either in the Assembly or in the Council; and if it also appears that the United States has not been able to find the submission of the question so important for the general good as to call upon the United States to forego its objection in that particular instance leaving the request to be acted upon by the Court without in any way binding the United States; then it shall be deemed that owing to a material difference of view regarding the proper scope of the practice of requesting advisory opinions the arrangement now agreed upon is not yielding satisfactory results and that the exercise of the powers of withdrawal provided in Art. 7 hereof will follow naturally without any imputation of unfriendliness or of unwillingness to cooperate generally for peace and good will.

The most important point to note in this paragraph is that it provides for a case which might never arise and that it was intended as an ultimate safeguard to "provide against a very rare and improbable contingency." [1] On

[1] Explanation of Mr. Root, *Minutes*, p. 13.

the basis of his long experience in international affairs, as a delegate to international conferences and especially as Secretary of State, Mr. Root was convinced that in the course of a full and friendly discussion such as he proposed, agreement would always be reached along one of the lines explained in his draft. The privilege of withdrawal would probably never need to be exercised.[1] The nature of the ultimate safeguard through withdrawal is suggested by the provision of Art. 7 of the Preliminary Draft of a Protocol adopted by the 1926 Conference of Signatories, which gave the Signatory States the privilege of restoring the *status quo ante* by withdrawing their acceptance of the American accession.

It is important to note the reason for the possible withdrawal of the United States as clearly described in this original plan. The description is not retained in the Final Draft which will be considered shortly, but is implicit in it, since it constitutes a statement of fact. It must not be erroneously assumed that Mr. Root proposed that we should withdraw from the Court because of a sense of pique over any failure to make our point of view prevail in a specific case or because of annoyance regarding the adoption of some particular request for an advisory opinion. If this were the basis, there might possibly be some justification for the feeling that a withdrawal under these circumstances would place us in an unfavorable light before the public opinion of the world, although this fear would seem to be dispelled by the proviso that the withdrawal would "follow naturally without any imputation of unfriendliness or of unwillingness to cooperate generally for peace and good will." The withdrawal contemplated by Mr. Root as an ultimate though remote safeguard would be due to a more fundamental difference of opinion. He believed that the cooperation of the United States in the work of the Court could be successfully carried on and that through this proposed friendly exchange of views, agreement could always be reached. If this were not the

[1] Explanation of Mr. Root, *Minutes*, p. 15.

case, it might as well be recognized that the proposed collaboration was impossible, "*owing to a material difference of view regarding the proper scope of the practice of requesting advisory opinions.*" In such a situation it would be best for all concerned if we returned to our present situation of a non-participating state.

Such was the nature of the original Root Plan as submitted to the Committee of Jurists on March 11. It has already been noted [1] that the project had already received the informal and general approval of the principal statesmen of Europe and that its basic principles had commended themselves also to certain official persons in the United States. Attention has also been called to the fact that the project was not drafted with the idea that it would form the ultimate text of a treaty. Mr. Root was too experienced in the ways of conferences and committees to ignore the fact that any primary proposal must be redrafted to meet the varying views and suggestions of those concerned. The draft was accordingly considered by him and laid before the Committee of Jurists as a basis for discussion. With this end in view it had been drafted so as to be self-explanatory and it had included details to the ultimate modification or omission of which Mr. Root had not the slightest objection.

One of the first suggestions made in the committee discussions was that of Sir Cecil Hurst which reverted to the 1926 protocol and Secretary Kellogg's note of February 19, 1929, and which proposed that the United States might freely withdraw if any modification were made in the Covenant of the League (presumably regarding unanimity) or in the rules or practice of the Court.[2]

The president, M. Scialoja, was insistent that the committee, under its terms of reference from the Council, should consider specifically Mr. Kellogg's note of February 19, 1929, in order that it might recommend to the Council the

[1] *Supra*, p. 6 [646].

[2] *Minutes*, p. 11.

nature of the reply to be made.[1] M. Gaus and others, however, believed that Mr. Root's proposal would itself contain the basis of a reply and that Mr. Kellogg's note need not be considered separately. This view prevailed.[2]

At the second session a new draft of the proposal prepared by Sir Cecil Hurst was circulated to the committee.[3] Mr. Root declared that, so far as he could see, it "fulfilled exactly the same purpose as his own. The essential point was that the United States should be promptly informed of the intentions of the Council in dealing with any matter in which the former might be interested, and that there should be some kind of informal conference in regard to any concrete case which might arise." [4] Before this Hurst draft was examined, M. van Eysinga of the Netherlands, vice chairman of the committee and formerly the president of the 1926 conference, had suggested that the procedure in Mr. Root's draft might be simplified and he suggested direct notice from the Council to the United States instead of indirect notice through the Court.[5] The Hurst draft, in fact, contained such a suggestion and the idea was acceptable to Mr. Root, who noted that in preparing his own draft he had felt it necessary to avoid any suggestion of interfering with the Council's procedure, but that if the other members felt such an arrangement would be welcome, he was quite willing to accept that arrangement.[6]

As bearing on the likelihood of agreement in an exchange of views with the Council, and on the improbability of withdrawal ever being necessary, it may be noted that the chairman drew attention to the fact that the Council would be most reluctant to take a step of so serious a character as to force the United States to withdraw. He accordingly considered this provision as a "species of sanctions" which would "be a kind of moral pressure on the Council." [7]

[1] *Minutes*, p. 12.

[2] See the Committee Report, p. 134.

[3] *Minutes*, p. 14; the text at p. 16.

[4] *Ibid.*, p. 13.

[5] *Ibid.*, p. 14, where are also the similar views of M. Osusky.

[6] *Ibid.*, p. 14.

[7] *Ibid.*, p. 5.

There was, however, such a very general feeling of assurance that agreement would always be possible that this consideration did not deter the ultimate acceptance of the plan.

The Hurst draft, in the interests of simplification, had combined the first two paragraphs of the Root draft, which, it will be recalled, separated disputes to which the United States was a party from those disputes or questions in which it merely had an interest. M. Raestad expressed himself forcefully as preferring the first form,[1] but the simpler redaction was ultimately adopted. M. Raestad feared that under the Hurst phrasing a situation might arise in which the Council and the United States might disagree and the United States might then withdraw. Subsequently, however, the Court might rule that the United States was a party to or had a legal interest in the dispute and that therefore the opinion could not be rendered. He wished, therefore, to leave the question of competency in the first place to the Court. This proposal failed to take account of what has been said above regarding the real reason for American withdrawal. It would, moreover, put the United States in the position of appearing before the Court as a litigant and then of withdrawing if it were defeated in the litigation. This would indeed be an awkward situation, to which the United States could never assent.

Other proposals were laid before the committee, some in formal drafts and some in informal oral suggestions.[2] The Hurst draft, however, seemed to afford the most satisfactory basis and no other draft was considered in great detail. On the other hand, numerous suggestions were made which were incorporated into the final text.[3] This final text may be studied in comparison with the original Root draft.[4]

[1] *Minutes*, p. 17.

[2] See especially those of M. Politis, *ibid.*, p. 21, and those of M. Fromageot, *ibid.*, p. 81.

[3] See *ibid.*, p. 22; Report of Subcommittee of Four, M. Politis, Reporter.

[4] The text in question is Art. 5 of the Draft Protocol adopted by the committee, *infra*, p. 136. Although Sir Cecil Hurst was designated as reporter to make the final draft, he was instructed to work closely with Mr. Root and as a matter of fact did so.

Instead of following Mr. Root's phraseology by starting with a statement as to what the Court may or may not do, the final text opens with a phrase taken from the fifth reservation itself and serves to emphasize the fact that it is concerned with providing a procedural device. It must be borne in mind that Mr. Root had first submitted a draft covering the second part of the fifth reservation only but that the final Draft Protocol covers all five reservations. The new provisions must therefore be considered with the rest of the protocol in mind, and especially the terms of Art. 1, in which the acceptance of all the reservations "upon the terms and conditions set out in the following articles" is agreed to. The acceptance of the second part of the fifth reservation is thus the underlying fact on which the text now considered hinges. The opening phrase is this: [1]

> With a view to insuring that the Court shall not, *without the consent of the United States, entertain any request for an advisory opinion touching any dispute or question in which the United States has or claims an interest. . . .*

The first step in accomplishing this result is for the Secretary-General of the League to inform the United States,

> " through any channel designated for that purpose by the United States," "of any proposal before the Council or the Assembly of the League for obtaining an advisory opinion from the Court."

It will be noted that, since the United States may designate the channel of communication, it can have a notification sent to Washington by cable; it can have its minister at Bern informed by telegraph or telephone; or it can have a representative present in Geneva who will receive a written or oral statement. The words "before the Council or the Assembly" were carefully chosen to preserve a certain measure of elasticity. It was realized that it would be unnecessary to put the machinery into

[1] The italics are inserted to show the precise words taken from the fifth reservation.

operation merely because some individual had suggested that he would like to have the Council request an opinion. On the other hand, it would not do to wait till the matter were placed on the agenda of the meeting since a request for an advisory opinion would probably never appear in that form. The agenda would merely include the subject matter of the dispute and the course of the discussion would bring out whether it should be settled by means of a request for an advisory opinion. In the light of the committee discussions it may be said that "before the Council" means "under serious consideration." [1]

The second step is that,

> if desired, an exchange of views as to whether an interest of the United States is affected shall proceed with all convenient speed between the Council or the Assembly of the League and the United States.

This preserves the essence of the Root Plan. It should be noted that the exchange of views shall take place "if desired," that is, by either party. Frequently and probably usually, the United States would be able to say at once that it had no interest and that discussion was therefor unnecessary. It is also important to note the expressed purpose of the exchange of views. This is not to decide whether the opinion should be requested, but merely whether "an interest of the United States is affected." When this provision is read in the light of Art. 1 which accepts the reservations, and in the light of the opening phrase of this Art. 5 — "with a view to insuring that the Court shall not without the consent of the United States entertain any request for an advisory opinion touching any dispute or question in which the United States has or claims an interest" — the inference is clear that if an interest of the United States is affected, the request will not be transmitted.

The article then continues with a new paragraph based largely on the original Root draft. It was pointed out

[1] *Minutes*, p. 77–79.

in the committee [1] that the Council sessions usually last only a week and that in a serious emergency it might be necessary for the Council to take some action before it would be possible to complete an exchange of views. The draft accordingly provides a solution for this difficulty. It requires the Registrar to notify the United States whenever a request for an advisory opinion comes to the Court. Like the Root draft it also emphasizes and crystallizes the present practice of the Court by a reference to Art. 73 of the Rules regarding notice and the fixing of a reasonable time limit within which a written statement by the United States will be received. The article of the Draft Protocol continues:

> . . . If for any reason no sufficient opportunity for an exchange of views upon such request should have been afforded, and the United States advises the Court that the question upon which the opinion of the Court is asked is one that affects the interests of the United States, proceedings shall be stayed for a period sufficient to enable such an exchange of views between the Council or the Assembly and the United States to take place.

Although this proviso is designed to cover especially the emergency just described, it is couched in general terms and thus affords the United States an additional safeguard in every case.

The next paragraph goes back to the idea contained in Art. 4 of the protocol of 1926, which was also incorporated in the original Root draft. It reads as follows:

> With regard to requesting an advisory opinion of the Court in any case covered by the preceding paragraphs, there shall be attributed to an objection of the United States the same force and effect as attached to a vote against asking for the opinion given by a Member of the League of Nations in the Council or in the Assembly.

This provision, it will be recalled, was originally adopted to afford a way out of the unsolved problem of unanimity

[1] See *Minutes*, p. 21, and Sir Cecil Hurst's Report, Hudson, *World Court*, p. 198.

or majority. In view of the other provisions in this new plan, this is no longer of vital importance, but at the same time it does give the United States one more safeguard. From the phraseology it will be apparent that both the Council and the Court must attribute this weight to the vote of the United States, since the text clearly refers to the preceding "paragraphs," one of which deals with the Council and the other with the Court. The Council might decide a majority vote was sufficient and transmit the request over the objection of the United States. The Court would then have to rule on the point and if it decided unanimity was necessary it would be forced to decide that the request was improperly before it and could not be answered. It is true also that, even if in some cases a majority vote was sufficient, the vote of the United States might turn a minority into a majority. In any event, we are assured a position of strict legal equality with the Members of the Council and Assembly and that without the correlative assumption of any of their obligations. Meanwhile, the fact that this safeguard is, while valuable and important, only subsidiary to the main plan, has made unnecessary the probably futile attempt to secure at this time a definitive interpretation of Art. 5 of the Covenant.

The last paragraph of this article in the Draft Protocol does not differ substantially from the corresponding part of Mr. Root's original draft, which provided for ultimate withdrawal, except that it is more condensed and does not fully state all the factual situations which Mr. Root found it appropriate to list in a preliminary proposal. It reads as follows:

> If, after the exchange of views provided for in pars. 1 and 2 of this article, it shall appear that no agreement can be reached, and the United States is not prepared to forego its objection, the exercise of the powers of withdrawal provided for in Art. 8 hereof will follow naturally without any imputation of unfriendliness or unwillingness to cooperate generally for peace and good will.

Attention is drawn to the fact that it is not only the United States which might withdraw in case of a disagreement. As in the Root draft, the words are "the powers of withdrawal provided for in Art. 8" and Art. 8, like Art. 7 of the 1926 protocol, provides for the withdrawal of the United States and of the other Signatory States.[1]

Since, as already noted, the acceptance of the fifth reservation is the basis for this whole article, and in view of the other points just elaborated, it would seem that no request for an advisory opinion could be entertained by the Court without the consent of the United States while this protocol is in force. In the improbable case of disagreement with the Council, for the reason already indicated, the United States would no doubt wish to withdraw from the whole arrangement, but on the other hand if the United States chose to stand on its objection, it would appear that proceedings in the Court would be stayed until the other parties exercised their rights under Art. 8 and brought the protocol to an end. This would throw upon them the *onus* of dissolving the partnership, but in reality there would be practically no factual difference. As M. Scialoja pointed out,[2] the Council would always be very slow to disagree with the United States, since the disagreement would probably cause American withdrawal. It is scarcely conceivable that a group of expert statesmen would not in such a situation find some different method of solution which would avoid such a calamity. A reframing of the form of submission or the putting forward of a different legal angle involved in the dispute would probably suffice to eliminate any American objection.

It has been suggested [3] that under the Root Plan, a veto power which would have been obtained under the fifth reservation has been abandoned. This statement requires analysis. In the first place, the theory of a veto power seems to have been based on the use of the words "claims

[1] This fact is not made clear in the Committee's Report; see Hudson, *op. cit.*, p. 198.

[2] See *supra*, p. 50 [690].

[3] *Minutes*, p. 20; see also Hudson, *American Reservations*, p. 13.

an interest." It was felt that a mere "claim" by the United States would be sufficient to block any opinion. But there are other words in the reservation. The claim of interest is sufficient to block the opinion if it is one "touching any dispute or question" in which that interest or alleged interest is involved. The reservation does not say it is sufficient if we "claim" that it touches such a matter. This is therefore a question of fact or of law for which the reservation provided no method of solution. It would seem that, if the Signatory States had in the first instance flatly accepted the fifth reservation, the following situation might have resulted: The Council would transmit a request to the Court. The United States would inform the Court that it claimed an interest. The Court, as a judicial body, acting in accordance with the treaties which govern its jurisdiction would say, even though that be true, where is the proof that this dispute or question "touches" that interest which you claim? The United States would have then been compelled to submit arguments to the Court, to explain and define the interest, and to allow the Court to pass upon it. This was just the result which the reservation intended to avoid, but to which it would almost certainly have led. The new protocol or Root Plan, therefore, not only fully protects every possible interest of the United States, but goes further in that direction than the reservation itself. Of course, under the withdrawal provisions, the power of control vested in the United States would cease when the protocol is terminated but no reservations which are always ultimately parts of a treaty can survive the existence of the treaty to which they are attached. One may echo the hope expressed in the report of the committee, that if any withdrawal ever materializes "it would in fact be followed or accompanied by the conclusion of some new and more satisfactory arrangement." [1]

[1] Hudson, *World Court*, p. 198.

III. PROPOSED AMENDMENTS TO THE STATUTE

When the Assembly, on September 20, 1928, adopted its resolution looking toward the revision of the Statute, it was made clear that there was "no question of recasting the Statute of the Court or of actually revising it. All we are proposing is that it should be examined with a view to remedying such defects as experience may have brought to light, and introducing amendments which could be effected by general agreement without undue delay." [1] For this reason, the proposal of M. Pella, the Rumanian delegate, to confer on the Court certain powers in penal matters was rejected. The Committee of Jurists fully recognized this limitation on the scope of its activities.[2]

The recommendations of the committee may be considered under the headings found in its report.[3]

Certain preliminary matters are first dealt with in the report. Among these is the question of the qualification of judges. Art. 2 of the Statute now requires them to be "persons of high moral character, who possess the qualifications required in their respective countries for appointment to the highest judicial offices, or are jurisconsults of recognized competence in international law." [4] M. Fromageot (France) believed that the word "competence" did not necessarily include practical experience and he wished to see this quality included among the required attributes.[5]

[1] Statement of René Cassin, rapporteur for the First Committee of the Assembly, *Records of the Ninth Ordinary Session of the Assembly*, p. 110, col. 2. For a discussion of the wisdom of proceeding to secure amendments to the Statute by this method without first obtaining the views of the Court, see the illuminating article by Mr. Hammarskjöld, Registrar of the Court, in *Revue de Droit international et de Législation comparée*, 1928, No. 6, p. 5 *ff.* at p. 7–9 and 17 *ff.* This article also includes valuable comments on some of the substantive changes discussed in the committee.

[2] *Minutes*, p. 24; also Committee Report, *infra*, p. 105 [745].

[3] League Document, C. 142. M. 52. 1929. V. 4; also *infra*, p. 104 [744]. The conference at Geneva, September 4–12, 1929, and the Assembly of the League of Nations approved the report of the Committee with only slight changes.

[4] *Infra*, p. 83 [723].

[5] *Minutes*, p. 24.

It was also proposed that every judge should have some familiarity with the official languages of the Court — French and English. Not only for the examination of the often voluminous records and pleadings submitted to the Court and for the understanding of the oral arguments, but also particularly for the Court's own private consultations, such a language requirement would seem to be essential. On the other hand, the committee felt it would be undesirable to lay down so strict a rule on this point as to exclude from the bench persons otherwise highly qualified to serve upon it. Accordingly it was finally decided to specify a reading knowledge of both the official languages and a speaking knowledge of one of them.[1]

It was at first suggested that Art. 5 of the Statute, which describes the manner of nomination, should be amended to include a definite requirement that each nomination should be accompanied by a statement indicating that the nominee possessed the required qualifications.[2] An alternate suggestion was for the amendment of Art. 8 dealing with the method of election, to provide an opportunity for speeches in support of the candidates.[3] The President pointed out, however, that this might result in an election being based on the eloquence of the advocate rather than on the merits of the nominee.[3] It was eventually decided that the best plan would be merely to advise that the Assembly approve the following recommendation:[4]

> The Secretary-General, in issuing the invitations provided for in Art. 5 of the Statute, will request the national groups to satisfy themselves that the candidates nominated by them possess recognized practical experience in international law and that they are at least able to read both the official languages of the Court and to

[1] See Committee Report, *infra*, p. 106 [746]; *Minutes*, p. 87–90, especially the statement of M. Anzilotti, President of the Court, p. 88.

[2] *Minutes*, p. 25.

[3] *Ibid.*, p. 26.

[4] Committee Report, *infra*, p. 106 [746]; also *Minutes*, p. 26, 39, 87–90; the compromise formula finally adopted was suggested by Mr. Root, *ibid.*, p. 27.

speak one of them; he will recommend the groups to attach to each nomination a statement of the career of the person nominated showing that he possesses the required qualifications.[1]

Composition of the Court

Many of the suggestions of the committee are based on a desire to improve the organization of the Court with a view to enabling it more easily to handle the steadily increasing volume of business confided to it. As Mr. Root has pointed out, when the Committee of Experts of which he was one framed the Court Statute in 1920, they were treading new paths and could not foresee the extent to which the new Court would be used. The committee of 1929, therefore, had to apply "the lessons, not of failure, but of success." [2]

With regard to the composition of the Court, the first matter considered was the position of deputy-judges. Art. 3 of the Statute now provides that the Court shall be composed of eleven regular judges and four deputy-judges. The committee decided that the class of deputy-judges should be abolished. M. Fromageot explained why this should be done.[3] The function of a deputy-judge was to act when a sufficient number of regular judges was not available to constitute a quorum. If it were inconvenient for a regular judge to attend a session, particularly if his home were at a great distance from The Hague, the realization that a deputy-judge was available to take his place might dissuade him from making a special effort to be present. But the need for having deputy-judges immediately available made it almost essential to elect to this position only persons residing reasonably

[1] The 1929 conference made this recommendation even milder, asserting its approval of the ideas but merely suggesting that the recommendation be transmitted to the Assembly "in order that eventually it may be brought by the Secretary-General to the knowledge of the national groups." The resolution adopted by the Assembly associates that body with the recommendation, which will be referred to by the Secretary-General in notices to the nominating groups. See *Report of the First Committee to the Assembly* (M. Politis, rapporteur) September 13, 1929, League Doc. A. 50. 1929. 5, p. 4, and *infra*, note p. 98 [738] (hereinafter referred to as "Report of First Committee, 1929").

[2] Prepared statement to the Press, Geneva, March 20, 1929.

[3] *Minutes*, p. 27.

near The Hague. This created a tendency to choose only Europeans, thus creating a privileged situation in their favor.[1] Furthermore, regular judges are placed under certain disabilities as to the activities in which they may engage,[2] while this restriction is not and could not fairly be imposed on the deputy-judges. Yet when sitting on the bench, both groups of judges are on a footing of equality; this did not seem an advantageous situation. In the words of the committee report, "practical experience thus points to assimilation of the two classes of judges and accordingly suggests the desirability of abolishing the deputy-judges and replacing them by an equal number of ordinary judges." [3] Art. 3 of the Statute now also provides that the number of judges and deputy-judges might be increased by the Assembly, on the proposal of the Council, to a total of fifteen judges and six deputy-judges. Since under the new amendment, this maximum number would be reached, the committee recommended omitting in this article all reference to increasing the bench. The new Art. 3 would thus read : "The Court shall consist of fifteen members." This abolition of deputy-judges of course would make necessary changes in other articles where they are referred to, but this being a matter of detail, it is not considered here.[4]

Permanent Functioning of the Court [5]

In noting the suggested abolition of the deputy-judges, it has been indicated that the need was felt for having the judges more readily available for service. Art. 23 of the Statute now provides that the Court shall hold a regular

[1] One of the present deputy-judges, however, is Wang Chung-hui of China.

[2] See Arts. 16 and 17 of the Statute, *infra*, p. 87 [727].

[3] *Infra*, p. 106 [746].

[4] The articles of the Statute affected are 8, 15, 16, 17, 25, 31 and 32; see Committee Report, *infra*, p. 107*ff*. [747*ff*.]. The proposed redraft of Art. 3 was accepted without change; see *Report of First Committee, 1929*, p. 2; *infra*, p. 83 [723].

[5] This is not the next subject in order in the committee report, which follows the order of the articles of the Statute. It seems, however, more convenient to shift the order here in order to draw together closely related matters.

session on June 15 of each year and that extraordinary sessions may be called if necessary. Up to June, 1929, the Court had held seven ordinary and nine extraordinary sessions.[1] This volume of business was far greater than had been anticipated when the Statute was framed in 1920 and it was probably for this reason that no requirement was laid down regarding the residence of the judges near the seat of the Court. In view of the experience of the Court, it seemed to the committee that this situation should be altered.[2] It was realized, however, that judges from non-European countries might be placed under a disadvantage if required to reside near The Hague and special provisions were made for such persons.[3]

The committee's final conclusion, after much discussion of detail, was that the Court should remain constantly in session except for judicial vacations and that the members of the bench should be continuously at the disposal of the Court. These provisions are all included in the suggested redraft of Art. 23 of the Statute, which is as follows:[4]

> The Court shall remain permanently in session except during the judicial vacations, the dates and duration of which shall be fixed by the Court at the end of each year for the following year.
>
> Members of the Court whose homes are situated at more than five days' normal journey from The Hague shall be entitled, apart from the judicial vacations, to six months' leave every three years.
>
> Members of the Court shall be bound, unless they are on regular leave or prevented from attending by illness or other serious reason duly explained to the President, to hold themselves permanently at the disposal of the Court.

[1] See *Fifth Annual Report of the Court*, Series E, No. 5, p. 167.

[2] Committee Report, *infra*, p. 110 [750]; *Minutes*, p. 28 *ff.* and 34–36.

[3] M. Urrutia, of Colombia, especially called attention to this situation; *Minutes*, p. 29–36.

[4] Committee Report, *infra*, p. 111 [751]. The conference made the following changes in the above text: At the end of the first paragraph the words "at the end of each year for the following year" are omitted. At the end of the second paragraph the following words are added: "not including the time spent in traveling." See *Report of First Committee, 1929*, p. 2; *infra*, p. 110 [750].

Functions and Occupations Incompatible with Membership of the Court

At the present time, under Arts. 16 and 17 of the Statute, the judges are permitted to carry on private occupations so long as they do not violate the express prohibitions against exercising political and administrative functions or taking part in international cases as agent, counsel or advocate. Not only were there certain fundamental objections to this activity of the judges, but it would evidently be impossible under the proposed new arrangement whereby the Court would be practically in continuous session.

Although the committee members were in agreement that some further restrictions on the outside activities of the judges were necessary, there were long debates as to the framing of an appropriate text. M. Fromageot proposed excluding them from any activity except that of serving as a judge of the Permanent Court of Arbitration.[1] Mr. Root opposed this suggestion on the ground that it was too broad. He felt that the caliber of man needed on the Court was one who would resent these restrictions on his liberty which would make him feel that he was "returning to a state of tutelage resembling that of a schoolboy."[2] Having already required the judges to be constantly available for the work of the Court, something, in Mr. Root's opinion, might be left to their own good judgment and conscience.

M. Fromageot agreed that perhaps his draft had been too broadly phrased, but felt that the occupation of barrister before national tribunals, for example, was incompatible with the function of a judge on the Permanent Court of International Justice. He also felt that a judge should not continue to act as a university professor, since in his lectures he would become known as favoring certain views and doc-

[1] *Minutes*, p. 42.

[2] *Ibid.*, p. 43.

trines which would consequently incline him to judge certain cases in a particular way.[1] As the result of further discussion, the phrase ultimately adopted for insertion in Art. 16 provides that a judge shall not "engage in any other occupation of a professional nature." [2]

Manner of Forming the Court

Another problem developing from those already discussed was that of the size of the Court. Sir Cecil Hurst suggested an amendment which would provide that so long as the number of judges was not reduced below eleven, the Court, by its rules, could provide that one or more judges should be from time to time relieved from sitting.[3] Mr. Root supported this idea, urging that fifteen was too large a number to have on the bench at one time. He suggested the adoption of a scheme of rotation based on the plan in force for the courts of New York State for over 30 years.[4] This system enabled a judge, while not sitting on one case, to be at work upon a case which he had previously heard. The result would be an economy of time and effort and a remedy for the disadvantage attendant upon having too large a bench. Although it was noted that some difficulty might be experienced in applying this system to an international court,[5] the suggestion was finally adopted in the following new redaction of Art. 25: [6]

[1] In response to a question from the president, M. Fromageot stated that a man should not be excluded from the bench because he had written a book on international law, *ibid.*, p. 43; see also further discussion, p. 44–45.

[2] Committee Report, *infra*, p. 108 [748]; which see for comments and slight drafting changes in Art. 17. The conference adopted and the Assembly approved the phrase proposed by the Committee of Jurists on the understanding that it was "to be interpreted in the widest sense, *i.e.*, cover, for example, such an activity as being director of a company." The conference also slightly altered the new phrasing of Art. 17. See *Report of First Committee, 1929*, p. 2; *infra*, p. 87 [727].

[3] *Minutes*, p. 70, 74.

[4] *Ibid.*, p. 74.

[5] *Ibid.*, p. 74. See also statement in the Report that the committee of course intended that the application of this provision should never be such as to give grounds for suspicion that the Court has been specially composed in a given case for the purpose of affecting the decision of that case.

[6] Committee Report, *infra*, *p.* 111 [751]. The article was approved without change; *Report of First Committee, 1929*, p. 2; *infra*, p. 89 [729].

The full Court shall sit except when it is expressly provided otherwise.

Subject to the condition that the number of judges available to constitute the Court is not thereby reduced below eleven, the Rules of Court may provide for allowing one or more judges, according to circumstances and in rotation, to be dispensed from sitting.

Provided always that a quorum of nine judges shall suffice to constitute the Court.

Resignation of a Judge

Quite a separate problem was the question of the resignation of a judge. The Statute at present contains no provision on the subject and when Judge Moore resigned he submitted his resignation through the Secretary-General to the Council and Assembly, but it was difficult to say whether a vacancy could be considered to have occurred before acceptance of the resignation by those bodies. It was considered desirable to remedy the omission by supplying a regular procedure.[1] The procedure adopted is for the judge to address his resignation to the President of the Court for transmission to the Secretary-General, the notification thus effected making the place vacant.[2]

Filling of Occasional Vacancies

A somewhat similar problem was that of filling occasional vacancies caused by death or resignation. Art. 14 of the Statute provides that such vacancies shall be filled in the same manner as provided for regular elections. But such elections are by the Assembly and Council and the former body meets only once a year in September. Since invitations to make nominations must, under Art. 5 of the Statute, be sent out at least three months prior to an election, it is obvious that a vacancy might exist for 15 months.[3] M.

[1] *Minutes*, p. 46.

[2] Committee Report, *infra*, p. 107 [747]; adopted with only a slight verbal change; *Report of First Committee, 1929*, p. 2; *infra*, p. 86 [726].

[3] See the statement of M. Fromageot, *Minutes*, p. 37. M. Fromageot called attention to the fact that Judge Weiss died in September, 1928, and that his place could not be filled till the meeting of the Assembly in September, 1929.

Fromageot suggested that perhaps an extraordinary session of the Assembly might be convened for the purpose of holding an election, but doubted the need for such action unless at least two vacancies occurred.

On this point the committee consulted the Secretary-General of the League, who expressed the opinion that this solution would present little real difficulty. If the Assembly were to act only on this one matter, it would be unnecessary for the states to send special representatives, since they could designate their diplomatic representatives in Bern or some other European capital.[1] The committee accordingly adopted the suggestion in the following form:[2]

> Vacancies which may occur shall be filled by the same method as that laid down for the first election, subject to the following provision: the Secretary-General of the League of Nations shall, within one month of the occurrence of the vacancy, proceed to issue the invitations provided for in Art. 5, and the date of the election shall be fixed by the Council at its next session.

Salaries of Judges

In line with the new provisions calling for more frequent sessions of the Court and more constant attendance of the judges, it was considered appropriate that the compensation of the judges should be increased. It had been found by experience that the arrangement now laid down in Art. 32 of the Statute for a fixed salary plus certain per diem allowances had caused great difficulties of administration and it was therefore proposed to give only a fixed annual salary of 45,000 florins — about $18,000. As before, the President and Vice-President would receive additional grants. The Statute empowers the Assembly to fix the compensation of the members of the Court so that this part of the committee's work takes the form of a suggested draft resolution of the Assembly, in addition to

[1] See the statement of M. Fromageot, *Minutes*, p. 37.

[2] Committee Report, *infra*, p. 107 [747]. The text was adopted as proposed by the committee; *Report of First Committee, 1929*, p. 2; *infra*, p. 86 [726].

the necessary changes in the text of Art. 32 of the Statute.[1] It should be noted that this amendment includes the provision that the remuneration received by the members of the Court "shall be free of all taxation." This being included in the Statute and thus forming part of a treaty would impose on all Signatory States a conventional obligation to grant exemption from such taxation.

National Judges

Under Art. 31 of the Statute, whenever the Court includes on the bench a judge of the nationality of only one of the parties to a case the other party is entitled to appoint one of its nationals to sit as a judge *ad hoc*. The committee felt that it should not interfere with this system, but recommended that it should be extended to the special Chambers of the Court for Labor, Communications and Transit, and Summary Procedure.[2] But with regard to this subject an interesting debate occurred. At the eleventh session, Sir Cecil Hurst raised the question of the status of the British Dominions.[3] He pointed out that the British Empire is a political unit of an exceptional type and called attention to the fact that the Dominions and Great Britain were separate Members of the League. He wished to be assured that all the members of the committee agreed that for the purpose of applying Art. 31 of the Statute, citizens of the Dominions were to be considered as having a nationality separate from that of Great Britain. Thus, if a case came before the Court involving Australia and Japan, under Sir Cecil's interpretation, the presence of an English judge on the bench would not prevent Australia from appointing a national judge *ad hoc*.

[1] See Committee Report, *infra*, p. 115 [755]; see *Minutes*, p. 55 *ff*. The schedule proposed was adopted by the Council and will be budgeted by the Assembly of the League in 1931; see resolution *infra*, note, p. 95 [735].

[2] Committee Report, *infra*, p. 112 *ff*. [752 *ff*.]; see *Minutes*, p. 53; adopted without change; *Report of First Committee, 1929*, p. 2; *infra*, p. 90 [730].

[3] *Minutes*, p. 70.

At this session only two members of the committee expressed any view on this theory. M. Raestad of Norway stated that Sir Cecil Hurst's interpretation seemed to be the logical one.[1] But M. Politis took vigorous exception. He considered it a matter of the highest importance which could not be disposed of by a mere interpretation.[1] Sir Cecil also responded with some force, but there the matter rested,[2] the committee passing on to another matter.

At the fourteenth session Sir Cecil raised the question again.[3] He stated that he had understood from the previous discussion that the committee, with the exception of M. Politis, shared his view, but it appeared that M. Politis believed that all but Sir Cecil and M. Raestad agreed with him. Sir Cecil accordingly made a careful technical argument based on various articles of the Statute and the distinction between "states" and "Members of the League of Nations," both of which may be parties before the Court. He asked that his interpretation be mentioned in the committee's report, but did not propose any amendment to the Statute.

M. Politis replied by saying that the adoption of such an interpretation would certainly prevent small states such as his own (Greece) from accepting the Optional Clause for the compulsory jurisdiction of the Court. He also opposed Sir Cecil's theory on legal grounds and asked that, if the committee inserted that interpretation in its report, it should also insert his formal reservations thereto.

M. Fromageot felt that the adoption of Sir Cecil's theory would open the door to grave abuses, while the acceptance of M. Politis' view would be a grave injustice to the Dominions. He, therefore, proposed a middle way whereby cases would be differentiated into those which concerned the whole Empire and those which concerned one Dominion only. But, in any case, M. Fromageot felt that any such attempt to interpret the Statute in advance of an actual

[1] *Minutes*, p. 71.
[2] *Ibid.*, p. 71–72.
[3] *Ibid.*, p. 84–87.

case arising would be outside the scope of the committee's functions.

M. Raestad then reaffirmed his agreement with Sir Cecil's position and expressed strong disapproval of M. Fromageot's compromise proposal.

M. Ito of Japan stated that the composition and status of the British Empire always perplexed him and that he did not wish to commit himself on the merits of the proposition. He believed, however, that this was not a matter on which the committee could pass judgment.

The only other speaker was M. Gaus of Germany who, while agreeing that the committee should not deal with the question at all, stated that he did not share the view of Sir Cecil Hurst as to the correct interpretation of the Statute.

In view of this divergency of opinion, the Vice-President, who was then in the chair, declared that the discussion should be closed. The only conclusion that one can reach from the discussion is that the matter was raised but not passed on by the committee. The views of the individual legal experts as to the correct interpretation of the Statute in this respect are of course most interesting but can not be taken as foreshadowing an ultimate decision either way. Probably the ultimate solution will not be reached for the time being. In this connection it may be noted that the United States has to a certain extent recognized the separate personality of the Dominions by exchanging ministers with Canada and with the Irish Free State.[1]

Advisory Opinions

One of the recommendations of the Committee of Jurists is of especial interest in connection with the accession of the United States. This recommendation is for the incorporation into the Statute of a new Chap. IV, dealing with advisory opinions. The Statute at present contains no reference to this part of the Court's jurisdiction and the Court has accordingly had to supply the deficiency by

[1] *Minutes*, p. 87.

framing appropriate rules. Many of the provisions of these rules contain matters analogous to those which, with respect to contested cases, are already in the Statute. It was accordingly proposed to transfer bodily into the Statute the appropriate provisions of the existing Rules.[1] The committee was throughout solicitous to avoid infringing upon the prerogatives of the Court in framing the rules of its own procedure, but M. Anzilotti, the President of the Court, on his own behalf and on that of M. Huber, the Vice-President of the Court, stated that they had no objection to the proposal.[2] It was pointed out by M. Huber that one reason for omitting reference to advisory opinions in the original Statute was the absence of any experience as to how this activity of the Court would operate, but this reason did not apply now after eight years of experience.[3] It was also noted that the proposal would be advantageous in connection with the anticipated accession of the United States.

In the discussions of the committee it became apparent that it would be useful to add to the rules which it was proposed to insert in the Statute a general article which would serve as a guide to the Court in exercising its advisory functions. Thus where an opinion was requested regarding an actual dispute, certain articles of the Statute would be applicable which it would not be appropriate to apply when the Court gave an opinion on a noncontentious question.

Thus, omitting matters which it was thought more proper to leave in the regulatory powers of the Court, the committee suggested inserting in the Statute four new articles, the first three of which correspond closely to Arts. 72, 73 and 74 of the Rules of Court, providing in particular for publicity and hearing in connection with advisory opinions. It is scarcely necessary to add that the adoption of this amendment would give complete sat-

[1] The discussion of the matter was opened by M. van Eysinga in the eleventh session; see *ibid.*, p. 66.

[2] *Ibid.*, p. 67.

[3] *Ibid.*, p. 68.

isfaction to the first part of the fifth reservation of the United States.[1]

Other Matters

In addition to what has been noted above, the committee made several other recommendations. With regard to the various special Chambers of the Court — for Labor cases, for Transit and Communications cases and for Summary Procedure — several drafting changes are advocated. For the first two it also made provision for summary procedure and to the Summary Procedure Chamber itself it made applicable the provisions of Art. 31 regarding national judges.[2]

Drafting amendments were also adopted for Arts. 38, 39, 40 and 45.[3] With regard to Art. 35, which provides that the Court may fix the amount of the contribution which should be paid by a state party to a dispute before the Court, but not a Member of the League, the committee thought no amendment necessary, but noted in its report that the third reservation of the United States would make this article inapplicable to that state if it should accede.[4]

[1] See Committee Report, *infra*, p. 119 [759]. In transferring the articles of the Rules into the Statute the Committee of Jurists omitted in the new Arts. 66 and 67 that part of the Rules which requires notice to interested international organizations as well as to interested States. The attention of the conference was called to this omission by the International Labor Office (League Doc. A. 22. 1929. V), which pointed out that with regard to advisory opinions concerning labor questions it seemed highly desirable to continue the present practice of the Court, whereunder notice is given to the International Labor Office. The conference accordingly restored these words in the new text. There is also a slight change in the wording of the new Art. 68 relative to the Court's cross-reference to other articles of the Statute. See *Report of First Committee, 1929*, p. 2; *infra*, p. 101 [741].

[2] *Ibid.*, p. 115 [755].

[3] *Ibid.*, p. 118 [758].

[4] Committee Report, *infra*, p. 117 [757]. This point was considered by the conference in the light of a communication from the Brazilian delegate. Brazil having withdrawn from the League, but having advised the Secretary-General that it desired to contribute to the expenses of the Court, wished to secure an arrangement permitting it to participate in elections. The conference proposed an amendment to Art. 4 providing that, "in the absence of a special agreement" (*e.g.*, such as that proposed with the United States), the Assembly should, on the proposal of the Council, lay down the conditions under which a state not a Member of the League might participate in the elections. As to Art. 35, the conference preferred to put into the text of the article the point suggested by the Committee in its report. It therefore recommended a new sentence in that article, to the effect that the Court's power to fix the contribution of a State not a Member of the League should not apply if such State "is bearing a share of the expenses of the Court." (*Report of First Committee, 1929*, p. 3; *infra*, p. 96 [736].)

Two other matters should be noted which were discussed but rejected by the committee and therefore do not appear in the report.

M. Fromageot proposed that the practice of rendering dissenting opinions should be abolished. In so doing he was merely advocating the continental European system in which the decision always appears merely as the judgment of the Court without any expression of opinions of individual judges, in place of the Anglo-American practice now actually in force in the Court.[1] M. Fromageot thought the continental system would give greater weight to the decisions of the Permanent Court of International Justice.

Sir Cecil Hurst and Mr. Root opposed this suggestion with great vigor, the former stating that "the effect of that proposal would be to destroy the Court." [2] Mr. Root felt that such a change would run counter to the whole modern trend of international affairs, which is moving in the direction of greater publicity. He also felt that in such a Court, no judge would be willing to "rest under an imputation of acquiescing in views which he did not hold" and that their dissenting opinions would thus come out privately. He felt that respect for, and the authority of, the Court "could not be founded on any suppression of the facts." He, too, felt that the suppression of dissenting opinions would be "disastrous." [3] M. Politis, M. Huber and M. Anzilotti, while trained in the continental school, rallied to the view of their English and American colleagues and M. Fromageot withdrew his proposal.

The other point of interest was the suggestion of M. Urrutia that Art. 34 of the Statute should be amended to make clear that the League of Nations as a judicial personality could be a party in a case before the Court.[4] This suggestion, of course, raised interesting questions as to

[1] *Minutes*, p. 50 *ff.*
[2] *Ibid.*, p. 50.
[3] *Ibid.*, p. 51.
[4] *Ibid.*, p. 57.

the nature and status of the League. It was noted that the League might be involved in a dispute with Switzerland as to its buildings or real property or it might be involved in a "public" dispute with a state. Mr. Root pointed out [1] that this was such an important and complex matter that a hasty decision in the limited time available to the committee would hardly seem proper. In view of these considerations and the great variety of views expressed by the members of the committee, it was thought best to leave Art. 34 unchanged in this respect.

There was a further matter on which the committee did not take action, but which gained added attention subsequently. M. Rundstein submitted a memorandum advocating the extension of the jurisdiction of the Court as a court of appeal.[2] Although the memorandum contained detailed proposals, M. Rundstein stated that he did not propose to have it discussed by the committee and he accepted the vice-chairman's suggestion that it be transmitted with the covering letter from the Committee to the Council.[3]

The same idea was adopted in a resolution of the Assembly on a proposal of the Government of Finland.[4] Again there was no suggestion for immediate consideration, but only for examination by the Council. It must be noted that the question involves some political complications, because of the situation now existing regarding the review of decisions of some of the Mixed Arbitral Tribunals of which so many are now set up in Europe.[5]

PROCEDURE ON AMENDING THE STATUTE

Attention has already been drawn to the fact that at its June session the Council decided to convene a con-

[1] *Minutes*, p. 60.

[2] See *Minutes*, Annex 6, p. 105.

[3] *Minutes*, p. 75.

[4] *Journal of the Tenth Assembly*, September 26, 1929, No. 22, p. 390.

[5] See, for example, the Hungarian-Rumanian dispute; see Deák, *The Hungarian-Rumanian Land Dispute* (1928), especially p. 77 *ff*.

ference of the Signatory States to meet in Geneva in September to consider these proposed amendments to the Statute.[1] As regards the United States, it is of interest to note the possible eventualities and the relation of these amendments to American accession.

Two contingencies are possible: in the first place, the various Signatory States may ratify the protocol for American accession before the amendments are ratified. In that case, the United States would itself be one of the contracting parties whose consent would be necessary before the amendments could take effect. In this situation the United States Senate would be called upon to pass on the amendments — which seem to offer no objectionable feature from the American standpoint — but this action would be wholly independent of the question of the accession of the United States to the Court.

In the second place, ratification of the protocol for American accession may not be completed before the amendments to the Statute are ratified by the present Signatory States and thus have come into force. In such a case the treaty to the ratification of which the Senate has given its consent, subject to the five reservations, would no longer be in existence, having been replaced by a new treaty, though, to be sure, the new treaty would be merely a modified form of the old one. The President would then have to submit this new treaty to the Senate, together with the protocol for American accession and ask anew for advice and consent to ratification. Since, however, the amendments would appear to be unobjectionable to the United States, this would not seem to present any new political obstacle.

With a view to avoiding the difficulties inherent in this situation, an ingenious plan was proposed. The conference suggested[2] that three instruments would be presented to the United States for its acceptance, namely: (1) The

[1] The conference met September 4–12, 1929; its activities have been alluded to above.

[2] See letter from the President of the conference to the First Committee of the Assembly, *infra*, p. 127 [767].

Protocol of Signature of 1920; (2) the Protocol regarding American Accession; and (3) the Protocol of Amendments. It was stated that "while it is of course not within the province of the . . . Conference to anticipate what procedure the United States may follow, it may be hoped that the United States will in due course sign and ratify all three above-mentioned instruments."

The form in which the matter is presented is as follows:[1] The amendments are set forth in an annex to a Protocol which declares that the signatories agree to the amendments thus set out. The Protocol is open for signature by the signatories of the original Protocol of Signature of December 16, 1920, and by the United States. The Protocol is to be ratified, but it will enter into force on September 1, 1930, "provided that the Council of the League of Nations has satisfied itself that those Members of the League of Nations and states mentioned in the Annex to the Covenant which have ratified the Protocol of December 16, 1920, and whose ratification of the present Protocol has not been received by that date, have no objection to the coming into force of the amendments to the Statute of the Court which are annexed to the present Protocol." For this purpose the United States "shall be in the same position as a state which has ratified the Protocol of December 16, 1920." This is a generous concession to the American Government, enabling it to have a voice in the adoption of the amendments regardless of any delay which might be incidental to securing general ratification of the Protocol of American Accession. It is further stipulated that "after the entry into force of the present Protocol, the new provisions shall form part of the Statute adopted in 1920 and the provisions of the original articles which have been made the subject of amendment shall be abrogated. It is understood that, until January 1, 1931, the Court shall continue to perform its functions in accordance with the Statute of 1920." "After the entry into force of the present Protocol, any acceptance of the Statute of the

[1] See League Doc. A. 50 (Annex). 1929. V. 16, and *infra*, p. 124 [764].

Court shall constitute an acceptance of the Statute as amended." [1]

This arrangement, contemplating that a treaty may come into force through failure to object, is rather novel and, if successful, may prove a useful precedent for the future. It is inspired by the necessity for quick action. It presents some possible difficulties. The Protocol of Signature of 1920 is a treaty and can be amended only by unanimous consent.[2] If a state whose constitutional system requires parliamentary approval for ratification signs the new Protocol but thereafter remains inactive and silent, can it be said that it has approved the amendments? If not, are the amendments effective? Can the state be bound by the signature of an agent, who under the national law of the state *ex hypothese* is not authorized so to bind the state? In practical effect, however, it is probable that if such a situation should develop, the executive branch of such government would inform the Council that due to the failure to secure timely ratification, it must be considered as objecting to the coming into force of the amendments on the date specified. So far as the Government of the United States is concerned, it would seem unlikely that that Government would care to exercise its privilege of blocking the amendments unless it first ratified the Statute.

The form in which the whole subject will be submitted to the Senate must be a matter of surmise. The simplest procedure would seem to be to follow the suggestion of the conference and to submit all three Protocols to the Senate. On the other hand, the Senate Resolution of January 27, 1926, might be construed as carrying consent to ratification of the Protocol of Signature of December 16, 1920, provided that the Senate gave its consent to the new Protocol of American Accession to fill the requirement of the five reservations. Unless the amendments are defeated

[1] Similarly, under Art. 6 of the Protocol of American Accession, any future signature of the Protocol of 1920 is declared to be an acceptance of the former Protocol as well.

[2] *Cf. supra*, p. 23 [663].

by the opposition of some state or states, consent to ratification of the 1920 Protocol would be illusory. Since any Senate debate on the Court would almost inevitably involve a consideration of the proposed amendments, it would seem likely that the two issues would not be separated in submission to that body.

APPENDIX I

DOCUMENTS CONCERNING THE COURT

STATES WHICH HAVE SIGNED THE PROTOCOL OF THE PERMANENT COURT OF INTERNATIONAL JUSTICE

(As of October 1, 1929)

States Signatory	Date of Ratification	States Signatory	Date of Ratification
Abyssinia	July 16, 1926	Irish Free State	Aug. 21, 1926[3]
Albania	July 13, 1921	Italy	June 20, 1921
Australia	Aug. 4, 1921	Japan	Nov. 16, 1921
Austria	July 23, 1921	Latvia	Feb. 12, 1924
Belgium	Aug. 29, 1921	Liberia	
Bolivia		Lithuania	May 16, 1922
Brazil	Nov. 1, 1921	Luxemburg	
Bulgaria	Aug. 12, 1921	Netherlands	Aug. 6, 1921
Canada	Aug. 4, 1921	New Zealand	Aug. 4, 1921
Chile	July 20, 1928	Nicaragua	
China	May 13, 1922	Norway	Aug. 20, 1921
Colombia		Panama	June 14, 1929
Costa Rica		Paraguay	
Cuba	Jan. 12, 1922	Persia	
Czechoslovakia	Sept. 2, 1921	Peru	
Denmark	June 13, 1921	Poland	Aug. 26, 1921
Dominican Republic[1]		Portugal	Oct. 8, 1921
		Rumania	Aug. 8, 1921
Estonia	May 2, 1923	Salvador	
Finland	April 6, 1922	Serb-Croat-Slovene State	Aug. 12, 1921
France	Aug. 7, 1921		
Germany	March 11, 1927	Siam	Feb. 27, 1922
Great Britain	Aug. 4, 1921	South Africa	Aug. 4, 1921
Greece	Oct. 3, 1921	Spain	Aug. 30, 1921
Guatemala[2]		Sweden	Feb. 21, 1921
Haiti	Sept. 7, 1921	Switzerland	July 25, 1921
Hungary	Nov. 20, 1925	Uruguay	Sept. 27, 1921
India	Aug. 4, 1921	Venezuela	Dec. 2, 1921

Total — 54

[1] National Congress approved the signature December, 1926.

[2] Signed at Geneva, December 17, 1926.

[3] Letter notifying "that the Irish Free State is to be included among those Members of the League of Nations which have ratified."

OTHER STATES TO WHICH THE COURT IS OPEN

AFGHANISTAN [1]
ARGENTINE REPUBLIC [2]
DANZIG [1]
ECUADOR [2]
EGYPT [1]
HONDURAS [2]
ICELAND [1]
LIECHTENSTEIN [1]
MEXICO [1]
MONACO [1]
SAN MARINO [1]
SOVIET UNION [1]
TURKEY [1]
UNITED STATES [2]

Total — 14

[1] Notified by the Court of the resolution of the Council of the League of Nations of May 17, 1922. It should be noted that the state to which the Court is opened must "undertake to carry out in full good faith the decision or decisions of the Court and not to resort to war against a state complying therewith" (Resolution, par. 1).

[2] Open by reason of membership in the League of Nations or mention in the Annex to the Covenant.

PERMANENT COURT OF INTERNATIONAL JUSTICE

PROTOCOL OF SIGNATURE [1]

The Members of the League of Nations, through the undersigned, duly authorized, declare their acceptance of the adjoined Statute of the Permanent Court of International Justice, which was approved by a unanimous vote of the Assembly of the League on the 13th December, 1920, at Geneva.

Consequently, they hereby declare that they accept the jurisdiction of the Court in accordance with the terms and subject to the conditions of the above-mentioned Statute.

The present Protocol, which has been drawn up in accordance with the decision taken by the Assembly of the League of Nations on the 13th December, 1920, is subject to ratification. Each Power shall send its ratification to the Secretary-General of the League of Nations; the latter shall take the necessary steps to notify such ratification to the other signatory Powers. The ratification shall be deposited in the archives of the Secretariat of the League of Nations.

The said Protocol shall remain open for signature by the Members of the League of Nations and by the States mentioned in the Annex to the Covenant of the League.

The Statute of the Court shall come into force as provided in the above-mentioned decision.

Executed at Geneva, in a single copy, the French and English texts of which shall both be authentic.

December 16, 1920.

[Here follow signatures of 52 Members of the League of Nations.]

[1] League of Nations, *Treaty Series*, VI, p. 380; XI, p. 404; XV, p. 304; XXIV, p. 152; XXVII, p. 416; XXXIX, p. 165; XLV, p. 96; L, p. 159; LIV, p. 387; LXIX, p. 70; LXXII, p. 452; LXXVIII, p. 435.

OPTIONAL CLAUSE

The undersigned, being duly authorized thereto, further declare, on behalf of their Government, that, from this date, they accept as compulsory, *ipso facto* and without special Convention, the jurisdiction of the Court in conformity with article 36, paragraph 2, of the Statute of the Court, under the following conditions:

[The declarations made by Signatory States are not here reprinted. They may be found in Hudson, *op. cit.*, p. 104, as compiled from *Treaty Series* volumes cited in note 1, p. 81 [721], *supra*.]

STATES WHICH HAVE SIGNED THE OPTIONAL CLAUSE

(AS OF OCTOBER 1, 1929)

(Asterisk (*) indicates states bound by the clause)

States Signatory	Date of Ratification [1]	States Signatory	Date of Ratification [1]
AUSTRALIA		INDIA	
* AUSTRIA	Mar. 13, 1927	IRISH FREE STATE	
* BELGIUM	Mar. 10, 1926	ITALY	
BRAZIL	– –[2]	LATVIA	
BRITISH EMPIRE		LIBERIA	
* BULGARIA	Aug. 12, 1921	*[LITHUANIA[3]	– –[2]]
CANADA		LUXEMBURG	
*[CHINA[3]	– –[2]]	* NETHERLANDS	– –[2]
COSTA RICA[4]	– –[2]	NEW ZEALAND	
CZECHOSLOVAKIA		NICARAGUA[4]	
* DENMARK	Mar. 28, 1926	* NORWAY	Oct. 3, 1921
DOMINICAN REPUBLIC		* PANAMA	June 14, 1929
		PERU	
* ESTONIA	– –[2]	* PORTUGAL	Oct. 8, 1921
* ETHIOPIA	July 16, 1926	SALVADOR[4]	– –[2]
* FINLAND	April 6, 1922	SIAM	
FRANCE		SOUTH AFRICA	
* GERMANY	Feb. 29, 1928	* SPAIN	– –[2]
* GREECE	Sept. 12, 1929	* SWEDEN	– –[2]
GUATEMALA		* SWITZERLAND	July 24, 1926
* HAITI	– –[2]	* URUGUAY	Sept. 27, 1921
* HUNGARY	Aug. 13, 1929		

Total — 42

[1] Ratification of the Optional Clause is not required by the document itself.

[2] Ratification not specified and not actually deposited.

[3] Five-year period specified has expired.

[4] Without condition as to ratification, but has not ratified the protocol of signature of the Statute.

STATUTE FOR THE PERMANENT COURT OF INTERNATIONAL JUSTICE, SHOWING AMENDMENTS PROVIDED FOR BY THE PROTOCOL OF SEPTEMBER 14, 1929[1]

Art. 1. A Permanent Court of International Justice is hereby established, in accordance with Article 14 of the Covenant of the League of Nations. This Court shall be in addition to the Court of Arbitration organized by the Conventions of The Hague of 1899 and 1907, and to the special Tribunals of Arbitration to which States are always at liberty to submit their disputes for settlement.

CHAPTER I

Organization of the Court

Art. 2. The Permanent Court of International Justice shall be composed of a body of independent judges, elected regardless of their nationality from among persons of high moral character, who possess the qualifications required in their respective countries for appointment to the highest judicial offices, or are jurisconsults of recognized competence in international law.

	Amendment
Art. 3. The Court shall consist of fifteen members: eleven judges and four deputy-judges. The number of judges and deputy-judges may hereafter be increased by the Assembly, upon the proposal of the Council of the League of Nations, to a total of fifteen judges and six deputy-judges.	**Art. 3.** The Court shall consist of fifteen members.

Art. 4. The members of the Court shall be elected by the Assembly and by the Council from a list of persons nominated by the national groups in the Court of Arbitration, in accordance with the following provisions.

[1] The Statute of December 16, 1920, is printed to embody the amendments called for by the annex to the protocol of September 14, 1929, which is printed in League of Nations Document A. 50. 1929. V. 16. These amendments will not in any case come into force before September 1, 1930.

In the case of Members of the League of Nations not represented in the Permanent Court of Arbitration, the list of candidates shall be drawn up by national groups appointed for this purpose by their Governments under the same conditions as those prescribed for members of the Permanent Court of Arbitration by Article 44 of the Convention of The Hague of 1907 for the pacific settlement of international disputes.[1]

Amendment

The conditions under which a state which has accepted the Statute of the Court but is not a member of the League of Nations, may participate in electing the members of the Court shall, in the absence of a special agreement, be laid down by the Assembly on the proposal of the Council.

Art. 5. At least three months before the date of the election, he Secretary-General of the League of Nations shall address a written request to the Members of the Court of Arbitration belonging to the states mentioned in the Annex to the Covenant or to the states which join the League subsequently, and to the persons appointed under paragraph 2 of Article 4, inviting them to undertake, within a given time, by national groups, the nomination of persons in a position to accept the duties of a member of the Court.

No group may nominate more than four persons, not more than two of whom shall be of their own nationality. In no case must the

[1] Article 44 of the convention of The Hague of 1907 for the pacific settlement of international disputes reads as follows:

"Each contracting power selects four persons at the most, of known competency in questions of international law, of the highest moral reputation, and disposed to accept the duties of arbitrator.

"The persons thus selected are inscribed, as members of the Court, in a list which shall be notified to all the contracting powers by the Bureau.

"Any alteration in the list of arbitrators is brought by the Bureau to the knowledge of the contracting powers.

"Two or more powers may agree on the selection in common of one or more members.

"The same person can be selected by different powers.

"The members of the Court are appointed for a term of six years. These appointments are renewable.

"Should a member of the Court die or resign, the same procedure is followed for filling the vacancy as was followed for appointing him. In this case the appointment is made for a fresh period of six years."

number of candidates nominated be more than double the number of seats to be filled.

Art. 6. Before making these nominations, each national group is recommended to consult its Highest Court of Justice, its Legal Faculties and Schools of Law, and its National Academies and national sections of International Academies devoted to the study of Law.

Art. 7. The Secretary-General of the League of Nations shall prepare a list in alphabetical order of all the persons thus nominated. Save as provided in Article 12, paragraph 2, these shall be the only persons eligible for appointment.

The Secretary-General shall submit this list to the Assembly and to the Council.

	Amendment
Art. 8. The Assembly and the Council shall proceed independently of one another to elect, firstly the judges, then the deputy-judges.	**Art. 8.** The Assembly and the Council shall proceed independently of one another to elect the members of the Court.

Art. 9. At every election, the electors shall bear in mind that not only should all the persons appointed as members of the Court possess the qualifications required, but the whole body also should represent the main forms of civilization and the principal legal systems of the world.

Art. 10. Those candidates who obtain an absolute majority of votes in the Assembly and in the Council shall be considered as elected.

In the event of more than one national of the same Member of the League being elected by the votes of both the Assembly and the Council, the eldest of these only shall be considered as elected.

Art. 11. If, after the first meeting held for the purpose of the election, one or more seats remain to be filled, a second and, if necessary, a third meeting shall take place.

Art. 12. If, after the third meeting, one or more seats still remain unfilled, a joint conference consisting of six members, three appointed by the Assembly and three by the Council, may be formed, at any time, at the request of either the Assembly or the Council, for the purpose of choosing one name for each seat still vacant, to submit to the Assembly and the Council for their respective acceptance.

If the Conference is unanimously agreed upon any person who fulfils the required conditions, he may be included in its list, even though he was not included in the list of nominations referred to in Articles 4 and 5.

If the joint conference is satisfied that it will not be successful in procuring an election, those members of the Court who have already been appointed shall, within a period to be fixed by the Council, proceed to fill the vacant seats by selection from among those candidates who have obtained votes either in the Assembly or in the Council.

In the event of an equality of votes among the judges, the eldest judge shall have a casting vote.

Art. 13. The members of the Court shall be elected for nine years.

They may be re-elected.

They shall continue to discharge their duties until their places have been filled. Though replaced, they shall finish any cases which they may have begun.

Amendment

Art. 13. The members of the Court shall be elected for nine years.

They may be re-elected.

They shall continue to discharge their duties until their places have been filled. Though replaced, they shall finish any cases which they may have begun.

In the case of the resignation of a member of the Court, the resignation will be addressed to the President of the Court for transmission to the Secretary-General of the League of Nations.

This last[1] notification makes the place vacant.

Art. 14. Vacancies which may occur shall be filled by the same method as that laid down for the first election. A member of the Court elected to replace a member whose period of ap-

Amendment

Art. 14. Vacancies which may occur shall be filled by the same method as that laid down for the first election, subject to the following provision: the Secretary-General of the League

[1] The word "last" was included in text adopted by the Assembly, as recommended by the conference of September 4-12, 1929.

pointment had not expired will hold the appointment for the remainder of his predecessor's term.

of Nations shall, within one month of the occurrence of the vacancy, proceed to issue the invitations provided for in Article 5, and the date of the election shall be fixed by the Council at its next session.

Art. 15. Deputy-judges shall be called upon to sit in the order laid down in a list.

This list shall be prepared by the Court and shall have regard firstly to priority of election and secondly to age.

Amendment

Art. 15. A member of the Court elected to replace a member whose period of appointment has not expired, will hold the appointment for the remainder of his predecessor's term.

Art. 16. The ordinary members of the Court may not exercise any political or administrative function. This provision does not apply to the deputy-judges except when performing their duties on the Court.

Any doubt on this point is settled by the decision of the Court.

Amendment

Art. 16. The members of the Court may not exercise any political or administrative function, nor engage in any other occupation of a professional nature.[1]

Any doubt on this point is settled by the decision of the Court.

Art. 17. No member of the Court can act as agent, counsel or advocate in any case of an international nature. This provision only applies to the deputy-judges as regards cases in which they are called upon to exercise their functions on the Court.

Amendment

Art. 17. No member of the Court may act as agent, counsel or advocate in any case.[2]

No member may participate in the decision of any case in which he has previously taken an active part as agent, counsel or advocate for one of the contesting parties, or as a member

[1] The words "occupation of a professional nature" are, according to the conclusion of the conference of September 4–12, 1929, "to be interpreted in the widest sense, *i.e.*, cover, for example, such an activity as being director of a company."

[2] The Committee of Jurists had specified "case of an international nature."

No member may participate in the decision of any case in which he has previously taken an active part, as agent, counsel or advocate for one of the contesting parties, or as a member of a national or international court, or of a commission of inquiry, or in any other capacity.

Any doubt on this point is settled by the decision of the Court.

of a national or international Court, or of a commission of inquiry, or in any other capacity.

Any doubt on this point is settled by the decision of the Court.

Art. 18. A member of the Court can not be dismissed unless, in the unanimous opinion of the other members, he has ceased to fulfil the required conditions.

Formal notification thereof shall be made to the Secretary-General of the League of Nations, by the Registrar.

This notification makes the place vacant.

Art. 19. The members of the Court, when engaged on the business of the Court, shall enjoy diplomatic privileges and immunities.

Art. 20. Every member of the Court shall, before taking up his duties, make a solemn declaration in open Court that he will exercise his powers impartially and conscientiously.

Art. 21. The Court shall elect its President and Vice-President for three years; they may be re-elected.

It shall appoint its Registrar.

The duties of Registrar of the Court shall not be deemed incompatible with those of Secretary-General of the Permanent Court of Arbitration.

Art. 22. The seat of the Court shall be established at The Hague.

The President and Registrar shall reside at the seat of the Court.

Art. 23. A session of the Court shall be held every year.

Unless otherwise provided by Rules of Court, this session shall begin on the 15th of June, and shall continue for so long as

Amendment

Art. 23. The Court shall remain permanently in session except during the judicial vacations, the dates and duration of which shall be fixed by the Court.

may be deemed necessary to finish the cases on the list.

The President may summon an extraordinary session of the Court whenever necessary.

Members of the Court whose homes are situated at more than five days' normal journey from The Hague shall be entitled, apart from the judicial vacations, to six months' leave every three years, not including the time spent in traveling.

Members of the Court shall be bound, unless they are on regular leave or prevented from attending by illness or other serious reason duly explained to the President, to hold themselves permanently at the disposal of the Court.

Art. 24. If, for some special reason, a member of the Court considers that he should not take part in the decision of a particular case, he shall so inform the President.

If the President considers that for some special reason one of the members of the Court should not sit on a particular case, he shall give him notice accordingly.

If in any such case the member of the Court and the President disagree, the matter shall be settled by the decision of the Court.

Art. 25. The full Court shall sit except when it is expressly provided otherwise.

If eleven judges can not be present, the number shall be made up by calling on deputy-judges to sit.

If, however, eleven judges are not available, a quorum of nine judges shall suffice to constitute the Court.

Amendment

Art. 25. The full Court shall sit except when it is expressly provided otherwise.

Subject to the condition that the number of judges available to constitute the Court is not thereby reduced below eleven, the Rules of Court may provide for allowing one or more judges, according to circumstances and in rotation, to be dispensed from sitting.

Provided always that a quorum of nine judges shall suffice to constitute the Court.

Art. 26. Labor cases, particularly cases referred to in Part XIII (Labor) of the treaty of Versailles and the corresponding portions of the other Treaties of Peace, shall be heard and determined by the Court under the following conditions:

The Court will appoint every three years a special chamber of five judges, selected so far as possible with due regard to the provisions of Article 9. In addition, two judges shall be selected for the purpose of replacing a judge who finds it impossible to sit. If the parties so demand, cases will be heard and determined by this chamber. In the absence of any such demand, the Court will sit with the number of judges provided for in Article 25. On all occasions the judges will be assisted by four technical assessors sitting with them, but without the right to vote, and chosen with a view to insuring a just representation of the competing interests.

If there is a national of one only of the parties sitting as a judge in the chamber referred to in the preceding paragraph, the President will invite one of the other judges to retire in favor of a judge chosen by the other party in accordance with Article 31.

The technical assessors shall be chosen for each particular

Amendment

Art. 26. Labor cases, particularly cases referred to in Part XIII (Labor) of the treaty of Versailles and the corresponding portions of the other Treaties of Peace, shall be heard and determined by the Court under the following conditions:

The Court will appoint every three years a special chamber of five judges, selected so far as possible with due regard to the provisions of Article 9. In addition, two judges shall be selected for the purpose of replacing a judge who finds it impossible to sit. If the parties so demand, cases will be heard and determined by this chamber. In the absence of any such demand, the full Court will sit. In both cases, the judges will be assisted by four technical assessors sitting with them, but without the right to vote, and chosen with a view to insuring a just representation of the competing interests.

The technical assessors shall be chosen for each particular case in accordance with rules of procedure under Article 30 from a list of "Assessors for Labor cases" composed of two persons nominated by each Member of the League of Nations and an equivalent number nominated by the Governing Body of the Labor Office. The Governing Body will nominate, as to one-case in accordance with rules of procedure under Article 30 from a list of "Assessors for Labor cases" composed of two persons nominated by each Member of the League of Nations and an equivalent number nominated by the Governing Body of the Labor Office. The Governing Body will nominate, as to one-half, representatives of the workers, and as to one-half, representatives of employers from the list referred to in Article 412 of the treaty of Versailles and the corresponding Articles of the other Treaties of Peace.

In Labor cases the International Labor Office shall be at liberty to furnish the Court with all relevant information, and for this purpose the Director of that Office shall receive copies of all the written proceedings.

half, representatives of the workers, and as to one-half, representatives of employers from the list referred to in Article 412 of the treaty of Versailles and the corresponding articles of the other Treaties of Peace.

Recourse may always be had to the summary procedure provided for in Article 29, in the cases referred to in the first paragraph of the present article, if the parties so request.

In Labor cases the International Office shall be at liberty to furnish the Court with all relevant information, and for this purpose the Director of that Office shall receive copies of all the written proceedings.

Art. 27. Cases relating to transit and communications, particularly cases referred to in Part XII (Ports, Waterways and Railways) of the treaty of Versailles and the corresponding portions of the other Treaties of Peace, shall be heard and determined by the Court under the following conditions:

The Court will appoint every three years a special chamber of five judges, selected so far as possible with due regard to the

Amendment

Art. 27. Cases relating to transit and communications, particularly cases referred to in Part XII (Ports, Waterways and Railways) of the treaty of Versailles and the corresponding portions of the other Treaties of Peace, shall be heard and determined by the Court under the following conditions:

The Court will appoint every three years a special chamber of five judges, selected so far as possible with due regard to the provisions of Article 9. In addition, two judges shall be selected for the purpose of replacing a judge who finds it impossible to sit. If the parties so demand, cases will be heard and determined by this chamber. In the absence of any such demand, the Court will sit with the number of judges provided for in Article 25. When desired by the parties or decided by the Court, the judges will be assisted by four technical assessors sitting with them, but without the right to vote.

If there is a national of one only of the parties sitting as a judge in the chamber referred to in the preceding paragraph, the President will invite one of the other judges to retire in favor of a judge chosen by the other party in accordance with Article 31.

The technical assessors shall be chosen for each particular case in accordance with rules of procedure under Article 30 from a list of "Assessors for Transit and Communications cases" composed of two persons nominated by each Member of the League of Nations.

provisions of Article 9. In addition, two judges shall be selected for the purpose of replacing a judge who finds it impossible to sit. If the parties so demand, cases will be heard and determined by this chamber. In the absence of any such demand, the full Court will sit. When desired by the parties or decided by the Court, the judges will be assisted by four technical assessors sitting with them, but without the right to vote.

The technical assessors shall be chosen for each particular case in accordance with rules of procedure under Article 30 from a list of "Assessors for Transit and Communication Cases" composed of two persons nominated by each Member of the League of Nations.

Recourse may always be had to the summary procedure provided for in Article 29, in the cases referred to in the first paragraph of the present article, if the parties so request.

Art. 28. The special chambers provided for in Articles 26 and 27 may, with the consent of the parties to the dispute, sit elsewhere than at The Hague.

Art. 29. With a view to the speedy dispatch of business, the Court shall form annually a chamber composed of three judges who, at the request of the contesting parties, may hear and determine cases by summary procedure.

Amendment

Art. 29. With a view to the speedy dispatch of business, the Court shall form annually a chamber composed of five judges who, at the request of the contesting parties, may hear and determine cases by summary procedure. In addition, two judges shall be selected for the purpose of replacing a judge who finds it impossible to sit.

Art. 30. The Court shall frame rules for regulating its procedure. In particular, it shall lay down rules for summary procedure.

Art. 31. Judges of the nationality of each contesting party shall retain their right to sit in the case before the Court.

If the Court includes upon the Bench a judge of the nationality of one of the parties only, the other party may select from among the deputy-judges a judge of its nationality, if there be one. If there should not be one, the party may choose a judge, preferably from among those persons who have been nominated as candidates as provided in Articles 4 and 5.

If the Court includes upon the Bench no judge of the nationality of the contesting parties, each of these may proceed to select or choose a judge as provided in the preceding paragraph.

Amendment

Art. 31. Judges of the nationality of each of the contesting parties shall retain their right to sit in the case before the Court.

If the Court includes upon the Bench a judge of the nationality of one of the parties, the other party may choose a person to sit as judge. Such person shall be chosen preferably from among those persons who have been nominated as candidates as provided in Articles 4 and 5.

If the Court includes upon the Bench no judge of the nationality of the contesting parties, each of these parties may proceed to select a judge as provided in the preceding paragraph.

The present provision shall

Should there be several parties in the same interest, they shall, for the purpose of the preceding provisions, be reckoned as one party only. Any doubt upon this point is settled by the decision of the Court.

Judges selected or chosen as laid down in paragraphs 2 and 3 of this Article shall fulfil the conditions required by Articles 2, 16, 17, 20, 24 of this Statute. They shall take part in the decision on an equal footing with their colleagues.

apply to the case of Articles 26, 27 and 29. In such cases the President shall request one or, if necessary, two of the members of the Court forming the chamber to give place to the members of the Court of the nationality of the parties concerned, and, failing such or if they are unable to be present, to the judges specially appointed by the parties.

Should there be several parties in the same interest, they shall, for the purpose of the preceding provisions, be reckoned as one party only. Any doubt upon this point is settled by the decision of the Court.

Judges selected as laid down in paragraphs 2, 3 and 4 of this article shall fulfil the conditions required by Articles 2, 17 (paragraph 2), 20 and 24 of this Statute. They shall take part in the decision on terms of complete equality with their colleagues.

Art. 32. The judges shall receive an annual indemnity to be determined by the Assembly of the League of Nations upon the proposal of the Council. This indemnity must not be decreased during the period of a judge's appointment.

The President shall receive a special grant for his period of office, to be fixed in the same way.

Amendment

Art. 32. The members of the Court shall receive an annual salary.

The President shall receive a special annual allowance.

The Vice-President shall receive a special allowance for every day on which he acts as President.

The judges appointed under Article 31, other than members of the Court, shall receive an

The Vice-President, judges and deputy-judges shall receive a grant for the actual performance of their duties, to be fixed in the same way.

Traveling expenses incurred in the performance of their duties shall be refunded to judges and deputy-judges who do not reside at the seat of the Court.

Grants due to judges selected or chosen as provided in Article 31 shall be determined in the same way.

The salary of the Registrar shall be decided by the Council upon the proposal of the Court.

The Assembly of the League of Nations shall lay down, on the proposal of the Council, a indemnity for each day on which they sit.

These salaries, allowances and indemnities shall be fixed by the Assembly of the League of Nations on the proposal of the Council.[1] They may not be decreased during the term of office.

The salary of the Registrar shall be fixed by the Assembly on the proposal of the Court.

Regulations made by the Assembly shall fix the conditions under which retiring pensions may be given to members of the Court and to the Registrar,[2] and the conditions under which members of the Court and the Registrar shall have their traveling expenses refunded.

[1] On September 13, 1929, the Council of the League of Nations adopted the following resolution, the substance of which had been proposed in the report of the Committee of Jurists:

"With reference to Art. 32 of the Court's Statute, the Council agrees with the suggestions of the Supervisory Commission and proposes that, subject to the entry into force of the amendments proposed in the Court's Statute, the Assembly should fix the salaries of the members of the Court from January 1, 1931, as follows:

		Dutch florins
"*President:*	Annual salary	45,000
	Special allowance	15,000
"*Vice-President:*	Annual salary	45,000
	Allowance of 100 florins for each day on which he acts as President, up to a maximum of	10,000
"*Members:*	Annual salary	45,000
"*Judges referred to in Art. 31 of the Statute:*	Allowance of 100 florins for each day of duty, plus a daily subsistence allowance of 50 florins."	

Appropriate Assembly action will take place in connection with the adoption of the budget for the financial year 1931.

[2] The Assembly of the League of Nations on September 14, 1929, adopted a report approving regulations for the repayment of traveling expenses to the members and to the registrar of the Court as recommended by the Supervisory Commission.

The report recorded that Art. 32 of the Statute as then in force provided that the regulation concerning retiring pensions of judges was to be fixed by the Assembly on the proposal of the Council. The article as amended provides for the determination of the regulations by the Assembly. In 1929, as the Council had not submitted special regulation fixing the conditions under which retiring pensions may be given to the personnel of the Court.

The above salaries, indemnities and allowances shall be free of all taxation.

Art. 33. The expenses of the Court shall be borne by the League of Nations, in such a manner as shall be decided by the Assembly upon the proposal of the Council.

CHAPTER II

Competence of the Court

Art. 34. Only States or Members of the League of Nations can be parties in cases before the Court.

Art. 35. The Court shall be open to the Members of the League and also to states mentioned in the Annex to the Covenant.

The conditions under which the Court shall be open to other states shall, subject to the special provisions contained in treaties in force, be laid down by the Council, but in no case shall such provisions place the parties in a position of inequality before the Court.

When a state which is not a Member of the League of Nations is a party to a dispute, the Court will fix the amount which that party is to contribute toward the expenses of the Court. This provision shall not apply if such state is bearing a share of the expenses of the Court.

Art. 36. The jurisdiction of the Court comprises all cases which the parties refer to it and all matters specially provided for in treaties and conventions in force.

The Members of the League of Nations and the states mentioned in the Annex to the Covenant may, either when signing or ratifying

a proposal, the Assembly did not act upon a revision of the regulations regarding retiring pensions proposed by the Committee of Jurists and reading as follows:

"The payment of a pension shall not begin until the person entitled to such pension has reached the age of 65. Should, however, the person entitled to a pension, before attaining that age, reach the end of his term of office without being re-elected, his pension may, by a decision of the Court, be made payable to him, in whole or part, as from the date on which his functions cease."

However, the Supervisory Commission in its session of June 21–25, 1929, proposed the following text:

"The payment of a pension shall not begin until the person entitled to such pension has reached the age of 65. In certain exceptional cases, however, the pension may, by a decision of the Court, be made payable in whole or in part to persons entitled thereto who have not reached that age."

the Protocol to which the present Statute is adjoined, or at a later moment, declare that they recognize as compulsory *ipso facto* and without special agreement, in relation to any other Member or State accepting the same obligation, the jurisdiction of the Court in all or any of the classes of legal disputes concerning:

(*a*) The interpretation of a Treaty;
(*b*) Any question of International Law;
(*c*) The existence of any fact which, if established, would constitute a breach of an international obligation;
(*d*) The nature or extent of the reparation to be made for the breach of an international obligation.

The declaration referred to above may be made unconditionally or on condition of reciprocity on the part of several or certain Members or States, or for a certain time.

In the event of a dispute as to whether the Court has jurisdiction, the matter shall be settled by the decision of the Court.

Art. 37. When a treaty or convention in force provides for the reference of a matter to a tribunal to be instituted by the League of Nations, the Court will be such tribunal.

Art. 38. The Court shall apply:

(1) International conventions, whether general or particular, establishing rules expressly recognized by the contesting States;
(2) International custom, as evidence of a general practice accepted as law;
(3) The general principles of law recognized by civilized nations;
(4) Subject to the provisions of Article 59, judicial decisions and the teachings of the most highly qualified publicists of the various nations, as subsidiary means for the determination of rules of law.[1]

This provision shall not prejudice the power of the Court to decide a case *ex aequo et bono*, if the parties agree thereto.

Chapter III

Procedure

Art. 39. The official languages of the Court shall be French and English. If the parties agree that the case shall be conducted in French, the judgment will be delivered in French. If the

[1] **A proposed amendment affects the French text only; see Committee Report, p. 118 [758].**

parties agree that the case shall be conducted in English, the judgment will be delivered in English.

In the absence of an agreement as to which language shall be employed, each party may, in the pleadings, use the language which it prefers; the decision of the Court will be given in French and English. In this case the Court will at the same time determine which of the two texts shall be considered as authoritative.[1]

	Amendment
The Court may, at the request of the parties, authorize a language other than French or English to be used.	The Court may, at the request of any party, authorize a language other than French or English to be used.

Art. 40. Cases are brought before the Court, as the case may be, either by the notification of the special agreement, or by a written application addressed to the Registrar. In either case the subject of the dispute and the contesting parties must be indicated.

The Registrar shall forthwith communicate the application to all concerned.

	Amendment
He shall also notify the Members of the League of Nations through the Secretary-General.	He shall also notify the Members of the League of Nations through the Secretary-General, and also any States entitled to appear before the Court.

Art. 41. The Court shall have the power to indicate, if it considers that circumstances so require, any provisional measures which ought to be taken to reserve the respective rights of either party.

Pending the final decision, notice of the measures suggested shall forthwith be given to the parties and the Council.

[1] The Tenth Assembly of the League of Nations on September 14, 1929, adopted the following:

"The Assembly associates itself with the following recommendation adopted by the Conference:

"'The Conference recommends that, in accordance with the spirit of Arts. 2 and 39 of the Statute of the Court, the candidates nominated by the national groups should possess recognized practical experience in international law and that they should be at least able to read both the official languages of the Court and to speak one of them; it also considers it desirable that to the nominations there should be attached a statement of the careers of the candidates justifying their candidature.'"

Art. 42. The parties shall be represented by agents.

They may have the assistance of counsel or advocates before the Court.

Art. 43. The procedure shall consist of two parts: written and oral.

The written proceedings shall consist of the communication to the judges and to the parties of cases, counter-cases and, if necessary, replies; also all papers and documents in support.

These communications shall be made through the Registrar, in the order and within the time fixed by the Court.

A certified copy of every document produced by one party shall be communicated to the other party.

The oral proceedings shall consist of the hearing by the Court of witnesses, experts, agents, counsel and advocates.

Art. 44. For the service of all notices upon persons other than the agents, counsel and advocates, the Court shall apply direct to the government of the state upon whose territory the notice has to be served.

The same provision shall apply whenever steps are to be taken to procure evidence on the spot.

	Amendment
Art. 45. The hearing shall be under the control of the President or, in his absence, of the Vice-President; if both are absent, the senior judge shall preside.	**Art. 45.** The hearing shall be under the control of the President or, if he is unable to preside, of the Vice-President; if neither is able to preside, the senior judge present shall preside.[1]

Art. 46. The hearing in Court shall be public, unless the Court shall decide otherwise, or unless the parties demand that the public be not admitted.

Art. 47. Minutes shall be made at each hearing, and signed by the Registrar and the President.

These minutes shall be the only authentic record.

Art. 48. The Court shall make orders for the conduct of the case, shall decide the form and time in which each party must conclude its arguments, and make all arrangements connected with the taking of evidence.

[1] The amendment is solely an improved version of the English text.

Art. 49. The Court may, even before the hearing begins, call upon the agents to produce any document, or to supply any explanations. Formal note shall be taken of any refusal.

Art. 50. The Court may, at any time, intrust any individual, body, bureau, commission or other organization that it may select, with the task of carrying out an inquiry or giving an expert opinion.

Art. 51. During the hearing, any relevant questions are to be put to the witnesses and experts under the conditions laid down by the Court in the rules of procedure referred to in Article 30.

Art. 52. After the Court has received the proofs and evidence within the time specified for the purpose, it may refuse to accept any further oral or written evidence that one party may desire to present unless the other side consents.

Art. 53. Whenever one of the parties shall not appear before the Court, or shall fail to defend his case, the other party may call upon the Court to decide in favor of his claim.

The Court must, before doing so, satisfy itself, not only that it has jurisdiction in accordance with Articles 36 and 37, but also that the claim is well founded in fact and law.

Art. 54. When, subject to the control of the Court, the agents, advocates and counsel have completed their presentation of the case, the President shall declare the hearing closed.

The Court shall withdraw to consider the judgment.

The deliberations of the Court shall take place in private and remain secret.

Art. 55. All questions shall be decided by a majority of the judges present at the hearing.

In the event of an equality of votes, the President or his deputy shall have a casting vote.

Art. 56. The judgment shall state the reasons on which it is based.

It shall contain the names of the judges who have taken part in the decision.

Art. 57. If the judgment does not represent in whole or in part the unanimous opinion of the judges, dissenting judges are entitled to deliver a separate opinion.

Art. 58. The judgment shall be signed by the President and by the Registrar. It shall be read in open Court, due notice having been given to the agents.

Art. 59. The decision of the Court has no binding force except between the parties and in respect of that particular case.

Art. 60. The judgment is final and without appeal. In the event of dispute as to the meaning or scope of the judgment, the Court shall construe it upon the request of any party.

Art. 61. An application for revision of a judgment can be made only when it is based upon the discovery of some fact of such a nature as to be a decisive factor, which fact was, when the judgment was given, unknown to the Court and also to the party claiming revision, always provided that such ignorance was not due to negligence.

The proceedings for revision will be opened by a judgment of the Court expressly recording the existence of the new fact, recognizing that it has such a character as to lay the case open to revision, and declaring the application admissible on this ground.

The Court may require previous compliance with the terms of the judgment before it admits proceedings in revision.

The application for revision must be made at latest within six months of the discovery of the new fact.

No application for revision may be made after the lapse of ten years from the date of the sentence.

Art. 62. Should a State consider that it has an interest of a legal nature which may be affected by the decision in the case, it may submit a request to the Court to be permitted to intervene as a third party.

It will be for the Court to decide upon this request.

Art. 63. Whenever the construction of a convention to which States other than those concerned in the case are parties is in question, the Registrar shall notify all such States forthwith.

Every State so notified has the right to intervene in the proceedings; but if it uses this right, the construction given by the judgment will be equally binding upon it.

Art. 64. Unless otherwise decided by the Court, each party shall bear its own costs.

Present Rules of Court

[The proposed amendments to the Statute are adaptations from the following articles of the Rules of Court:]

Art. 72. Questions upon which the advisory opinion of the Court is asked shall be laid

Amendment to Statute

CHAPTER IV

Advisory Opinions

Art. 65. Questions upon which the advisory opinion of the Court is asked shall be laid before the Court by means of a before the Court by means of a written request, signed either by the President of the Assembly or the President of the Council of the League of Nations, or by the Secretary-General of the League under instructions from the Assembly or the Council.

The request shall contain an exact statement of the question upon which an opinion is required, and shall be accompanied by all documents likely to throw light upon the question.

Art. 73. 1. The Registrar shall forthwith give notice of the request for an advisory opinion to the members of the Court, to the Members of the League of Nations, through the Secretary-General of the League, and to any states entitled to appear before the Court.

The Registrar shall also, by means of a special and direct communication, notify any Member of the League or state admitted to appear before the Court or international organization considered by the Court (or, should it not be sitting, by the President) as likely to be able to furnish information on the question, that the Court will be prepared to receive, within a time-limit to be fixed by the President, written statements, or to hear, at a public sitting to be held for the purpose, oral statements relating to the question.

written request, signed either by the President of the Assembly or the President of the Council of the League of Nations, or by the Secretary-General of the League under instructions from the Assembly or the Council.

The request shall contain an exact statement of the question upon which an opinion is required, and shall be accompanied by all documents likely to throw light upon the question.

Art. 66. The Registrar shall forthwith give notice of the request for an advisory opinion to the Members of the League of Nations, through the Secretary-General of the League, and to any states entitled to appear before the Court.

The Registrar shall also, by means of a special and direct communication, notify any Member of the League or State admitted to appear before the Court or international organization considered by the Court (or, should it not be sitting, by the President) as likely to be able to furnish information on the question, that the Court will be prepared to receive, within a time-limit to be fixed by the President, written statements, or to hear, at a public sitting to be held for the purpose, oral statements relating to the question.

Should any Member or state referred to in the first paragraph have failed to receive the com-

Should any state or Member referred to in the first paragraph have failed to receive the communication specified above, such state or Member may express a desire to submit a written statement, or to be heard; and the Court will decide.

2. States, Members and organizations having presented written or oral statements or both shall be admitted to comment on the statements made by other states, Members or organizations, in the form, to the extent and within the time-limits which the Court or, should it not be sitting, the President shall decide in each particular case. Accordingly, the Registrar shall in due time communicate any such written statements to states, Members and organizations having submitted similar statements.

Art. 74. Advisory opinions shall be read in open Court, notice having been given to the Secretary-General of the League of Nations and to the representatives of states, of Members of the League and of international organizations immediately concerned. . . . [1]

munication specified above, such Member or state may express a desire to submit a written statement, or to be heard; and the Court will decide.

Members, States and organizations having presented written or oral statements or both shall be admitted to comment on the statements made by other Members, States or organizations in the form, to the extent and within the time-limits which the Court or, should it not be sitting, the President shall decide in each particular case. Accordingly, the Registrar shall in due time communicate any such written statements to Members, States and organizations having submitted similar statements.

Art. 67. The Court shall deliver its advisory opinions in open Court, notice having been given to the Secretary-General of the League of Nations and to the representatives of Members of the League, of states and of international organizations immediately concerned.

Art. 68. In the exercise of its advisory functions, the Court shall further be guided by the provisions of the Statute which apply in contentious cases to the extent to which it recognizes them to be applicable. [2]

[1] The remainder of Art. 74 of the Rules of Court stipulates duties of the Registrar.

[2] *Cf.* Committee Report, League Doc. A. 50. 1929. V. 16, p. 3.

II. REPORT ADOPTED BY THE COMMITTEE OF JURISTS ON THE QUESTION OF THE AMENDMENT OF THE STATUTE, MARCH 19, 1929 [1]

On September 20, 1928, the Assembly of the League of Nations adopted the following resolution:

The Assembly,

Considering the ever increasing number of matters referred to the Permanent Court of International Justice;

Deeming it advisable that, before the renewal of the term of office of the members of the Court in 1930, the present provisions of the Statute of the Court should be examined with a view to the introduction of any amendments which experience may show to be necessary;

Draws the Council's attention to the advisability of proceeding, before the renewal of the term of office of the members of the Permanent Court of International Justice, to the examination of the Statute of the Court with a view to the introduction of such amendments as may be judged desirable and to submitting the necessary proposals to the next ordinary session of the Assembly.

In pursuance of this resolution the Council decided on December 13 and 14, 1928, to set up a committee consisting of Jonkheer van Eysinga, M. Fromageot, M. Gaus, Sir Cecil Hurst, M. Ito, M. Politis, M. Raestad, M. Rundstein, M. Scialoja, M. Urrutia and a jurist of the United States of America, to be appointed by the President of the Council and the Rapporteur, who selected M. Elihu Root. The Council further invited the President and the Vice-President of the Court, M. Anzilotti and M. Huber and the chairman of the Supervisory Commission, M. Osusky, to participate in the work of the committee. M. Pilotti was added to the committee on March 9, 1929.

The Council Rapporteur had pointed out that, having regard to the terms of the Assembly's decision, the committee should have wide terms of reference, namely, "to report what amendments appear desirable in the various provisions of the Court's Statute." He further stated "that the committee would, of course, be competent to examine such suggestions as may reach it, during its work,

[1] Reprinted from Document C. 142, M. 52. 1929, V. 4, p. 2.

from authoritative sources" and "that it would fall to the committee to ascertain the opinion of the Permanent Court of International Justice in respect of the working of the Court."

As may be seen from the discussion in the Assembly, the latter did not contemplate recasting completely the Statute of the Court; it had merely in view the possibility of supplementing or improving the Statute in the light of the experience already acquired.

It is in this spirit that the committee, which met at Geneva on March 11, 1929, under the chairmanship of M. Scialoja, has pursued its work, which was completed on March 19 under the chairmanship of Jonkheer van Eysinga, the vice-chairman.

In the proposals which the committee has the honor to submit to the Council, it has been in general actuated by the desire to give the States full assurance that the Permanent Court of International Justice established by the League of Nations is a real *judicial* body which is constantly at their disposal for the purpose of hearing and determining their disputes and which possesses alike the necessary juristic competence and experience of international affairs.

It would appear that effect can be given to some of the committee's proposals by means of *vœux* or recommendations; other proposals would appear to call for an amendment of the existing text of the Statute.

In the first place, the committee examined the qualifications which members of the Court should possess in order to satisfy the expectations of Governments in regard to the Permanent Court of International Justice. These conditions will be found in Art. 2 of the Statute. The committee has thought that it would be desirable to mention, in addition to recognized competence in international law which is mentioned in Art. 2 of the Statute, the requirement of practical experience in this sphere.

Similarly, the national groups, when nominating their candidates in accordance with Art. 5, should attach to each nomination a statement of the career of the person nominated, showing that he possesses the required qualifications.

Further, as the official languages of the Court are French and English, it appears essential that the judges should be at least able to read these languages and to speak one of them. Though this may be self-evident, the committee has thought that it would be desirable to draw the special attention of the national groups to the point.

The committee is of opinion that, despite their importance, none of these three questions necessitates a modification of the existing texts, and that it would be sufficient to proceed by way of a recommendation, as follows:

"*The Committee decides to advise the Assembly to adopt the following recommendation:*

" '*The Secretary-General, in issuing the invitations provided for in Art. 5 of the Statute, will request the national groups to satisfy themselves that the candidates nominated by them possess recognized practical experience in international law and that they are at least able to read both the official languages of the Court and to speak one of them; he will recommend the groups to attach to each nomination a statement of the career of the person nominated showing that he possesses the required qualifications.*' "

On the other hand it appeared necessary to deal with the following questions by means of amendments:

1. Composition of the Court

Experience has shown that deputy-judges have been called upon almost constantly to sit on the Court, the reason being that the majority of them are resident in Europe and were consequently more readily available than judges belonging to other continents; this has tended to give the Europeans a privileged position. On the other hand, as the deputy-judges have in fact been placed on a footing of equality with the ordinary judges in regard to the work performed, without being subject to the same disabilities, the difference in treatment in this latter respect has not been without its disadvantages. Finally, a further difference between the two classes of judges — that relating to their emoluments — has actually disappeared, since the allowances granted to deputy-judges have placed them in a situation almost equal to that of the ordinary judges.

Practical experience thus points to assimilation of the two classes of judges and accordingly suggests the desirability of abolishing the deputy-judges and replacing them by an equal number of ordinary judges.

The committee proposes, therefore, to increase the number of ordinary judges from eleven to fifteen and to omit all mention of deputy-judges in Art. 3. The disappearance of the deputy-judges naturally involves consequential amendment of various articles in the Statute in which they are mentioned. These changes will be indicated below in connection with Arts. 8, 15, 16, 17, 25, 31 and 32. To avoid the risk of an exaggeration which might cause misconception, it also appeared desirable to omit in the new text of Art. 3 the reference to a possible increase of the members of the Court above the number of fifteen.

As a result, the new text of Art. 3 would be as follows:

The Court shall consist of fifteen members.

2. Election of Judges

As already stated the text of Art. 8 will, as a result of the disappearance of the deputy-judges, read as follows:

The Assembly and the Council shall proceed independently of one another to elect the members of the Court.

3. Resignation of a Judge

The resignation of a judge is not provided for in the present existing text of the Statute. The question has, however, arisen in practice, and doubts have been felt as to the procedure to be adopted in such cases. The committee considered that it would be desirable to supply the omission and to take the view that, once a resignation has been transmitted to the League of Nations, it must be regarded as final; but that, nevertheless, the resignation should be transmitted to the League by the President of the Court in order that he may, if desirable, be able to satisfy himself that the decision of the judge concerned is irrevocable.

Consequently, the committee proposes to add two paragraphs to Art. 13, which would read as follows:

The members of the Court shall be elected for nine years.

They may be re-elected.

They shall continue to discharge their duties until their places have been filled. Though replaced, they shall finish any cases which they may have begun.

In the case of the resignation of a member of the Court, the resignation will be addressed to the President of the Court for transmission to the Secretary-General of the League of Nations.

This notification makes the place vacant.

4. Filling of Occasional Vacancies

Art. 14 of the Statute merely provides that vacancies which may occur shall be filled by the same method as that laid down for the renewal of the entire Court. Experience has shown that there is a serious disadvantage in waiting for the annual meeting of the Assembly before filling a vacancy, as this may cause a delay of as much as fifteen months. During this period the Court might be deprived of its essential characteristic — that of a body representative of the various juridical systems — while at the same time the uninterrupted and regular working of this high tribunal might be rendered more difficult.

To remedy this defect the committee has thought it desirable to establish a somewhat elastic system which, especially in cases deemed by the Council of the League of Nations to be urgent, would allow of the filling even of a single vacancy within the shortest possible space of time. Under this system the Secretary-General of the League of Nations would address the prescribed request, within one month after the occurrence of any vacancy, to the national groups, in accordance with Art. 5, and the Council would be in a position at its next session to decide whether the election was of a sufficiently urgent character to necessitate the convening of the Assembly in extraordinary session before its ordinary September session.

The system would be embodied in the following new draft of Art. 14:

Vacancies which may occur shall be filled by the same method as that laid down for the first election, subject to the following provision: the Secretary-General of the League of Nations shall, within one month of the occurrence of the vacancy, proceed to issue the invitations provided for in Art. 5, and the date of the election shall be fixed by the Council at its next session.

5. New Article 15

As Art. 15 of the Statute disappears with the disappearance of the deputy-judges, the committee proposes to make a new Art. 15 out of the unaltered part of Art. 14, reading as follows:

A member of the Court elected to replace a member whose period of appointment has not expired, will hold the appointment for the remainder of his predecessor's term.

6. Functions and Occupations Incompatible with Membership of the Court

In accordance with the guiding idea of the committee's work, namely, that the Court, by its composition and its operation, should inspire in the states the highest possible degree of confidence, the committee has thought that it would be necessary to amplify the rules of Art. 16 as to what functions and occupations are incompatible with membership of the Court and for this purpose to indicate clearly that the members of the Court must not only refrain from exercising any political or administrative function but also may not engage in any other occupation of a professional nature. Naturally, it would be permissible for members of the Court to be included on the list of members of the Permanent Court of Arbitration and to exercise, if their duties on the Court allowed them the necessary leisure, the functions of arbitrators or conciliators, provided always that the instrument under which they were appointed did not provide for a reference to the Court following upon the arbitration or upon the failure of the conciliation proceedings.

With the disappearance of the deputy-judges, the second sentence in Par. 1 of Art. 16 naturally disappears as well.

Art. 16 would thus read as follows:

The members of the Court may not exercise any political or administrative function, nor engage in any other occupation of a professional nature.

Any doubt on this point is settled by the decision of the Court.

7. Article 17

The second sentence of the first paragraph of Art. 17 referring to deputy-judges becomes meaningless and is to be omitted.

At this point, the committee feels it should observe that while it is stated that no member of the Court can act as agent, counsel or advocate in any case of an international nature, it will not henceforth, in view of the new Art. 16, be possible to infer *a contrario* that he is free to exercise the said functions in a case which is national in character. It has not seemed necessary to redraft the text of the second paragraph.

The same consideration applies to the end of the second paragraph, which states that no member of the Court may participate personally in any case in which he has previously taken an active part as agent, counsel or advocate for one of the contesting parties, or as a member of a national or international court, or of a commission of inquiry, or in any other capacity. Obviously, the same would hold good as to their participation in a commission of conciliation; this appeared to be indicated clearly enough in the expression "or in any other capacity."

Art. 17 would therefore read as follows:

No member of the Court may act as agent, counsel or advocate in any case of an international nature.

No member may participate in the decision of any case in which he has previously taken an active part as agent, counsel or advocate for one of the contesting parties, or as a member of a national or international Court, or of a commission of inquiry, or in any other capacity.

Any doubt on this point is settled by the decision of the Court.

8. Permanent Functioning of the Court

Under the system at present laid down, the Court holds one session annually, beginning on June 15, and it is convened, in exceptional cases, in extraordinary session when circumstances so require.

In practice, the Court has often been obliged, on account of the increase in the cases referred to it, to hold several extraordinary sessions annually. In so doing, it has occasionally encountered serious practical difficulties. The repeated holding of extraordinary sessions has, in this way, tended, in fact, to bring the Court nearer to that permanent character which its title denotes, and which its promoters had contemplated in order to advance the progress of international justice.

The committee accordingly considers that it is desirable to bring the written rules into harmony with the facts and to indicate, in a new draft of Art. 23, a more regular working of the Court by providing, in imitation of national Courts, for a real international judicial year. It therefore proposes to state that the Court shall, in principle, remain constantly in session, except during the judicial vacations, the dates and duration of which shall be fixed by the Court.

On the other hand, in order to enable members of the Court whose ordinary residence is in a country at a considerable distance from its seat, to return occasionally to their homes during their term of office, it is suggested that they should be granted the right to six months' leave every three years in addition to the ordinary vacations.

Apart from exceptional cases, such as that of illness or other good reason for absence, the judges must be permanently at the disposal of the Court.

It is to be understood that this principle applies even during the judicial vacations, in the sense that it will be for the Court, when fixing the length of the vacation, to provide for the possibility of convening at The Hague, in an urgent case, such a number of judges as would be necessary to allow it to discharge its duties.

It would also be for the Court to provide in its Rules for the organization of a vacations procedure for the cases in which a full meeting of the Court would not be necessary.

Art. 23 would accordingly be redrafted as follows:

The Court shall remain permanently in session except during the judicial vacations, the dates and duration of which shall be fixed by the Court at the end of each year for the following year.

Members of the Court whose homes are situated at more than five days' normal journey from The Hague shall be entitled, apart from the judicial vacations, to six months' leave every three years.

Members of the Court shall be bound, unless they are on regular leave or prevented from attending by illness or other serious reason duly explained to the President, to hold themselves permanently at the disposal of the Court.

9. Manner of Forming the Court

As a result of the disappearance of the deputy-judges the present Par. 2 of Art. 25 must be deleted.

The committee proposes to replace it by a provision which would enable judges, when there is a heavy cause-list, to sit in turn in order to insure the prompt dispatch of business and would at the same time make it possible to remove the disadvantages that might arise from the cooperation in one and the same case of fifteen members of the Court.

Under this provision the Court would have the power to provide in its Rules that, according to circumstances and in rotation, a judge or judges might be dispensed from sitting.

The intention of the committee has of course been that the right just mentioned should in no case be so exercised as to give grounds for any suspicion that the Court has in a given case been specially composed for the purpose of affecting the decision of the case.

The deletion of Par. 2 of Art. 25 necessarily involves the redrafting of Par. 3. There is no longer any point in providing that a certain number of judges must be available since, as previously stated, all judges are in principle constantly at the disposal of the Court. It is therefore sufficient to retain the essential sentence in the third paragraph relating to the quorum.

The new Art. 25 would be worded as follows:

The full Court shall sit except when it is expressly provided otherwise.

Subject to the condition that the number of judges available to constitute the Court is not thereby reduced below eleven, the Rules of Court may provide for allowing one or more judges, according to circumstances and in rotation, to be dispensed from sitting.

Provided always that a quorum of nine judges shall suffice to constitute the Court.

10. Special Chamber for Labor Cases

The redrafting of Art. 25 involves a change in Par. 2 of Art. 26, which states that the Court will sit with the number of judges provided for in Art. 25. It should now be said that the full Court will sit.

In the next sentence of the same paragraph, the committee is of opinion that, for the sake of clearness, it is necessary to read "In both cases," that is to say, the cases which are referred to, instead of "on all occasions," because, as is suggested later on, the summary procedure without the assistance of the technical assessors becomes possible in labor cases.

Par. 3 of Art. 26 should be deleted in consequence of the modification proposed later in Art. 31 in regard to national judges.

The committee would suggest replacing this paragraph by inserting, as the last paragraph but one of Art. 26, a stipulation allowing the parties, should they so desire, to resort to the summary procedure provided for in Art. 29.

It is the committee's intention that, whenever resort is had to this right, the Court constituted as a chamber for summary procedure should consist of five judges only, as will be stated later in connection with Art. 29, without the presence of technical assessors.

Art. 26 would accordingly be drafted as follows:

Labor cases, particularly cases referred to in Part XIII (Labor) of the treaty of Versailles and the corresponding portions of the other Treaties of Peace, shall be heard and determined by the Court under the following conditions:

The Court will appoint every three years a special chamber of five judges, selected so far as possible with due regard to the provisions of Art. 9. In addition, two judges shall be selected for the purpose of replacing a judge who finds it impossible to sit. If the parties so demand, cases will be heard and determined by this Chamber. In the absence of any such demand, the full Court will sit. In both cases the judges will be assisted by four technical assessors sitting with them, but without the right to vote and chosen with a view to insuring a just representation of the competing interests.

The technical assessors shall be chosen for each particular case in accordance with rules of procedure under Art. 30 from a list of "Assessors for Labor Cases" composed of two persons nominated by each Member of the League of Nations and an equivalent number nominated by the Governing Body of the Labor Office. The Governing Body will nominate, as to one-half, representatives of the workers and as to one-half, representatives of employers from the list referred to in Art. 412 of the treaty of Versailles and the corresponding articles of the other Treaties of Peace.

Recourse may always be had to the summary procedure provided for in Art. 29, in the cases referred to in the first paragraph of the present article, if the parties so request.

In labor cases the International Office shall be at liberty to furnish the Court with all relevant information, and for this purpose the Director of that Office shall receive copies of all the written proceedings.

11. Special Chamber for Transit and Communications Cases

The committee considered whether it might not be well to delete Art. 27, seeing that no application has yet been received and that in the opinion of certain persons it is unlikely that any will ever be received. Nevertheless, the committee thought it preferable to retain the article, modifying it, however, in the same way as Art. 26, *i.e.*, by substituting in Par. 2 the words "the full Court will sit" for the present text "the Court will sit with the number of judges provided for under Art. 25;" by omitting paragraph 3; and, finally, by inserting as the last paragraph of Art. 27 the same new provision as is contained in the previous article with regard to summary procedure.

The new draft of Art. 27 would therefore be as follows:

Cases relating to transit and communications, particularly cases referred to in Part XII (Ports, Waterways and Railways) of the treaty of Versailles and the corresponding portions of the other Treaties of Peace shall be heard and determined by the Court under the following conditions:

The Court will appoint every three years a special chamber of five judges, selected so far as possible with due regard to the provisions of Art. 9. In addition, two judges shall be selected for the purpose of replacing a judge who finds it impossible to sit. If the parties so demand, cases will be heard and determined by this chamber. In the absence of any such demand, the full Court will sit. When desired by the parties or decided by the Court, the judges will be assisted by four technical assessors sitting with them, but without the right to vote.

The technical assessors shall be chosen for each particular case in accordance with rules of procedure under Art. 30 from a list of "Assessors for Transit and Communications Cases" composed of two persons nominated by each Member of the League of Nations.

Recourse may always be had to the summary procedure provided for in Art. 29, in the cases referred to in the first paragraph of the present article, if the parties so request.

12. Chamber for Summary Procedure

As indicated below in connection with Art. 31, the committee considered that, as the system of national judges exists, it should apply to the Chamber for Summary Procedure as well as to any other form of the Court. It will, therefore, be necessary to bring Art. 29 into harmony with the new draft of Art. 31 and for this purpose to make the Chamber for Summary Procedure consist of five judges instead of three. Provision must also be made, as in the case of the other special chambers (Arts. 26 and 27), for the selection of two judges to replace a judge who finds it impossible to sit.

Art. 29 would therefore read as follows:

With a view to the speedy dispatch of business, the Court shall form annually a chamber composed of five judges who, at the request of the contesting parties, may hear and determine cases by summary procedure. In addition two judges shall be selected for the purpose of replacing a judge who finds it impossible to sit.

13. National Judges

The committee considered that it was no part of its duty to deal with the institution of national judges, which is regarded by certain states as one of the essential principles of the organization of the Court.

It also considered that, in view of the importance which certain states attach to this system, its application should not be limited, as is at present done in Art. 31, to the single case in which the full Court sits, but that, on the contrary, it should be extended to the Court in all its forms.

With this object, the committee proposes to insert as a fourth paragraph in Art. 31 a provision making the system of national judges apply to the Special Chambers for Labor, for Communications and Transit and for Summary Procedure (Arts. 26, 27 and 29).

Moreover, the disappearance of the deputy-judges necessitates redrafting Par. 2 of Art. 31. There must be a slight change in Par 2 and changes of minor importance in Pars. 3 and 5 of Art. 31.

The new Art. 31 would read as follows:

Judges of the nationality of each of the contesting parties shall retain their right to sit in the case before the Court.

If the Court includes upon the Bench a judge of the nationality of one of the parties, the other party may choose a person to sit as judge. Such person shall be chosen preferably from among those persons who have been nominated as candidates as provided in Arts. 4 and 5.

If the Court includes upon the Bench no judge of the nationality of the contesting parties, each of these parties may proceed to select a judge as provided in the preceding paragraph.

The present provision shall apply to the case of Arts. 26, 27 and 29. In such cases, the President shall request one or, if necessary, two of the members of the Court forming the Chamber to give place to the members of the Court of the nationality of the parties concerned, and, failing such or if they are unable to be present, to the judges specially appointed by the parties.

Should there be several parties in the same interest, they shall, for the purpose of the preceding provisions, be reckoned as one party only. Any doubt upon this point is settled by the decision of the Court.

Judges selected as laid down in Pars. 2, 3 and 4 of this article shall fulfil the conditions required by Arts. 2, 17, Par. 2, 20 and 24 of this Statute. They shall take part in the decision on terms of complete equality with their colleagues.

14. Salaries of Judges

The permanent character of the Court having been more firmly established, and the requirements as to the selection of judges and the rules regarding the other occupations which they may not follow concurrently having been more clearly stated, it has been thought expedient to abandon the mixed system at present in force, which consists in an annual indemnity and allowances for each day of service. Payment for the services and subsistence expenses of members of the Court at The Hague will now take the form of a fixed inclusive annual salary which, in fact, will correspond approximately to the maximum obtainable by the judges under the present system.

This will be a simplification of a system which at present is particularly complicated.

Accordingly, the committee proposes to redraft Art. 32 completely and to submit to the Assembly a draft resolution to be substituted for the resolution of December 18, 1920, concerning the salaries of members of the Court.

It has not, however, been thought expedient to include in the annual salary the traveling expenses of members attending the Court or their traveling expenses while on duty.

In the committee's view, it is for the Assembly to lay down special regulations on this point. The committee considers, however, that the members of the Court and the Registrar should, apart from journeys made on duty, be reimbursed for only one journey every year from the seat of the Court to their homes and back again.

The final paragraph of the present Art. 32 deals with retiring pensions for the personnel of the Court. It refers to a special regulation which was made by the Assembly in 1924. This regulation will require revision; the Supervisory Commission will lay the matter before the Assembly, but on account of certain proposed amendments to the Statute of the Court, of which a brief summary was given at the head of this section, the committee is of opinion that the Assembly's attention should be specially drawn to the desirability of redrafting Par. 5 of Art. 1 of the 1924 regulation in the terms indicated in the attached draft resolution as to pensions.

The new text of Art. 32 and the accompanying draft resolutions, referred to above, would be as follows:

The members of the Court shall receive an annual salary.

The President shall receive a special annual allowance.

The Vice-President shall receive a special allowance for every day on which he acts as President.

The judges appointed under Art. 31, other than members of the Court, shall receive an indemnity for each day on which they sit.

These salaries, allowances and indemnities shall be fixed by the Assembly of the League of Nations on the proposal of the Council. They may not be decreased during the term of office.

The salary of the Registrar shall be fixed by the Assembly on the proposal of the Court.

Regulations made by the Assembly shall fix the conditions under which retiring pensions may be given to members of the Court and to the Registrar, and the conditions under which members of the Court and the Registrar shall have their traveling expenses refunded.

The above salaries, indemnities and allowances shall be free of all taxation.

Draft resolution concerning salaries:

In accordance with the provisions of Art. 32 of the Statute, the Assembly of the League of Nations fixes the salaries, allowances and indemnities of the members and judges of the Permanent Court of International Justice as follows:

	Dutch florins		Dutch florins
President:		*Members:*	
Annual salary	45,000	Annual salary	45,000
Special indemnity	15,000		
		Judges referred to in Article 31 of the Statute:	
Vice-President:			
Annual salary	45,000	Indemnity for each day on duty	100
Allowance for each day on duty (100 x 100)	10,000 (maximum)	Allowance for each day of attendance	50

Draft resolution amending Par. 5 of Art. 1 of the regulation regarding pensions.[1]

The payment of a pension shall not begin until the person entitled to such pension has reached the age of 65. Should, however, the person entitled to a pension, before attaining that age, reach the end of his term of office without being re-elected, his pension may, by a decision of the Court, be made payable to him, in whole or part, as from the date on which his functions cease.

15. Contributions of States not Members of the League of Nations

The committee does not propose any amendment to Art. 35, but thinks that an observation is called for on paragraph 3 of that article.

In view of the third reservation attached by the United States to their accession to the Protocol of Signature, Par. 3 of Art. 35 should not apply to the special case of the United States, if they accede to the Court Statute.

[1] The original paragraph reads as follows:

"The payment of a pension shall not begin until the person entitled to such pension has reached the age of 65. Nevertheless, in exceptional cases and by a special decision of the Court, in consideration of the state of health or the means of the beneficiary, pensions may be paid to such beneficiary before he reaches the age of 65." (*League of Nations, Resolutions and Recommendations Adopted by the Assembly during its Fifth Session*, p. 36 (*Official Journal*, Spec. Supp. No. 21)).

16. Amendment to No. 4 of Article 38

The committee has only a very slight and purely formal amendment to propose to No. 4 of Art. 38. It consists in restoring in the French text a few words which appear in the English text. In the said No. 4 of Art. 38, after the words "*la doctrine des publicistes les plus qualifiés,*" the words "*des différentes nations*" shou d be added.

Art. 38, No. 4, would then read in the French text as follows:

4. *Sous réserve de la disposition de l'article 59, les décisions judicaires et la doctrine des publicistes les plus qualifiés des différentes nations, comme moyen auxiliaire de détermination des régles de droit.*

17. Procedure

In the final paragraph of Art. 39, where reference is made to the power of the Court to authorize, at the request of the parties, the use of a language other than French or English, the committee thinks it should be more clearly stated that such authorization may be granted without agreement between the parties, provided one of them so requests. Experience has shown that it might be desirable to make this clearer.

Art. 39, paragraph 3, would then read as follows:

The Court may, at the request of any party, authorize a language other than French or English to be used.

18. Communication of Applications

In Par. 3 of Art. 40, the committee thinks it would be desirable to bring the text of the Statute into line with Art. 73 of the present Rules of Court, which latter provision, as will be seen, the committee proposes to embody in the new draft of the Statute.

Art. 40, Par. 3, would then read as follows:

He shall also notify the Members of the League of Nations through the Secretary-General, and also any States entitled to appear before the Court.

19. Direction of the Hearing

The English text of Art. 45 does not quite correspond to the French text, which here is better.

In order to bring the two texts into concordance, the committee proposes to replace the words "in his absence" by the words "if he is unable to preside," and the words "if both are absent" by the words "if neither is able to preside."

The English text of this article would then read as follows:

The hearing shall be under the control of the President or, if he is unable to preside, of the Vice-President; if neither is able to preside, the senior judge present shall preside.

20. Advisory Opinions

The present Statute contains no explicit reference to advisory opinions. The Court has been compelled by circumstances to remedy this omission to a certain extent in Arts. 71, 72, 73 and 74 of the Rules of Court.

The committee considers that the essential parts of these provisions should be transferred to the Statute of the Court in order to give them a permanent character, which seems particularly desirable to-day in view of the special circumstances attending the possible accession of the United States to the Protocol of Signature of the Statute of the Court.

The committee therefore proposes to add at the end of the present Statute a new chapter numbered IV and headed "Advisory Opinions," the first three articles of which, numbered 65, 66 and 67, would reproduce the substance of Arts. 72, 73 and 74 of the present Rules of Court.

It also proposes that a final article numbered 68 should be added to this chapter in order to take account of the fact that the Court may be called upon to give advisory opinions both in contentious and in noncontentious matters. The effect would be that, in the former case, the Court would apply the provisions relating to contentious procedure referred to in the previous chapters of the Statute, whereas those provisions would not always be applicable when the Court gave an opinion on a noncontentious matter. Thus, for example, Arts. 57 and 58 should apply in all cases, but Art. 31 would only apply when an advisory opinion was asked on a question relating to a dispute which had already arisen.

The new Arts. 65, 66, 67 and 68 would be worded as follows:

Chapter IV

Advisory Opinions

Art. 65. Questions upon which the advisory opinion of the Court is asked shall be laid before the Court by means of a written request, signed either by the President of the Assembly or the President of the Council of the League of Nations, or by the Secretary-General of the League under instructions from the Assembly or the Council.

The request shall contain an exact statement of the question upon which an opinion is required and shall be accompanied by all documents likely to throw light upon the question.

Art. 66. The Registrar shall forthwith give notice of the request for an advisory opinion to the Members of the League of Nations, through the Secretary-General of the League, and to any States entitled to appear before the Court.

The Registrar shall also, by means of a special and direct communication, notify any Member of the League or State admitted to appear before the Court considered by the Court (or, should it not be sitting, by the President) as likely to be able to furnish information on the question, that the Court will be prepared to receive, within a time-limit to be fixed by the President, written statements, or to hear, at a public sitting to be held for the purpose, oral statements relating to the question.

Should any State or Member referred to in the first paragraph have failed to receive the communication specified above, such State or Member may express a desire to submit a written statement, or to be heard; and the Court will decide.

States or Members having presented written or oral statements or both shall be admitted to comment on the statements made by other States or Members in the form, to the extent and within the time-limits which the Court or, should it not be sitting, the President shall decide in each particular case. Accordingly, the Registrar shall in due time communicate any such written statements to States or Members having submitted similar statements.

Art. 67. The Court shall deliver its advisory opinions in open Court, notice having been given to the Secretary-General of the League of Nations and to the representatives of States and Members of the League immediately concerned.

Art. 68. In the exercise of its advisory functions the Court shall apply Arts. 65, 66 and 67. It shall further be guided by the provisions of the preceding Chapters of this Statute to the extent to which it recognizes them to be applicable to the case.

Such are the proposals which the committee has the honor to submit for the Council's consideration.

The committee has to observe that, in the course of its work, it has found somewhat inappropriate expressions used in the French and in the English texts of several articles of the Statute; it has, however, felt it unnecessary to propose corrections, as it does not wish to encumber the present report with suggestions which are not clearly of practical value.

Finally, the committee has considered what would be the appropriate procedure for bringing into force the amendments proposed in the present report.

On this subject the committee ventures to make the following suggestions:

If the Council approves the conclusions of the report, it will no doubt find it convenient to communicate them to the Members of the League of Nations and the states mentioned in the Annex to the Covenant and to transmit them to the Assembly; it would be desirable that, if the amendments secure general approval, the protocol accepting them which must be concluded between the parties which have ratified the 1920 Statute should be made in the course of next Assembly.

On this point the committee must call the attention of the Council to the necessity for taking appropriate measures to secure the entry into force of the amendments a sufficient time before the election of the members of the Court in September, 1930, on account, more particularly, of the changes which are made in regard to the number of the members of the Court and the rules as to the occupations which are incompatible with membership.

III. CONVOCATION OF A CONFERENCE: REPORT AND RESOLUTION OF THE COUNCIL OF THE LEAGUE OF NATIONS, JUNE 12, 1929[1]

[Excerpt]

The Committee of Jurists, which sat from March 11–19, 1929, embodied the results of its examination in two separate reports, corresponding to the two parts of its task. These reports, of which members of the Council have already taken note (C. 142. M. 52. 1929)[2] deal in detail with the questions referred to the committee. My colleagues will have found in them the proposals put forward by the committee, together with a statement of the grounds on which those proposals are based.

One of the reports, relating to the revision of the Statute of the Permanent Court of International Justice, recommends certain amendments to that Statute. The report contains the following suggestions in regard to the procedure to be followed in this matter:

> If the Council approves the conclusions of the report, it will no doubt find it convenient to communicate them to the Members of the League of Nations and the states mentioned in the Annex to the Covenant and to transmit them to the Assembly; it would be desirable that, if the amendments secure general approval, the protocol accepting them, which must be concluded between the parties which have ratified the 1920 Statute, should be made in the course of the next Assembly.
>
> On this point, the committee must call the attention of the Council to the necessity for taking appropriate measures to secure the entry into force of the amendments a sufficient time before the election of the members of the Court in September, 1930, on account, more particularly, of the changes which are made in regard to the number of the members of the Court and the rules as to the occupations which are incompatible with membership.

Although the Assembly's resolution of September 20, 1928, asks the Council "to submit the necessary proposals to the next ordinary session of the Assembly," it seems clear that the intentions of the

[1] *Official Journal*, X, p. 996.
[2] *Ibid.*, p. 1113.

Assembly will be fulfilled only if measures are taken by the Council forthwith for the early consideration by the states parties to the Court's Statute of the proposed amendments. I think that the Council would be correctly interpreting the wishes of the Assembly in deciding, in accordance with the committee's suggestion, that such a consultation should take place concurrently with the next session of the Assembly. I propose, therefore, that the Council decide to convoke a conference of the states parties to the Statute to meet at a date that would enable it to consult with the Assembly, whose intervention is also required. For similar reasons the Council might agree to ask the Supervisory Commission to examine and report to the Assembly at its next session on the financial proposals contained in Par. 14 of the report of the committee.

. . . .

I venture, therefore, to submit to the Council the following draft resolution:

The Council adopts the considerations and suggestions put forward by its Rapporteur. In view of the report which the Committee of Jurists has submitted to it on the question of the revision of the Statute of the Permanent Court of International Justice,

The Council decides:

To instruct the Secretary-General to communicate the report of the committee to the Members of the League of Nations and to the states mentioned in the Annex to the Covenant;

To convoke a conference of states parties to the Statute of the Permanent Court of International Justice to meet at Geneva on [Wednesday, September 4,[1]] 1929, with a view to examining the amendments to the Statute and recommendations formulated by the Committee of Jurists;

To request the Supervisory Commission to present to the Assembly at its next ordinary session its opinion as to the measures proposed in paragraph 14 of the report of the Committee of Jurists.

The draft resolution was adopted.

[1] Tuesday, September 10, was the date in the resolution as adopted; however, a reconsideration of the date by the Council resulted in advancing it to Wednesday, September 4 (*Official Journal*, X, p. 1031).

IV. PROTOCOL CONCERNING REVISION OF THE STATUTE OF THE PERMANENT COURT OF INTERNATIONAL JUSTICE, OPENED FOR SIGNATURE AT GENEVA, SEPTEMBER 14, 1929[1]

1. The undersigned, duly authorized, agree, on behalf of the Governments which they represent, to make in the Statute of the Permanent Court of International Justice the amendments which are set out in the Annex to the present Protocol and which form the subject of the resolution of the Assembly of the League of Nations of September 14, 1929.

2. The present Protocol, of which the French and English texts are both authentic, shall be presented for signature to all the signatories of the Protocol of December 16, 1920, to which the Statute of the Permanent Court of International Justice is annexed, and to the United States of America.

3. The present Protocol shall be ratified. The instruments of ratification shall be deposited, if possible before September 1, 1930, with the Secretary-General of the League of Nations, who shall inform the Members of the League of Nations and the States mentioned in the Annex to the Covenant.

4. The present Protocol shall enter into force on September 1, 1930, provided that the Council of the League of Nations has satisfied itself that those Members of the League of Nations and States mentioned in the Annex to the Covenant which have ratified the Protocol of December 16, 1920, and whose ratification of the present Protocol has not been received by that date, have no objection to the coming into force of the amendments to the Statute of the Court which are annexed to the present Protocol.

5. After the entry into force of the present Protocol, the new provisions shall form part of the Statute adopted in 1920 and the

[1] Reprinted from the protocol in League Document C. 492. M. 156. 1929. V. The Protocol was opened for signature following the adoption of a resolution by the Assembly of the League of Nations which read in part:

"1. The Assembly adopts the amendments to the Statute of the Permanent Court of International Justice and the draft Protocol which the Conference convened by the Council of the League of Nations has drawn up after consideration of the report of the Committee of Jurists, which met in March 1929 at Geneva and which included among its members a jurist of the United States of America. The Assembly expresses the hope that the draft Protocol drawn up by the Conference may receive as many signatures as possible before the close of the present session of the Assembly and that all the Governments concerned will use their utmost efforts to secure the entry into force of the amendments to the Statute of the Court before the opening of the next session of the Assembly, in the course of which the Assembly and the Council will be called upon to proceed to a new election of the members of the Court."

provisions of the original articles which have been made the subject of amendment shall be abrogated. It is understood that, until January 1, 1931, the Court shall continue to perform its functions in accordance with the Statute of 1920.

6. After the entry into force of the present Protocol, any acceptance of the Statute of the Court shall constitute an acceptance of the Statute as amended.

7. For the purposes of the present Protocol, the United States of America shall be in the same position as a State which has ratified the Protocol of December 16, 1920.

DONE at Geneva, the fourteenth day of September, nineteen hundred and twenty-nine, in a single copy which shall be deposited in the archives of the Secretariat of the League of Nations. The Secretary-General shall deliver authenticated copies to the Members of the League of Nations and to the States mentioned in the Annex to the Covenant.

[Up to October 1, 1929, the Protocol had been signed on behalf of the following states:

Australia
Austria
Belgium
Bolivia
Brazil
Bulgaria
Canada
Chile
China
Colombia
Czechoslovakia
Denmark
Dominican Republic
Estonia
Finland
France
Germany
Great Britain and Northern Ireland and all Parts of the British Empire not separate Members of the League of Nations
Greece
Guatemala
Haiti
Hungary
India
Irish Free State
Italy
Latvia
Liberia
Luxemburg
Netherlands
New Zealand
Nicaragua
Norway
Panama
Paraguay
Persia
Peru
Poland
Portugal
Rumania
Salvador
Serb-Croat-Slovene State
Siam
South Africa, Union of
Spain
Sweden
Switzerland
Uruguay
Venezuela]

Annex to the Protocol of September 14, 1929

Amendments to the Statute of the Permanent Court of International Justice

Arts. 3, 4, 8, 13, 14, 15, 16, 17, 23, 25, 26, 27, 29, 31, 32 and 35 are replaced by the following provisions:

[The new texts are here set forth *in extenso;* for them see the Statute, p. 83 [723], *supra.*]

Arts. 39 and 40 are replaced by the following provisions:

[The new text of these articles as printed in the Statute.]

The English text of Art. 45 is replaced by the following provision:

[The text as printed in the Statute.]

The following new chapter is added to the Statute of the Court:

[New Arts. 65–68 are set forth as printed in the Statute.][1]

[1] *Supra*, p. 101 [741].

V. THE UNITED STATES AND REVISION

LETTER FROM THE PRESIDENT OF THE CONFERENCE OF SIGNATORY STATES TO THE ASSEMBLY OF THE LEAGUE OF NATIONS[1]

[Excerpt]

The Conference associates itself with the following observations made by its Drafting Committee upon the draft Protocol:

As regards the special position of the United States, it may perhaps prevent misunderstanding if it is pointed out that three instruments relating to the Court will be presented for acceptance to that power, namely:

> The Protocol destined to satisfy the reservations attached by the United States Senate to the accession of the United States of America to the Statute of the Court;
>
> The Protocol of Signature of 1920; and
>
> The new Protocol relating to the amendment of the Statute.

There could, of course, be no question of the United States being a party to the unamended Statute while the other states concerned were parties to the Statute in its amended form, but the draft Protocol relating to the amendment of the Statute is believed to safeguard entirely the situation of the United States with regard to the amendments (see par. 7 of the Protocol); and, while it is, of course, not within the province of the Drafting Committee or the Conference to anticipate what procedure the United States may follow, it may be hoped that the United States will in due course sign and ratify all three above-mentioned instruments. It would, in fact, be possible for the United States at the moment when it signs the Protocol dealing with its reservations to sign also the Protocol of Signature of 1920 and that relating to the amendments, subject to the eventual entry into force of the first-mentioned agreement.

[1] Reprinted from League of Nations Document A. 50. 1929. V. 16, p. 3.

APPENDIX II

ACCESSION OF THE UNITED STATES

I. SENATE RESOLUTION GIVING ADVICE AND CONSENT OF THE SENATE TO THE ADHESION BY THE UNITED STATES TO THE PROTOCOL OF DECEMBER 16, 1920, WITH RESERVATIONS, JANUARY 27, 1926[1]

Whereas the President, under date of February 24, 1923, transmitted a message to the Senate, accompanied by a letter from the Secretary of State, dated February 17, 1923, asking the favorable advice and consent of the Senate to the adherence on the part of the United States to the Protocol of December 16, 1920, of Signature of the Statute for the Permanent Court of International Justice, set out in the said message of the President (without accepting or agreeing to the optional clause for compulsory jurisdiction contained therein), upon the conditions and understandings hereafter stated, to be made a part of the instrument of adherence: Therefore, be it

Resolved (*two-thirds of the Senators present concurring*), That the Senate advise and consent to the adherence on the part of the United States to the said Protocol of December 16, 1920, and the adjoined Statute for the Permanent Court of International Justice (without accepting or agreeing to the optional clause for compulsory jurisdiction contained in said Statute), and that the signature of the United States be affixed to the said Protocol, subject to the following reservations and understandings, which are hereby made a part and condition of this resolution, namely:

1. That such adherence shall not be taken to involve any legal relation on the part of the United States to the League of Nations or the assumption of any obligations by the United States under the treaty of Versailles.

[1] S. Res. 5, 69th Cong. 1st sess., as modified in open executive session, January 16 (calendar day, January 23), 1926, and passed January 16 (calendar day, January 27), 1926.

2. That the United States shall be permitted to participate through representatives designated for the purpose and upon an equality with the other states, members, respectively, of the Council and Assembly of the League of Nations, in any and all proceedings of either the Council or the Assembly for the election of judges or deputy-judges of the Permanent Court of International Justice or for the filling of vacancies.

3. That the United States will pay a fair share of the expenses of the Court as determined and appropriated from time to time by the Congress of the United States.

4. That the United States may at any time withdraw its adherence to the said Protocol and that the Statute for the Permanent Court of International Justice adjoined to the Protocol shall not be amended without the consent of the United States.

5. That the Court shall not render any advisory opinion except publicly after due notice to all states adhering to the Court and to all interested states and after public hearing or opportunity for hearing given to any state concerned; nor shall it, without the consent of the United States, entertain any request for an advisory opinion touching any dispute or question in which the United States has or claims an interest.

The signature of the United States to the said Protocol shall not be affixed until the powers signatory to such Protocol shall have indicated, through an exchange of notes, their acceptance of the foregoing reservations and understandings as a part and a condition of adherence by the United States to the said Protocol.

Resolved, further, As a part of this act of ratification that the United States approve the Protocol and Statute hereinabove mentioned, with the understanding that recourse to the Permanent Court of International Justice for the settlement of differences between the United States and any other state or states can be had only by agreement thereto through general or special treaties concluded between the parties in dispute; and

Resolved, further, That adherence to the said Protocol and Statute hereby approved shall not be so construed as to require the United States to depart from its traditional policy of not intruding upon, interfering with, or entangling itself in the political questions of policy or internal administration of any foreign state; nor shall adherence to the said Protocol and Statute be construed to imply a relinquishment by the United States of its traditional attitude toward purely American questions.

II. PRELIMINARY DRAFT OF A PROTOCOL ADOPTED BY THE CONFERENCE OF STATES SIGNATORIES, SEPTEMBER 23, 1926 [1]

The states signatories of the Protocol of Signature of the Permanent Court of International Justice, dated December 16, 1920, and the United States of America, through the undersigned duly authorized representatives, have agreed upon the following provisions regarding the adherence by the United States of America to the said Protocol, subject to the five reservations formulated by the United States.

Article 1

The United States shall be admitted to participate, through representatives designated for the purpose and upon an equality with the signatory states, Members of the League of Nations, represented in the Council or in the Assembly, in any and all proceedings of either the Council or the Assembly for the election of judges or deputy-judges of the Permanent Court of International Justice, provided for in the Statute of the Court. The vote of the United States shall be counted in determining the absolute majority of votes required by the Statute.

Article 2

No amendment of the Statute annexed to the Protocol of December 16, 1920, may be made without the consent of all the contracting states.

Article 3

The Court shall render advisory opinions in public session.

Article 4

The manner in which the consent provided for in the second part of the fifth reservation is to be given, will be the subject of an understanding to be reached by the Government of the United States with the Council of the League of Nations.

[1] Annex B of the Final Act of the conference, *Minutes of the Conference* (1926. V. 26), p. 81; Hudson, *op. cit.*, p. 181.

The states signatories of the Protocol of December 16, 1920, will be informed as soon as the understanding contemplated by the preceding paragraph has been reached.

Should the United States offer objection to an advisory opinion being given by the Court, at the request of the Council or the Assembly, concerning a dispute to which the United States is not a party or concerning a question other than a dispute between states, the Court will attribute to such objection the same force and effect as attaches to a vote against asking for the opinion given by a Member of the League of Nations either in the Assembly or in the Council.

Article 5

Subject to the provisions of Art. 7 below, the provisions of the present Protocol shall have the same force and effect as the provisions of the Statute annexed to the Protocol of December 16, 1920.

Article 6

The present Protocol shall be ratified. Each State shall forward the instrument of ratification to the Secretary-General of the League of Nations, who shall inform all the other signatory states. The instruments of ratification shall be deposited in the archives of the Secretariat of the League of Nations.

The present Protocol shall come into force as soon as all the states which have ratified the Protocol of December 16, 1920, including the United States, have deposited their ratifications.

Article 7

The United States may at any time notify the Secretary-General of the League of Nations that it withdraws its adherence to the Protocol of December 16, 1920. The Secretary-General shall immediately communicate this notification to all the other states signatories of the Protocol.

In such case the present Protocol shall cease to be in force as from the receipt by the Secretary-General of the notification by the United States.

On their part, each of the contracting states may at any time notify the Secretary-General of the League of Nations that it desires to withdraw its acceptance of the special conditions attached by the United States to its adherence to the Protocol of December 16, 1920, in the second part of its fourth reservation and in its fifth reservation. The Secretary-General shall immediately give communication of this notification to each of the states signatories of the present Protocol. The present Protocol shall be considered as ceasing to be in force if and when, within one year from the receipt of the said notification, not less than two-thirds of the contracting states other than the United States shall have notified the Secretary-General of the League of Nations that they desire to withdraw the above-mentioned acceptance.

Article 8

The present Protocol shall remain open for signature by any state which may in the future sign the Protocol of Signature of December 16, 1920.

Done at............., the.............day of............., 19...., in a single copy, of which the French and English texts shall both be authoritative.

III. RESOLUTION OF THE COUNCIL OF THE LEAGUE OF NATIONS, MARCH 9, 1929[1]

Sir AUSTEN CHAMBERLAIN submitted the following proposal and draft resolution:[2]

My Government received a few days ago a note from the Secretary of State of the United States of America relating to the accession of the United States to the Protocol of Signature of the Statute of the Permanent Court of International Justice. I understand that similar notes have been received by the Governments of the other signatories.

The Secretary of State's communication relates more particularly to the reply made to the communication of 1926 by 24 Governments as a result of the conference which was held at the end of that year at Geneva.

My Government has observed with satisfaction that the United States Government feels that a further informal exchange of views, such as was contemplated by the conference, ought to lead to an agreement which would be satisfactory to all parties.

The Secretary of State's note has reached the Governments at the moment at which the Committee of Jurists, appointed under the Council's resolution of December 14, 1928,[3] is about to commence its study of the question of eventual amendment of the Statute of the Court. The task with which this committee has been entrusted makes it, in my opinion, possible that it might be able to furnish valuable assistance toward reaching the agreement which is contemplated in the Secretary of State's note, and which I am sure is greatly desired by all the present signatories of the Protocol of Signature of the Court's Statute.

I venture, therefore, to suggest that the Council should invite the committee to examine this question and to offer any advice upon it which it feels it can usefully give. I therefore propose the adoption of the following resolution:

"The Council requests the Committee appointed by its resolution of December 14, 1928, to consider the present situation as regards accession of the United States of America to the Protocol of Signature of the Statute of the Permanent Court of International Justice and to

[1] League of Nations, *Official Journal*, X, p. 564.

[2] Document C. 120. 1929. V.

[3] *Ibid.*, p. 56.

make any suggestions which it feels able to offer with a view of facilitating such accession on conditions satisfactory to all the interests concerned."

He added that he was sure his colleagues would have observed with great pleasure the very sympathetic reference, made in Mr. Kellogg's note, to the Council and its work.

The Government of the United States [he writes] desires to avoid, in so far as may be possible, any proposal which would interfere with or embarrass the work of the Council of the League of Nations, doubtless often perplexing and difficult, and it would be glad if it could dispose of the subject by a simple acceptance of the suggestions embodied in the Final Act and Draft Protocol adopted at Geneva on September 23, 1926. There are, however, some elements of uncertainty in the bases of these suggestions which seem to require further discussion.

The note concluded with the following friendly and hopeful statement:

The Government of the United States feels that such an informal exchange of views as is contemplated by the 24 Governments should, as herein suggested, lead to agreement upon some provision which, in unobjectionable form, would protect the rights and interests of the United States as an adherent to the Court Statute, and this expectation is strongly supported by the fact that there seems to be but little difference regarding the substance of these rights and interests.

It was in the confident hope that the above expectation would be realized that the British representative made his proposal to invite the Committee of Jurists to consider the suggestion. It was a most fortunate circumstance that among the gentlemen who had accepted the invitation of the Council to serve on that committee was the very eminent jurist and statesman, Mr. Elihu Root, than whom no one could be more competent to assist the committee in its task, since he was himself one of the framers of the Statute of the Court.

M. de Agüero y Bethancourt said that, as representative of the Government of Cuba, he wholeheartedly associated himself with the proposal made by the British representative. His Government welcomed all the more cordially the new step taken by the Government of the United States since the Cuban Government had from the beginning adhered to the amendment presented by that Government. He believed with Sir Austen Chamberlain that the presence of the distinguished jurist, Mr. Elihu Root, could not fail to have a considerable influence in achieving an agreement which was extremely desirable, not only in the interests of the Permanent Court of International Justice but also in the interests of the League of Nations.

M. Briand said that, as representative of France, he fully approved the proposal made by the representative of Great Britain and associated himself with the hope that had been expressed to the effect that the Committee of Jurists, whose terms of reference were to be enlarged, might be able, after an exchange of views with the distinguished American statesman then at Geneva, Mr. Elihu Root, to reach an agreement which was warmly desired by every one.

Dr. Stresemann associated himself with the proposal made by the Rapporteur and in particular, with the appreciation expressed by him, in common with the other speakers, of the intention of the United States of America to adhere to the Permanent Court of International Justice at The Hague. The adherence on the part of so great a state would constitute a considerable progress in the development of international life and would be an important supplement to the pact for the outlawry of war signed at Paris. He was confident that the Committee of Jurists, with the cooperation of the distinguished American lawyer, would find means of removing any difficulties which might still subsist, so that the intention of the Government at Washington might be carried out as quickly as possible. The accession of the United States would not only help to increase the prestige of the supreme international jurisdiction but would also be a further encouragement to the principle of international arbitration.

Mr. Dandurand said he was expressing the views of the Canadian Government in cordially adhering to the proposal of the British representative.

M. Zumeta, on behalf of the Government of Venezuela, fully associated himself with the proposal which had just been made by the British representative and particularly with the declarations and hopes expressed by him and the other speakers.

M. Titulesco said that the accession of the United States to the Permanent Court of International Justice would be a world event of such importance that he could very warmly support the proposal of the British representative and associate himself with the hopes that had been expressed.

M. PROCOPÉ also associated himself very sincerely with the words of the British representative. He was sure that his Government earnestly hoped that means would be found to render possible the accession of the United States to the Permanent Court of International Justice.

M. VALDÉS-MENDEVILLE said he fully agreed with the proposal of the British representative and particularly with the declarations which had been made. He further indorsed the hopes which had just been expressed, as his country would be extremely glad if a formula could be found which would render possible the accession of the United States to the Permanent Court of International Justice.

He was glad to note that the endeavor to reach a solution which was so greatly desired had been intrusted to Mr. Elihu Root working in cooperation with the Committee of Jurists. Mr. Root's qualities were very widely respected and appreciated in Chile.

M. QUIÑONES DE LEÓN associated himself with the report of the British representative and with the observations which had been added by him.

M. ADATEI cordially agreed with the proposal of the British representative and expressed the hope that the Committee of Jurists would succeed in its new task of settling this question, which was of cardinal importance.

M. ZALESKI, on behalf of Poland, warmly associated himself with the proposals of the British representative.

H. H. MOHAMMAD ALI KHAN FOROUGHI added his approval of the words which had just been spoken, in order to emphasize that the Council was unanimous on the subject.

The PRESIDENT thought it was superfluous to take a vote on the proposal, since all the members of the Council had declared themselves in favor of it. He would be the only member to abstain if he did not add a few words. As a very old delegate to the League of Nations he would remind the Council that, when the Permanent Court of International Justice had first been constituted, the Council had felt it desirable to appoint as a member of that Court a distinguished American lawyer, although the United States had not yet adhered to the Statute of the Court. That had been a solemn invitation addressed to a great country, which now declared itself ready to accept the proposal of the Council. It only remained to settle certain technical legal problems and he hoped the solution would easily be found.

The draft resolution was adopted.

Sir AUSTEN CHAMBERLAIN said that the note originally addressed to the Governments concerned was also by the courtesy of the United States Government, communicated to the League through the intermediary of the United States Legation at Bern,[1] and he would venture to propose that the Council should request the Secretary-General to send a copy of the Minutes of the present discussion to the United States Government through the same intermediary.

The proposal was approved.

[1] *Official Journal*, X, p. 779.

IV. ELIHU ROOT'S SUGGESTED REDRAFT OF ART. 4 OF THE PROTOCOL OF 1926 [1]

(The original form of the Root Plan)

The Court shall not, without the consent of the United States, render an advisory opinion touching any dispute to which the United States is a party.

The Court shall not, without the consent of the United States, render an advisory opinion touching any dispute to which the United States is not a party but in which it claims an interest or touching any question other than a dispute in which the United States claims an interest.

The manner in which it shall be made known whether the United States claims an interest and gives or withholds its consent shall be as follows:

Whenever, in contemplation of a request for an advisory opinion, it seems to them desirable, the Council or the Assembly may invite an exchange of views with the United States and such exchange of views shall proceed with all convenient speed.

Whenever a request for an advisory opinion comes to the Court, the Registrar shall notify the United States thereof, among other states mentioned in the new existing Art. 73 of the Rules of the Court, stating a reasonable time limit fixed by the President within which a written statement by the United States concerning the request will be received.

In case the United States shall, within the time fixed, advise the Court in writing that the request touches a dispute or question in which the United States has an interest and that the United States has not consented to the submission of the question, thereupon all proceedings upon the question shall be stayed to admit of an exchange of views between the United States and the proponents of the request, and such exchange of views shall proceed with all convenient speed.

If after such exchange of views, either while a question is in contemplation or after a question has gone to the Court, it shall appear:

[1] Committee of Jurists. *Minutes*, p. 9.

(1) that no agreement can be reached as to whether the question does touch an interest of the United States within the true meaning of the second paragraph of this article; and (2) that the submission of the question is still insisted upon after attributing to the objections of the United States the same force and effect as attaches to a vote against asking for the opinion given by a Member of the League of Nations either in the Assembly or in the Council; and if it also appears that the United States has not been able to find the submission of the question so important for the general good as to call upon the United States to forego its objection in that particular instance, leaving the request to be acted upon by the Court without in any way binding the United States; then it shall be deemed that, owing to material difference of view regarding the proper scope of the practice of requesting advisory opinions, the arrangement now agreed upon is not yielding satisfactory results and that the exercise of the powers of withdrawal provided in Art. 7 hereof will follow naturally without any imputation of unfriendliness or of unwillingness to cooperate generally for peace and good will.

V. REPORT ADOPTED BY THE COMMITTEE OF JURISTS, MARCH 18, 1929[1]

On February 19, 1929, the Secretary of State of the United States addressed to each of the Governments which had signed the Protocol of Signature of the Statute for the Permanent Court of International Justice, dated December 16, 1920, and also to the Secretary-General of the League of Nations, a note suggesting that an exchange of views might lead to an agreement with regard to the acceptance of the stipulation set forth in the resolution adopted by the Senate of the United States on January 27, 1926, as the conditions upon which the United States would adhere to the said Protocol. This note was considered by the Council of the League of Nations at its meeting on March 9, 1929, and cordial satisfaction was expressed at the prospect which the note held out that a solution might be found for the difficulties which had prevented the adherence of the United States in 1926. On the same date a resolution was adopted by the Council, requesting the Committee of Jurists, which had been appointed by the Council at its meeting on December 14, 1928, to consider the revision of the Statute of the Permanent Court of International Justice, to deal with this question as well as those with which it was already charged and to make any suggestions which it felt able to offer, with a view to facilitating the accession of the United States on conditions satisfactory to all the interests concerned.

It has been of the greatest assistance to the committee in the accomplishment of this additional task that among its members was to be found the Hon. Elihu Root, former Secretary of State of the United States, and one of the members of the committee which in 1920 framed the original draft of the Statute of the Court. His presence in the committee has enabled it to re-examine with good results the work accomplished by the special conference which was convoked by the Council in 1926, after the receipt of the letter of March 2 of that year from the then Secretary of State of the United States informing the Secretary-General of the League that the United States was disposed to adhere to the Protocol of December

[1] Reprinted from Document C. 142. M. 52. 1929. V. 4, p. 15. *Official Journal*, X, p. 1113.

16, 1920, on certain conditions enumerated in that letter. The United States did not see its way to participate, as it was invited to do, in the special conference of 1926, and, unfortunately, the proposals which emanated from that conference were found not to be acceptable to the United States. Nevertheless, as is shown by the note of February 19, 1929, from Mr. Kellogg, the margin of difference between the requirements of the United States and the recommendations made by the special conference to the powers which had signed the protocol of December 16, 1920, is not great. For this reason, the committee adopted as the basis of its discussions the preliminary draft of a protocol annexed to the Final Act of that conference, and has introduced into the text the changes which it believes to be necessary to overcome the objections encountered by the draft of 1926 and to render it acceptable to all parties. This revised text is now submitted to the Council of the League.

The discussions in the committee have shown that the conditions with which the Government of the United States thought it necessary to accompany the expression of its willingness to adhere to the protocol establishing the Court owed their origin to apprehension that the Council or the Assembly of the League might request from the Court advisory opinions without reference to the interests of the United States which might in certain cases be involved. Those discussions have also shown that the hesitation felt by the delegates to the conference of 1926 as to recommending the acceptance of those conditions was due to apprehension that the rights claimed in the reservations formulated by the United States might be exercised in a way which would interfere with the work of the Council or the Assembly and embarrass their procedure. The task of the committee has been to discover some method of insuring that neither on the one side nor on the other should these apprehensions prove to be well founded.

No difficulty has at any time been felt with regard to the acceptance of the conditions laid down by the United States, except in so far as they relate to advisory opinions, and the task of the committee would have been simplified if its members had felt able to recommend that the system of asking the Court for an advisory opinion upon any particular question should be abandoned altogether. The committee, however, is of opinion that it can not recommend any such drastic solution. The system of asking the Court for an advisory opinion has proved to be of substantial utility in securing a solution of questions which could not conveniently be submitted to the Court in any other form. It has also on occasions enabled parties to a dispute to ask for the submission of their difference to the Court in the form of a request for an advisory opinion when they were for various reasons unwilling to submit it in the form of international litigation.

The committee has also felt obliged to reject another method by which satisfaction might without difficulty be given to the conditions laid down by the United States. It is that of recommending the adoption of a rule that in all cases a decision on the part of the Council or Assembly to ask for an advisory opinion from the Court must be unanimous.

As is pointed out in the Final Act of the special conference of 1926, it was not then possible to say with certainty whether a decision by a majority was not sufficient. It is equally impossible to-day. All that is possible is to guarantee to the United States a position of equality in this matter with the states which are represented in the Council or the Assembly of the League.

Furthermore, mature reflection convinced the committee that it was useless to attempt to allay the apprehensions on either side, which have been referred to above, by the elaboration of any system of paper guaranties or abstract formulæ. The more hopeful system is to deal with the problem in a concrete form, to provide some method by which such questions as they arise may be examined and views exchanged, and a conclusion thereby reached after each side has made itself acquainted with the difficulties and responsibilities which beset the other.

It is this method which the committee recommends should be adopted, and to provide for which it now submits a text of a Protocol to be concluded between the States which signed the Protocol of 1920 and the United States of America.

The note of February 19, 1929, from the Secretary of State of the United States makes it clear that the Government of the United States has no desire to interfere with or to embarrass the work of the Council or the Assembly of the League, and that that Government realizes the difficulties and responsibilities of the tasks with which the League is from time to time confronted. It shows that there is no intention on the part of the United States Government of hampering upon unreal or unsubstantial grounds the machinery by which advisory opinions are from time to time requested.

The committee is thereby enabled to recommend that the states which signed the Protocol of 1920 should accept the reservations formulated by the United States upon the terms and conditions set out in the articles of the draft Protocol. This is the effect of Art. I of the draft now submitted.

The next three articles reproduce without substantial change the corresponding articles of the draft of 1926.

The fifth article provides machinery by which the United States will be made aware of any proposal before the Council or the Assembly for obtaining an advisory opinion and will have an opportunity of indicating whether the interests of the United States are affected, so that the Council or the Assembly, as the case may be, may decide its course of action with full knowledge of the position. One may hope with confidence that the exchange of views so provided for will be sufficient to insure that an understanding will be reached and no conflict of views will remain.

The provisions of this article have been worded with due regard to the exigencies of business in the Council of the League. The desirability of obtaining an advisory opinion may only become apparent as the session of the Council is drawing to a close and when it may not be possible to complete the exchange of views before the members of that body separate. In that case, it will be for the Council to give such directions as the circumstances may require in order to insure that the intentions of the article are carried out. The request addressed to the Court may, for instance, be held up temporarily, or may be dispatched with the request that the Court will nevertheless suspend action on the request until the exchange of views with the United States has been completed. The provisions of the article have purposely been framed so as to afford a measure of elasticity in its application. Similarly, if the Court has commenced the preliminary proceedings consequent upon the receipt of a request for an advisory opinion and has given notice of the request to the United States in the same way as it has to the other Governments, the proceedings may, if necessary, be interrupted in order that the necessary exchange of views may take place. What is said in this paragraph with regard to requests for advisory opinions made by the Council would also apply to requests by the Assembly in the event of the Assembly making any such request.

The provisions of this article should in practice afford protection to all parties in all cases, but, if they do not, it must be recognized that the solution embodied in the present proposal will not have achieved the success that was hoped, and that the United States would be fully justified in withdrawing from the arrangement. It is for this eventuality that provision is made in the last paragraph of the article. It may be hoped that should any such withdrawal by the United States materialize, it would in fact be followed or accompanied by the conclusion of some new and more satisfactory arrangement.

The remaining provisions of the draft Protocol do not call for detailed comment, because they are in substance similar to the corresponding provisions of the draft Protocol of 1926.

It is necessary to consider what steps will be required to bring the Protocol, of which the text is now submitted, into force in the event of the recommendations of the committee being accepted.

If the terms of the protocol are approved by the Council, it will be advisable that the Secretary General should be directed, when answering Secretary Kellogg's note of February 19, 1929, to communicate the draft to the Government of the United States. Since the Protocol, if approved, covers the entire ground of Secretary Kellogg's note, its transmission with a statement of the Council's approval would seem to constitute an adequate reply to that note. It should at the same time be communicated to all the states which signed the Protocol of December 16, 1920, together with a copy of the resolution of the Senate of the United States, dated January 27, 1926, containing the reservations of the United States.

It should also be communicated to the Assembly, in which the proposal for the appointment of this committee originated, in order that, if its terms are acceptable to that body, a resolution approving it may be passed by the Assembly in the course of its ensuing session. Any action taken by the Assembly should be communicated to the signatory states which are called upon to determine whether or not to sign the new Protocol now proposed.

If the replies from the various Governments indicate a desire for a further exchange of views in regard to the nature of the proposed arrangement with the United States or to the terms of the draft protocol, it will be for the Council to decide whether such exchange of views should proceed through the diplomatic channel or whether it is necessary to convoke a further special conference for the purpose, at which states not Members of the League might be represented. In any event, such exchange of views should, if possible, be completed before the conclusion of the Assembly, in order that the approval by the Assembly may be obtained in 1929. A copy of the Protocol in the terms approved will then be prepared for signature, and every effort should be made to secure that delegates to the meeting of the Assembly or of the special conference, if there should be one, should be authorized to sign the instrument, and should actually sign it before they leave Geneva. The signature of representatives of states not Members of the League should be obtained at the same time.

As provided in Art. 7 of the draft, the protocol will come into force as soon as it has been ratified by the states which have ratified the Protocol of December 16, 1920, and by the United States, and, as soon as it comes into force, it will be possible for the United States to take the necessary steps to become a party to the Protocol of December 16, 1920, and to any further protocol which may have been concluded for introducing amendments into the Statute of the Court.

When that happy result has been achieved, it will be possible to feel that further progress has been made in establishing the reign of law among the nations of the world and in diminishing the risk that there may be a resort to force for the solution of their conflicts.

VI. ACTION OF THE COUNCIL OF THE LEAGUE OF NATIONS: REPORT AND RESOLUTION, JUNE 12, 1929 [1]

Referring to a letter from the Secretary of State of the United States of America, dated February 19, 1929, the Council of the League of Nations, on March 9 following, requested the Committee of Jurists mentioned in its resolutions of December 13 and 14, 1928, to make any suggestions which it felt able to offer with a view to facilitating the accession of the United States of America to the Protocol of Signature of the Statute of the Permanent Court of International Justice.

The Committee of Jurists, which sat from March 11–19, 1929, set forth in a report, to which is annexed a draft Protocol, the results of its study of the question. My colleagues have seen this report, which follows the Committee's report on the examination of the Statute of the Court in document C. 142. M. 52. 1929. The members of the Council will have found in the report, together with the proposals submitted, a statement of the grounds on which those proposals are based.

The procedure proposed by the committee seems to constitute the best means of realizing the end in view. The Jurists in their report have contemplated that:

> If the terms of the Protocol are approved by the Council, it will be advisable that the Secretary-General should be directed, when answering Mr. Kellogg's note of February 19, 1929, to communicate the draft to the Government of the United States. Since the Protocol, if approved, covers the entire ground of Mr. Kellogg's note, its transmission with a statement of the Council's approval would seem to constitute an adequate reply to that note. It should, at the same time, be communicated to all the States which signed the Protocol of December 16, 1920, together with a copy of the resolution of the Senate of the United States, dated January 27, 1926, containing the reservations of the United States.

As the Assembly is called upon to pronounce upon the matter at its next session, the procedure recommended gives the states which

[1] *Official Journal*, X, p. 997. (Document C. 275. 1929. V.)

are parties to the Court's Statute and the United States time to proceed in the interval to the necessary study of the question.

In view of what I have said, I have the honor to submit to the Council the following resolution: [1]

The Council adopts, together with the draft Protocol annexed thereto, the report submitted to it by the Committee of Jurists on the question of the accession of the United States of America to the Protocol of Signature of the Statute of the Permanent Court of International Justice.

Accordingly, it instructs the Secretary-General:

1. To reply to Mr. Kellogg's note of February 19, 1929, and communicate to the United States Government, together with the present Council resolution, the text of the said report and of the said draft Protocol;

2. To make the same communication to the states signatories of the Protocol of December 16, 1920, and to transmit also to those states the text of the resolution of the Senate of the United States, dated January 27, 1926, embodying the latter's reservations.

In order that the Assembly, being, like the Council, a body whose procedure in regard to the method of seeking Advisory Opinions from the Court would be affected by the adoption of the Protocol proposed by the Committee of Jurists, may have an opportunity of expressing its opinion thereon, the Council decides to instruct the Secretary-General to transmit to the Assembly the report of the committee and the draft Protocol and to place the question on the supplementary agenda of the tenth ordinary session of the Assembly.

[1] This resolution was transmitted on the same day by the Secretary-General to the Secretary of State.

VII. ASSENT OF UNITED STATES GOVERNMENT

1. Aide Mémoire presented on August 14, 1929, by the American Minister at Bern to the Secretary-General of the League of Nations [1]

The Minister of the United States to Switzerland has been instructed to acknowledge in person the courtesy of the Secretary-General of the League of Nations in forwarding his informal note of May 2, 1929,[2] and his formal note from Madrid dated June 12, 1929,[3] the latter inclosing the Council's resolution of June 12, 1929, League Document C. 142. M. 52. 1929. V, containing the texts of the report of the Committee of Jurists adopted at their session in Geneva, March 11 to March 19, 1929, and the annexed draft protocol as mentioned in the resolution regarding the question of American accession to the protocol of organization of the statute of the Permanent Court of International Justice.

The minister has been instructed at the same time to inform the Secretary-General that after careful examination the Secretary of State considers that the said draft protocol would effectively meet the objections represented in the reservations of the United States Senate and would constitute a satisfactory basis for the adherence of the United States to the Protocol and Statute of the Permanent Court of International Justice dated December 16, 1920, and that after the draft protocol has been accepted by the states signatory to the Protocol of Signature and the Statute of the Permanent Court he will request the President of the United States for the requisite authority to sign and will recommend that it be submitted to the Senate for its consent to ratification.

2. Statement by the Secretary of State, September 5, 1929 [4]

I have carefully examined the draft protocol recommended by the Committee of Jurists last spring for the purpose of meeting the objections represented by the reservations of the United States

[1] Reprinted from Department of State release, September 5, 1929.

[2] *Ad interim* note not here reproduced.

[3] Not here reproduced.

[4] Reprinted from Department of State release.

Senate in regard to the entry of the United States into the World Court and I have satisfied myself that this draft protocol, if ratified by the other signatory powers, would meet the objections raised by the Senate and fully protect the United States against the dangers anticipated by the Senate. Accordingly, last month I notified the Secretary-General of the League of Nations, who is presenting this to the other signatory powers, that the draft protocol met with my approval and that if it was accepted by the other states I would recommend to the President of the United States that it be signed and submitted to the Senate for its consent to ratification.

VIII. REPORT OF THE FIRST COMMITTEE TO THE ASSEMBLY OF THE LEAGUE OF NATIONS[1]

Rapporteur: M. Politis (Greece)

After the resolution adopted by the Senate of the United States on January 27, 1926, with regard to the adherence of the United States to the Protocol of Signature of the Statute of the Permanent Court of International Justice of December 16, 1920, a Conference of the Signatories of the said Protocol was held at Geneva in September, 1926, for the purpose of considering how effect might be given to the reservations and understandings embodied in the Senate resolution. The conference of 1926 prepared the draft of a protocol which it was believed would meet all the requirements of the situation, but unfortunately the Government of the United States, which had not been represented in the Conference, did not see its way to accept the protocol.

On February 19, 1929, the Government of the United States intimated by means of a note addressed to all the interested parties that an exchange of views might lead to an agreement with regard to the conditions upon which the United States desired to adhere to the Statute of the Court. Arrangements were accordingly made by the Council of the League that the Committee of Jurists which it had appointed in pursuance of the resolution of the Assembly dated September 20, 1928, on the subject of the examination of the Statute of the Court to see whether any amendments were necessary, should deal also with the question raised by the note from the United States Government and should make any suggestions which it felt able to offer with a view to facilitating the accession of the United States on conditions satisfactory to all the interests concerned.

It was of the greatest assistance to the Committee in the accomplishment of this additional task that among its members was to be found the Hon. Elihu Root, formerly Secretary of State of the United States, and one of the members of the committee which in 1920 framed the original draft of the Statute of the Court. His presence in the committee enabled it to re-examine with good

[1] Reprinted from A. 49. 1929. V. 15.

results the work accomplished by the Special Conference which met in 1926. The note from the United States Government to which reference is made above had shown that the margin of difference between the requirements of the United States and the recommendations made by the Special Conference was not great. For this reason, the Committee of Jurists adopted as the basis of its discussions the preliminary draft of a protocol which was annexed to the Final Act of that conference and introduced into it the changes which it believed were necessary in order to overcome the objections encountered by the draft of 1926 and to render it acceptable to all parties.

The revised draft protocol was submitted to the Council of the League and adopted by that body at its session at Madrid on June 12, 1929. It was placed on the agenda of the present session of the Assembly and also, in consequence of a resolution of the Council of August 31, 1929, upon that of the conference convened to consider the revision of the Court's Statute. This conference has now informed the Assembly that the text of the protocol has been approved by all the Governments represented in the conference and that there is every reason to believe that it will meet with unanimous acceptance. It is necessary, however, that the protocol should be formally approved by the Assembly of the League before it is opened for signature, as the agreement which it embodies will affect the right of the Assembly to ask for an advisory opinion from the Court.

No difficulty has at any time been felt with regard to the acceptance of the conditions laid down by the United States in the Senate resolution of January 27, 1926, except in so far as they relate to advisory opinions. A simple solution of these difficulties would have been found had it been possible to agree that the system of asking the Court for an advisory opinion upon any particular question should be abandoned altogether. So drastic a solution, however, is not at present feasible. The system of asking the Court for an advisory opinion has proved to be of substantial utility in securing a solution of questions which could not conveniently be submitted to the Court in any other form. It has also on occasions enabled the parties to a dispute to ask for the submission of their differences to the Court in the form of a request for an advisory opinion when they were for various reasons unwilling to submit them in the form of international litigation.

Another method by which satisfaction might easily have been given to the conditions laid down by the United States would have been that of adopting a rule that in all cases a decision on the part of the Council or of the Assembly to ask for an advisory opinion from the Court must be unanimous. As was pointed out in the Final Act of the special conference of 1926, it is not possible to say with certainty whether a decision by a majority is not sufficient. On this point, all that is possible is to guarantee to the United States a position of equality with the states which are represented in the Council or the Assembly of the League.

The investigation of the whole subject which was made by the Committee of Jurists showed that the conditions with which the Government of the United States thought it necessary to accompany the expression of its willingness to adhere to the protocol establishing the Court owed their origin to apprehension that the Council or the Assembly of the League might request from the Court advisory opinions without reference to the interests of the United States, which might in certain cases be involved. Those discussions also showed that the hesitation felt by the delegates to the conference of 1926 as to recommending the acceptance of those conditions was due to apprehension that the rights claimed in the reservations formulated by the United States might be exercised in a way which would interfere with the work of the Council or the Assembly and embarrass their procedure.

The system of asking a judicial tribunal for advisory opinions is one which does not exist at all in the Constitution of the United States of America, and it is not unnatural that some misapprehension should be entertained in that country as to the rôle which the Permanent Court of International Justice fulfils in giving advisory opinions on questions submitted to it by the Council or the Assembly of the League. The procedure followed by the Court in dealing with the questions submitted to it for an advisory opinion is in fact almost identical with the procedure which is followed in dealing with contentious cases.

Misapprehension appears also to exist in the United States as to the powers of the Council to give effect to the opinions rendered by the Court on questions submitted to it by the Council or the Assembly. It has, for instance, been suggested that the provisions of the concluding paragraph of Art. 13[1] of the Covenant would

[1] The article relates to settlement of disputes between Members of the League by arbitration or judicial methods. The concluding paragraph reads:

"4. The Members of the League agree that they will carry out in full good faith any award *or decision* that may be rendered, and that they will not resort to war against a Member of the League which complies therewith. In the event of any failure to carry out such an award *or decision*, the Council shall propose what steps should be taken to give effect thereto."

enable the Council to oblige the Members of the League to resort to war for the purpose of enforcing such an opinion.

This view is erroneous. The last paragraph of Art. 13 relates only to awards or decisions, not to advisory opinions. Advisory opinions are given by the Court at the request only of the Council or the Assembly of the League and in general only for the purpose of guiding the organs of the League or the International Labor Office in questions which come before those bodies in the execution of their duties. They are opinions only and in theory are not binding. Even in cases where an advisory opinion was asked for by the Council or the Assembly at the request of individual States which preferred to submit their disputes to judicial settlement through the machinery of an advisory opinion rather than by direct submission to the Court, the powers of the Council would not go beyond its general duty of securing respect for treaty engagements by insuring that parties which submit their dispute for decision by a tribunal shall execute in good faith the decision which may be rendered. The power of the Council under Art. 13, par. 4, in connection with awards or judicial decisions, is limited to "*proposing*" measures for the purpose of giving effect to them. It can not do more. It certainly could not oblige states to take measures which would violate their treaty engagements.

The discussions which took place in the Committee of Jurists showed that it was useless to attempt to allay the apprehensions on either side referred to above by the elaboration of any system of paper guarantees or abstract formulae. The only satisfactory method would be to deal with the problem in a concrete form, to provide some method by which the parties might be brought into contact so that questions as they arise might be examined and views exchanged and a conclusion thereby reached after each side had made itself acquainted with the difficulties and responsibilities which beset the other. This is the method which the committee recommended should be adopted and to provide for which it submitted the text of a protocol to be concluded between the states which signed the Protocol of 1920 and the United States of America. This view has been endorsed by the Conference which has recently concluded its labors, and the First Committee now recommends that it should be adopted by the Assembly.

The note of February 19, 1929, from the United States had made it clear that that Government has no desire to interfere with the work of the Council or the Assembly of the League and that there is no intention on the part of that Government to hamper, upon unreal or unsubstantial grounds, the machinery by which advisory opinions are from time to time requested. This rendered it possible for the committee to recommend that the states which signed the Protocol of 1920 should accept the reservations formulated by the United States upon the terms and conditions set out in the articles of the draft protocol which the committee prepared and which is now annexed to this report.[1] The important article is No. 5, which provides machinery by which the United States will be made aware of any proposal before the Council or the Assembly for obtaining an advisory opinion and will have an opportunity of indicating whether the interests of the United States are affected, so that the Council or the Assembly, as the case may be, may decide its course of action with full knowledge of the position. It may be expected that the exchange of views so provided for will be sufficient to insure that an understanding will be reached and no conflict of views will remain.

The provisions of this article have been worded with due regard to the exigencies of business in the Council of the League. The desirability of obtaining an advisory opinion may only become apparent as the session of the Council is drawing to a close and when it may not be possible to complete the exchange of views before the members of that body separate. In that case, it will be for the Council to give such directions as the circumstances may require, in order to insure that the intentions of the article are carried out. The request addressed to the Court may, for instance, be held up temporarily, or it may be dispatched with a request that the Court will nevertheless suspend action on the request until the exchange of views with the United States has been completed. The provisions of the article have purposely been framed so as to afford a measure of elasticity in its application. Similarly, if the Court has commenced the preliminary proceedings consequent upon the receipt of the request for an advisory opinion and has given notice of the request to the United States in the same way as to the other Governments, the proceedings may, if necessary, be interrupted in order that the necessary exchange of views may take place. What is said in this paragraph with regard to requests for advisory opinions made by the Council would also apply to requests by the Assembly in the event of the Assembly making any such request.

The provisions of this article should in practice afford protection to all parties in all cases; but, if they do not, it must be recognized

[1] This document in its completed form is No. IX, following.

that the solution embodied in the present proposal will not have achieved the success that was hoped for and that the United States would be fully justified in withdrawing from the arrangement. It is for this eventuality that provision is made in the last paragraph of the article. It may be hoped that, should any such withdrawal by the United States materialize, it would in fact be followed or accompanied by the conclusion of some new and more satisfactory arrangement.

In order to insure so far as possible that the parties to the Protocol of 1920 shall be identical with the parties to the new Protocol, Art. 6 provides that any State which in future signs the Protocol of 1920 shall be deemed to accept the new Protocol.

The remaining provisions of the draft Protocol do not call for detailed comment, because they are in substance similar to the corresponding provisions of the Draft Protocol of 1926.

For these reasons the First Committee submits the following resolution to the Assembly:

"The Assembly adopts the draft Protocol relating to the adherence of the United States of America to the Protocol of Signature of the Statute of the Permanent Court of International Justice."

It is understood that, if this resolution is adopted by the Assembly, the Secretary-General will proceed forthwith to open the Protocol for signature.

IX. PROTOCOL REGARDING THE ACCESSION OF THE UNITED STATES OF AMERICA TO THE PROTOCOL OF SIGNATURE OF THE PERMANENT COURT OF INTERNATIONAL JUSTICE OPENED FOR SIGNATURE AT GENEVA, SEPTEMBER 14, 1929[1]

The states signatories of the Protocol of Signature of the Statute of the Permanent Court of International Justice, dated December 16, 1920, and the United States of America, through the undersigned duly authorized representatives, have mutually agreed upon the following provisions regarding the adherence of the United States of America to the said Protocol, subject to the five reservations formulated by the United States in the resolution adopted by the Senate on January 27, 1926.

ART. 1. The states signatories of the said Protocol accept the special conditions attached by the United States in the five reservations mentioned above to its adherence to the said Protocol upon the terms and conditions set out in the following articles.

ART. 2. The United States shall be admitted to participate, through representatives designated for the purpose and upon an equality with the signatory states Members of the League of Nations represented in the Council or in the Assembly, in any and all proceedings of either the Council or the Assembly for the election of judges or deputy-judges of the Permanent Court of International Justice, provided for in the Statute of the Court. The vote of the United States shall be counted in determining the absolute majority of votes required by the Statute.

ART. 3. No amendment of the Statute of the Court may be made without the consent of all the contracting states.

ART. 4. The Court shall render advisory opinions in public session after notice and opportunity for hearing substantially as provided in the now existing Arts. 73 and 74 of the Rules of Court.

ART. 5. With a view to insuring that the Court shall not, without the consent of the United States, entertain any request for an advisory opinion touching any dispute or question in which the United States has or claims an interest, the Secretary-General of the League of Nations shall, through any channel designated for that purpose by the United States, inform the United States of any

[1] Reprint from the certified copy in League Document C. 493. M. 157. 1929. V. The text is identically that drawn up by the Committee of Jurists, March 18, 1929. The Council of the League submitted it to the Conference of Signatory States held September 4–12, which adopted it without change, as did the Assembly on September 14.

roposal before the Council or the Assembly of the League for obaining an advisory opinion from the Court, and thereupon, if esired, an exchange of views as to whether an interest of the Jnited States is affected shall proceed with all convenient speed beween the Council or the Assembly of the League and the United States.

Whenever a request for an advisory opinion comes to the Court, the Registrar shall notify the United States thereof, among other States mentioned in the now existing Art. 73 of the Rules of Court, stating a reasonable time limit fixed by the President within which a written statement by the United States concerning the request will be received. If for any reason no sufficient opportunity for an exchange of views upon such request should have been afforded, and the United States advises the Court that the question upon which the opinion of the Court is asked is one that affects the interests of the United States, proceedings shall be stayed for a period sufficient to enable such an exchange of views between the Council or the Assembly and the United States to take place.

With regard to requesting an advisory opinion of the Court in any case covered by the preceding paragraphs, there shall be attributed to an objection of the United States the same force and effect as attaches to a vote against asking for the opinion given by a Member of the League of Nations in the Council or in the Assembly.

If, after the exchange of views provided for in pars. 1 and 2 of this article, it shall appear that no agreement can be reached and the United States is not prepared to forego its objection, the exercise of the powers of withdrawal provided for in Art. 8 hereof will follow naturally without any imputation of unfriendliness or unwillingness to cooperate generally for peace and good will.

ART. 6. Subject to the provisions of Art. 8 below, the provisions of the present Protocol shall have the same force and effect as the provisions of the Statute of the Court and any future signature of the Protocol of December 16, 1920, shall be deemed to be an acceptance of the provisions of the present Protocol.

ART. 7. The present Protocol shall be ratified. Each state shall forward the instrument of ratification to the Secretary-General of the League of Nations, who shall inform all the other signatory states. The instruments of ratification shall be deposited in the archives of the Secretariat of the League of Nations.

The present Protocol shall come into force as soon as all states which have ratified the Protocol of December 16, 1920, and also the United States, have deposited their ratifications.

ART. 8. The United States may at any time notify the Secretary-General of the League of Nations that it withdraws its adherence to the Protocol of December 16, 1920. The Secretary-General shall immediately communicate this notification to all the other states signatories of the Protocol.

In such case the present Protocol shall cease to be in force as from the receipt by the Secretary-General of the notification by the United States.

On their part, each of the other contracting states may at any time notify the Secretary-General of the League of Nations that it desires to withdraw its acceptance of the special conditions attached by the United States to its adherence to the Protocol of December 16, 1920. The Secretary-General shall immediately give communication of this notification to each of the states signatories of the present Protocol. The present Protocol shall be considered as ceasing to be in force if and when, within one year from the date of receipt of the said notification, not less than two-thirds of the contracting states other than the United States shall have notified the Secretary-General of the League of Nations that they desire to withdraw the above-mentioned acceptance.

Done at Geneva, the fourteenth day of September, nineteen hundred and twenty-nine, in a single copy, of which the French and English texts shall both be authoritative.

[Up to October 1, 1929, the Protocol had been signed on behalf of the following states:

Australia
Austria
Belgium
Bolivia
Brazil
Bulgaria
Canada
Chile
China
Colombia
Cuba
Czechoslovakia
Denmark
Dominican Republic
Estonia
Finland
France
Germany
Great Britain and Northern Ireland and all Parts of the British Empire not separate Members of the League of Nations
Greece
Guatemala
Haiti
Hungary
India
Irish Free State
Italy
Japan
Latvia
Liberia
Luxemburg
Netherlands
New Zealand
Nicaragua

Norway
Panama
Paraguay
Persia
Peru
Poland
Portugal
Rumania
Salvador
Serb-Croat-Slovene State
Siam
South Africa, Union of
Spain
Sweden
Switzerland
Uruguay
Venezuela]

WHAT'S WRONG WITH INTERNATIONAL LAW?

By

DR. W. FRIEDMANN, LL.M.
Quain Lecturer in Laws, University College, London

LONDON:
WATTS & CO.,
5 & 6 JOHNSON'S COURT, FLEET STREET, E.C.4

THE THINKER'S LIBRARY

Each clothette, 1s. 3d. net

(With the exception of No. 62, which is 2s. 6d. net, cloth bound)

FULL LIST OF TITLES

1. **First and Last Things** — H. G. Wells
2. **Education: Intellectual, Moral, and Physical** — Herbert Spencer
3. **The Riddle of the Universe** — Ernst Haeckel
4. **Humanity's Gain from Unbelief** — Charles Bradlaugh
5. **On Liberty** — J. S. Mill
6. **A Short History of the World** (Revised edition to 1938) — H. G. Wells
7. **Autobiography of Charles Darwin**
9. **Twelve Years in a Monastery** — Joseph McCabe
10. **History of Modern Philosophy** — A. W. Benn
11. **Gibbon on Christianity**
12. **The Descent of Man** — Charles Darwin
13. **History of Civilization in England** (Vol. I) — H. T. Buckle
14, 15. **Anthropology** (In 2 vols.; Illus.) — Sir E. B. Tylor, Kt.
16. **Iphigenia** — Two Plays by Euripides
17. **Lectures and Essays** — T. H. Huxley
18. **The Evolution of the Idea of God** — Grant Allen
19. **An Agnostic's Apology** — Sir Leslie Stephen, K.C.B.
20. **The Churches and Modern Thought** — Vivian Phelips
21. **Penguin Island** — Anatole France
22. **The Pathetic Fallacy** — Llewelyn Powys
23. **Historical Trials** (A Selection) — Sir John Macdonell, K.C.B.
24. **A Short History of Christianity** — J. M. Robertson
25. **The Martyrdom of Man** — Winwood Reade
26. **Head-Hunters** (Illus.) — A. C. Haddon
27. **The Evidence for the Supernatural** — Dr. Ivor Ll. Tuckett
28. **The City of Dreadful Night** — James Thomson ("B.V.")
29. **In the Beginning** (Illus.) — Prof. Sir G. Elliot Smith
30. **Adonis** — Sir J. G. Frazer, O.M.
31. **Our New Religion** — Rt. Hon. H. A. L. Fisher
32. **On Compromise** — John Viscount Morley, O.M., P.C.
33. **A History of the Taxes on Knowledge** — Collet Dobson Collet
34. **The Existence of God** — Joseph McCabe
35. **The Story of the Bible** — Macleod Yearsley
36. **Savage Survivals** (Illus.) — J. H. Moore
37. **The Revolt of the Angels** — Anatole France
38. **The Outcast** — Winwood Reade
39. **Penalties Upon Opinion** — H. Bradlaugh Bonner
40. **Oath, Curse, and Blessing** — Ernest Crawley
41. **Fireside Science** (Illus.) — Sir E. Ray Lankester
    Prepared by Surg. Rear-Admiral Beadnell
42. **History of Anthropology** (with Portraits) — Dr. A. C. Haddon
43. **The World's Earliest Laws** — Chilperic Edwards
44. **Fact and Faith** — Prof. J. B. S. Haldane

Continued on p. 3 of cover

WHAT'S WRONG WITH INTERNATIONAL LAW?

By

Dr. W. FRIEDMANN

6d.

First published 1941

Printed and Published in Great Britain by C. A. Watts & Co. Limited,
5 & 6 Johnson's Court, Fleet Street, London, E.C.4

WHAT'S WRONG WITH INTERNATIONAL LAW?

EVEN in more normal times the man in the street was disinclined to regard International Law very seriously. He associated it with a lot of high-sounding phrases without much reality. Exaggerated and ignorant as many such opinions may have been, popular judgment is seldom quite without substance. For the last five to ten years, long before the outbreak of the war, it should have become patent to every one that there was something radically wrong with International Law. Everybody knows that International Law forbade Japan to attack China, Italy to attack Abyssinia, Russia to attack Finland, Germany to remilitarize the Rhineland, to annex Austria, not to speak of the invasion of all the countries which are now under her heel. The Non-Intervention Pact in the Spanish Civil War prohibited the supply of arms to either side by the signatories; yet the war was decided by the amount of supplies of 'planes, other arms, and troops from Germany and Italy to Franco. Since 1928 the Kellogg Pact, signed by practically all States of the world, outlawed war altogether. This pact, formally still in force, is now not even mentioned.

To come to the present war itself, there is no doubt that International Law forbids attacks upon civilians; the sinking of merchant ships without warning and adequate precautions for the safety of the crew, the use of poison gas, and so forth. Yet civilians are attacked, ships torpedoed daily—virtually every rule is flouted. The fact that we are officially directed to carry gas-masks well expresses the degree of confidence in the sanctity of international treaties.

According to International Law neutrals can trade with both belligerents, subject to their right of search for so-called contraband. Yet both sides in the war stop, as far as in their power, all neutral trade with the other side. The law of neutrality demands impartiality. Yet neither Japan nor the U.S.A., nor a number of other States, while not actually at war with Britain or Germany, can be called neutral, for they are far from being impartial. They deliberately support the cause of one side only.

What is the meaning of all this? It is disturbing that all these rules, so entirely ignored, should still be presented as law on paper. Only a few months ago the leading textbook on International Law recited these and innumerable other rules which are completely ignored as being part of International Law. If this were to happen in any country such a state of affairs would rightly be called revolutionary. What, then, is the position in international society?

The first task is to be clear about the particular character of International Law. International Law means a body of rules of conduct valid between the States which are members of the family of nations, imposing upon them certain obligations. Now three facts appear to stand out as distinguishing this body of rules of conduct from the law as we know it in our everyday life :—

(*a*) There is no legislator to give law, as Parliament legislates in Great Britain or Hitler with his Cabinet in Germany;

(*b*) There is no authority to enforce the law against States which do not observe it, as the police do within the State;

(*c*) Compared with what the law within a State commands or forbids the citizen to do, only a very small number of social relations are regulated by International Law. Until the League of Nations was formed, International Law did not forbid any State to go to war in order to enforce its demands, and thus to take the law into its own hands. The League Covenant outlawed certain, but not all, wars—broadly speaking, wars of aggression—and it imposed an obligation upon the members to delay war in all cases until a certain period after arbitration would have elapsed. It also provided for a certain type of sanctions in case of unlawful aggression. The Kellogg Pact outlawed war altogether, but made no provision at all as to what would happen if war nevertheless occurred. Apart from this, however, International Law contained only a limited number of rules. Most of these are of a predominantly formal character: they concern diplomatic representation, respect for national territory, territorial waters, etc.

Now most of these rules derive their alleged validity from custom. Custom means that a particular rule, without being formally laid down anywhere, is considered to be habitually observed by the members of the community (in the case of International Law, the States as members of the family of nations), with the conviction that they are not free to abandon the rule when they like. Apart from customary rules, a number of international treaties between some, or most, or all States regulate special matters. The International Postal Union, for example, is such a general international treaty. The Locarno Treaties were concluded between a small number of States, and consequently were binding only upon those. In some cases there was originally a treaty between certain States, but the rules laid down in the treaty became gradually so well-established that they eventually were recognized as general custom. In the Treaty of Paris (1856), for example, a number of Powers, among them Great Britain and France, undertook to observe certain rules in regard to neutral trade in time of war. These rules have gradually developed into general custom. On the other hand, certain rules developed by custom have eventually been formulated and signed in a general convention. The best-known example are the Hague Conventions on the laws of warfare and neutrality. Further there is a large number of treaties on special matters, such as the peaceful settlement of disputes between two States.

All these rules make up International Law, but nevertheless the number of matters regulated in this manner between the States is very small indeed, compared with the liberty of action preserved in most matters. Within the States we observe an increasing measure of legal regulation of all aspects of life. There are obligations to go to school, to do military service, to pay rates and taxes, to maintain highways, to observe certain standards of wages or hygiene in industry, there are civil remedies as well as penalties for a large number of actions which the Law declares illegal, and so forth. But little if any corresponding regulation exists as yet in the relations between States which form the substance of International Law. There are no international taxes, no international military service duties, only very limited obligations to maintain international highways, few actions committed by one State against another are made illegal, and altogether liberty of action is the predominant principle. Correspondingly the legal machinery is primitive. All the essential legal organs of a State are missing; the rudiments of international legislation envisaged by the League Covenant and of international jurisdiction undertaken by the Permanent Court of International Justice have now faded out. Only in a few instances have we seen the emergence of something like an international authority. Most of these, like the International Postal Union, derive from predominantly technical co-operation. A much more far-reaching attempt at international organization was the International Labour Office, designed to regulate labour conditions internationally. For reasons described below, this organization was never allowed to live up to its potentialities.

It will be obvious from all this that International Law, as it stands at present, is in many ways different from Municipal Law.

Two points in particular are made by those who wish to defend the present structure of International Law, either to justify its present condition, or to discourage further bold development, both designed to stress the difference between International Law and State Law :—

1. International Law is in a more primitive stage of development than State Law;

2. Law between collective entities such as States cannot be of the same character as law binding individuals.

Both arguments can easily be refuted.

At one time custom was generally the principal type of law. When people lived in smaller and more primitive communities, the central State authority, which we take for granted to-day, did not exist. The history of all States shows the gradual emergence of central authority, mostly at first in the form of monarchy, with its attributes, an army, a body of permanent officials, and a system of law and jurisdiction centrally controlled throughout the country. This took the place of the many smaller communities which before lived under their own law and settled their mutual disputes by force. Since the State became the acknowledged supreme authority in the life of the individual, law has almost universally been understood to mean a body of rules which derives its validity from the highest authority that is, the State—and which is enforced by sanctions imposed by the State. It is true that a number of jurists emphasize the law that people actually observe in their lives as against the external element of State authority. This controversy, however, has but little meaning for our purposes. Few would seriously deny to-day that no rule of conduct within a State can be law unless it is backed by State authority.

Against this, International Law is in a much more primitive stage. There is no legislative authority, no international Parliament, or even a dictator with international legislative authority. The States follow what rules there are by custom, and when they choose to depart from them the ultimate settlement is by war. We may call this Law if we like—primitive law, perhaps—as long as we are clear that this is a law of a very imperfect type, a law with which we should feel extremely unsafe in our daily life, a law without a legislator to determine what is Law and what has ceased to be Law, without Law Courts to interpret it authoritatively, without a police to enforce it. This difference is, of course, so vital and patent that it is difficult to argue it away. Yet many prominent jurists have insisted that such an order is Law, and given it the same name as those rules within the State which have so vitally different characteristics. To justify this they have resorted to most astonishing theories. A famous German jurist has established a widely accepted theory of the so-called self-limitation of the State. It says that the State is really sovereign, free to act as it likes, but voluntarily (and without any superior authority to compel it not to change its mind) agrees to observe certain rules in international affairs. If this is Law, it has nothing to do with what we otherwise call Law. But the literature of International Law abounds with expositions which, in one form or another, maintain this "have-it-both-ways" conception of the Law. There is one criterion, clear-cut and definite, for the citizen to follow within the State, and another, vague and non-committal, for international relations.

The explanation of this inconsistency appears to be mainly psychological. The men who put forward these theories were almost exclusively representatives of the nineteenth-century middle-class, obedient citizens and nationalists at heart. But at the same time the expansion of international relations in the nineteenth century, mainly as a consequence of growing international trade and commerce, made a certain measure of international understanding and rules of conduct respectable. Co-operation was accepted as long as it did not hamper the State's freedom of action in decisive questions. The result is this hybrid conception of Law.

The League Covenant seemed at first to mark a definite advance. Certain obligations were imposed upon the member States by the Covenant, and it seemed possible that the League Assembly and the League Council might develop into proper international authorities. Moreover, sanctions were provided for at least some of the obligations. But half-way counsels again prevailed. National sovereignty was saved by the requisite of unanimity in practically all decisions of importance, and Article 16, which decreed sanctions in case of aggression, refrained from establishing any machinery by which a clear decision, emanating from the League as a superior authority, would compel members to apply sanctions. The case of Abyssinia showed that this defect could on exceptional occasions be overcome by a sufficiently strong will to act, but this is a matter for which International Law can certainly claim no credit, for it happened despite the law, not because of it. The Abyssinian crisis at the same time revealed a fundamental weakness of the League, again due to the half-way character of almost all Covenant provisions—the unwillingness of those who framed it to decide clearly between national and international sovereignty. In particular, Article 16, while making economic sanctions against an aggressor compulsory, left the application of military sanctions to the discretion of the members. This solution, which courted disaster, was one of those "realistic" solutions which, under the guise of realism, in fact mean compromise for the present at the expense of the future, mean escape from hard facts, and invariably prove calamitous in times of crisis. No authority within a State would be so foolish as to deprive a tradesman of his licence because of an offence against the law, without making provisions for police action if the trader chose to ignore the punishment or to resort to private vengeance.

If illusions were still possible in 1919, the experience of the last twenty years proves clearly that there must be a definite choice between national sovereignty, with the consequence that there can be no international legal order but at best a prolonged armistice, and international sovereignty, which means the supremacy of International Law and the subordination of the State. All solutions which wanted to have it both ways have proved disastrous. Again and again the so-called realists, diplomats, lawyers, economists, and others, have told us that this is rigid theory, and that in actual life compromises are inevitable and preferable. This realism has contributed to the bloodshed and destruction through which we live at present. In times of comparative stability compromises are not so harmful, because there is agreement on fundamentals; but in times of crisis compromise is as disastrous as indecision, with which it is usually associated.

But it is secondly alleged that the principles of law which govern the conduct of individuals cannot be applied to relations between States, each of which comprises many millions of individuals. The simple answer to this is provided by the existence of Federal States. In a Federal State the Federal Legislative and Executive are endowed with certain overriding authority to which the member States submit. This does not mean that it is possible overnight to form a Federation of any given number of States, according to requirements. Federation is the result of a strong degree of cohesion between a number of States which are linked by many ties, political, geographical, military, cultural, social, economic, etc. What no international lawyer should fail to notice, however, is that federations are not a matter of Utopian theory, but exist and have existed for many centuries, that some of the biggest organized communities in existence, such as the United States of America and the Union of Socialist Soviet Republics, are Federal States, and that a Federal Organization provides the possibility of clearly applying law and sanction to States linked in the Federation without destroying their individuality. The progress from tribe to State, from individual States to Federations, and, in some cases (e.g., Germany), from Federations to unitary States, has been and must be a gradual one. What is important for our purposes is that the problem of legal authority exercised over a number of collective units is in no way a new one. It has been solved before, politically and legally. The history of Federal Unions shows that half-way solutions do not for long prevail. Loose Confederations, like the Deutsche Zollverein or the American or Swiss Confederations, have developed into closer units. On the other hand, the League of Nations had no alternative but to develop into a closer and more strictly organized unit, or to disintegrate with the first serious crisis. It was impossible for the League to maintain itself, except on paper, in the condition in which it was created, when it was never clear whether it was a loose aggregate of States or an international body. Whatever attempts may have been made in the past, out of sentimentalism or of cynicism, to hide this fact, to-day it is past denying.

With the League collapsing and the Kellogg Pact still-born, a number of international lawyers thought that it was possible to revert, with certain modifications, to the system prevailing before 1914. Two principal trends of thought are discernible :—

(*a*) Some strenuously maintained the fiction of an effective legal authority of the League of Nations when, for reasons of balance of power, ideology, economics, it had long ceased to function;

(*b*) Others were saying, " I told you so," and enthusiastically reverted to the previously existing condition of International Law, thinking that on the whole it was possible to resume where International Law had stopped in 1914.

Now this " realism " has proved as fallacious as the League idealism maintained after its foundation had gone. The international anarchy has developed far beyond the limits reached or even imagined as possible by international society as it was in 1914. As has been shown, it was not correct even then to speak of an International Law proper. But while fundamentally States retained their liberty of action, no State, including Germany, would have risked abandoning the whole code of rules of behaviour fixed in the Hague Conventions and other documents, at least as a standard to be adhered to as far as practicable. If the term " Family of Nations " was certainly euphemistic, there existed a certain community between the States which might be vaguely but not inaccurately described as being based on " Western Civilization."

Things are radically different to-day. If we go through the whole body of rules of International Law, we find that large parts, if not most of them, just have no more meaning. In the twenty-five years between 1914 and 1939 more has happened than a big war and the rise and eclipse of the League of Nations. The world has passed into a state of social crisis, which has shaken international society to its very foundations, and with it the basis and growth of International Law. This international social revolution is still in full swing, and it is therefore difficult to give a final verdict upon its principal features. But already at its present stage two aspects of its profound effect upon International Law appear to stand out :—

1. The process of the increasingly total organization of the people, as it has been described from different angles by politicians, economists, historians, and social philosophers of many nations. Society is transformed from one in which the State had limited functions—mainly of a protective character and where, under this protection, the individual moved freely, developed trade, industry, and business, thought, spoke, and believed with considerable if not unlimited liberty, lived a personal life apart from his obligations as a citizen—to one where the individual is thoroughly and completely organized in society, his life is largely standardized, where a huge working machinery is directed by a few master wills and master brains, where work is planned, divided, directed by such central authority, where food, family, education, and attainment are more and

more controlled and standardized. This means more and more government, and accordingly more and more law. Symbolic of the former state of society is the American Constitution, with its guarantee of the fundamental rights of life, liberty, and property of the individual, with its complicated and carefully balanced constitutional machinery, with its Supreme Court, guarding those liberties, even at the expense of crying social needs. Of the latter type, National Socialist Germany, thoroughly organized, controlled, regimented, and efficient, directed by a few men who are ruthless and active, is as yet the most perfect expression. The contrast is not a new one in history, but the change from the one to the other is certainly new for modern Western society, and it should need no argument to show that it is bound to have a profound effect upon the rules of behaviour framed for a different state of society. The most important effect of this transition from the angle of International Relations and International Law is that one activity after another which was formerly private and of no direct concern to the State now becomes a matter of State responsibility. Industries are nationalized, trade and currency controlled, opinion and education supervised. Consequently the State can no longer affect indifference when any of these activities causes international friction or other problems.

This process, however, popularly described as totalitarian, is internationally gradual and largely, although not entirely, dependent on the extent to which the different States have planned for war. For example, at the outbreak of the war, Russian trade was socialized and therefore fully State controlled; German, Italian, and Japanese trade was indirectly controlled, through a combination of currency regulations, control of imports and exports, and political supervision over all branches of economic life. At the same time British export trade was subject only to limited licence restrictions, while American trade was free except for the restrictions of the Neutrality Act of 1937. This state of affairs was, as we shall see, sufficient to make existing rules of neutrality unworkable in case of war, but on the other hand not sufficiently uniform to make the application of an alternative rule of conduct practicable.

On the whole we may say that the new social technique, which has been almost everywhere in evidence since 1914 and which is still continually developing, stimulated through two wars, consequent social troubles and parallel changes in ideology, has upset those legal rules which were based on the old social technique. But a new common international social technique has not yet developed. Socialist and capitalist ideas, planning and *laisser-faire*, liberal and absolutist tendencies are everywhere in conflict, in an unequal mixture. This state of affairs certainly affords no sufficiently stable basis for a code of legal rules between the different States of the world, in view of the difference in the degree of change they have internally produced.

2. But apart from this "horizontal" split—horizontal because it creates a dividing line between the international society of some decades ago and the society of to-day—there is also a "vertical" split which has created an abyss between different groups of States and destroyed the social and legal community between them. Outwardly this split is characterized by the conflict between aggressor and non-aggressor States, between those which deliberately defy International Law as an order of peace and believe in force as the instrument of change, and those which either defend the existing order of things or at any rate advocate a change within the methods and forms of the law—that is, by peaceful means. There is, however, underneath this superficial difference a deeper and more fundamental issue which cannot fail to affect the very basis of International Law. Much as we may mistrust the frequent use of ideological phrases—words like liberty, tyranny, progress, and so forth—as a disguise for very much more materialistic

interests, the conflict of ideas has always been deeply real, particularly in periods of social revolution. The present struggle goes to the foundations of Western civilization as a form of life, and, since what exists of International Law is one of the many manifestations of Western civilization, the reaction of this struggle upon International Law is bound to be profound. It is true that the issues are not quite as clear cut as they are often made to appear. Essentially, however, it is a conflict between different ways of life based upon antagonistic philosophies of life. It is no answer to this to assert, as a good many people do, that the whole world is moving towards totalitarianism, and therefore the alleged issue is a fictitious one. Totalitarianism, in the sense outlined above, is a technique of social life. It is determined by the changing conditions of collective life, and in our own time above all by the conditions created by the industrial revolution in its later stages. All States affected by this industrial revolution are gradually being compelled to adjust their methods and technique of government. But the identical technique is capable of being used for very different purposes. State control of the means of production, for example, may be on the one hand an instrument of dictatorship, of a few, the most efficient way of satisfying personal ambition and lust for power, or it may, on the other hand, be used to make individual liberty a reality, by giving equality of opportunity not only in the political, but also in the social and economic spheres.

In a broad sense such rules as exist to-day—or, as we should rather say, existed until a few years ago—are based on certain principles of Christian Ethics. Their main expressions in the field of International Law may be briefly summarized as follows :—

(1) An indispensable basis is a cosmopolitan outlook on international affairs which includes the conception of humanity as real and at least existing in addition to that of the nation. Although successive generations of diplomats and positivists have attempted to whittle down International Law to a point when it might seem little more than a formalized manner of diplomatic relations, the possibility at least of a world-wide law, binding all men, must be implicit in International Law as it was established by Grotius. Above all it is implicit in the whole structure of International Law as we know it that every nation, every human being, every race, every religion, should be considered as basically equal, provided a certain homogeneity of values is attained. Needless to say this ideal has as yet been very imperfectly realized. Under many different guises, such as concert of powers, protectorates, mandates

and League of Nations Council, etc., inequality in fact has prevailed. But unless humanity as a whole, rather than any particular nation or nations as being superior to others, is recognized as a reality, the present structure of International Law must collapse. It is, however, this very conception of mankind which Fascism and National Socialism assail. To the equality of man, to the very conception of humanity which they deride, they oppose the differentiation of human beings according to nationality, race, and other distinctive criteria. The law is conceived accordingly, and National-Socialist lawyers have made repeated attempts to establish a new international legal order which will take into account these differences, and thus be based on a hierarchy—that is, on domination of some over others instead of equality of all under a common law. It is clear that between these two conceptions there can be no compromise.

(2) The issue is often put as one of Democracy *versus* Dictatorship. But in so far as certain particular forms of constitutional life are meant by this contrast, it may well be doubted whether this is not much more a matter of social technique than of fundamental issues of life. The International Law which we know has developed for the last three hundred years regardless of differences in internal government. Grotius

himself advocated absolute government internally, in order to give greater power to those who conducted international negotiations to represent their peoples regardless of internal restrictions. The difficulties to which such restrictions may lead are well illustrated by the position of the United States of America in international affairs. It seems likely that Parliamentary Democracy in the leisurely form which it has adopted during the last century may not survive—or not without substantial modifications. Particular forms of conducting government have to evolve in accordance with the need for a more comprehensive and speedier machinery of social control. It is therefore better to put the issue not in terms of specific forms of constitutional government, but in terms of the fundamental human aims at stake. And this leads us to the issue of

(3) Individual Autonomy *versus* Absolutism. Indeed, State control over the individual is to-day fundamentally no longer a matter of controversy. It is a fact, accepted to a lesser or greater extent by all States. The real issue is whether such socialization will serve the development of fuller individuality or, on the contrary, lead to the complete merger of the individual in the collective, which is nothing but an efficiently organized machinery for the pursuit of the limitless ambitions of a few

individuals. On this issue again no compromise is possible between the conflicting political ideologies. International Law as it has developed during the past century in particular, reflects, if imperfectly, the ideal of individual autonomy that has been one of the principal creeds of Western civilization. Freedom of man has been denounced with no less vehemence by the apostles of Fascism and National Socialism than the fundamental equality of man. Whereas the latter is anathema to those who exalt the supremacy of the strong over the weak, of force over law, the former would gravely impair the absolute subservience of the social machine to the pursuit of power. That is why any conception of individual right, whether of life, liberty, property, or any right which has the individual being in mind as an end in himself, must, from the point of view of Fascism and National Socialism, be destroyed. Now International Law is based on the recognition of the protection of the individual no less than on the fundamental equality of nations and individuals. Only a few years ago a learned writer on International Law could write, with some measure of justification, the following words :—

> "This recognition of the paramount importance of the individual gives a broader basis for International Law, and the pressure

> of that Law on behalf of individuals is tending towards such a uniformity of standard in domestic laws that he may more and more expect to receive a fixed minimum of rights and protection, no matter where he goes."[1]

To give some illustrations, the individual was expected to be protected in his physical integrity wherever he went, inside the family of nations. The life of an alien must not be taken arbitrarily—that is, not without adequate cause, such as murder—and not without a judicial procedure by which he is given sufficient protection and defence. The same applies to any curtailment of his liberty. Lynch justice, for example, is as illegal internationally as a sentence of imprisonment arrived at without proper judicial procedure—for example, by judges who are not independent—or after a procedure which has not given the accused proper opportunities of defence. If these standards are not observed, the State responsible for the deficiencies is answerable to the State to whom the injured individual belongs, claiming on behalf of the latter.

Now it is obvious that the institution of a Gestapo or any other police organ with undefined and unlimited powers, the establishment of special political tribunals, the removal of any guarantee of judicial independence, the introduction of penal statutes with retro-

[1] Eagleton, *Responsibility of States*, 1928, p. 222.

spective effect, the discrimination, legally and politically, between nationals and foreigners—that these and many other institutions and measures characteristic of totalitarian States are incompatible with such standards. A common law between those States which advocate the one and those which advocate the other principle, is an impossibility.

(4) It is only a reinforcement of the divergences already apparent from the above considerations that those States which challenge the existing international order, and with it the existing International Law, advocate, like any rebel, the substitution of force for law, whether the object of law be the maintenance of the existing order of things or a peaceful process of change by legal means. This in itself is not new, but the challenge has been accentuated by the philosophy which praises force, power, and war as the sole means and test of international relations as between State and State. The issue and the conflict are age-old, as the conflicting philosophies of Plato and the Stoics, of Hobbes and Grotius, of Kant and Hegel, and many others show. But it is new for our present generation. Yet many scholars and jurists, who are well versed in and fully aware of such issues in the past, nevertheless fail to take note of them when they occur before their eyes.

A word must be said about the extent to which this conflict has really made the further existence of the former system of International Law, as applicable to all States, impossible. It has been and is even now argued that the breach of law by a criminal does not invalidate the law but, on the contrary, may test it and prove its strength. International Law in particular, so it is argued, has survived many breaches. This is, of course, true; but there is in every legal order a point at which a breach becomes so widespread and fundamental that it demolishes the law which is powerless to prevent or punish the breach. When that happens within a State one speaks of revolution, and the revolutionary authority becomes the source of a new legal order when it has succeeded in establishing itself with sufficient permanency. In international affairs the process of revolution is not so definite, because the legal organization of the international community is so very much looser and the whole process of revolt against the existing order so much less visible, owing to the size of international society. As long as the law can assert itself against a law-breaker there is no reason to maintain that it has ceased to be valid. Owing to the particular nature of International Law, as described at the beginning of this pamphlet, it has always been difficult to test whether International Law did or did not assert itself against a breach. But whatever may have been the case in the past, it cannot very well be denied that the present challenge to the existing international, political, and legal order is of a magnitude and breadth which have never before been equalled. The challenge to-day does not come from one or the other State which pursues certain expansionist aims in a shifting system of balance of power, but from a large group of States who not only numerically represent a very great proportion of mankind, but conceive this challenge to be of a fundamental character, designed to substitute a new order for the old one. Moreover this challenge occurs at a time when International Law, primitive as it still is in comparison with the stage reached by State Law, has attained a much greater comprehensiveness than ever before. Not only does it profess to embrace practically the whole of mankind, but, owing to modern conditions, International Law at present covers an infinitely bigger field than at any previous period. A large number of matters of transport, economics, cultural relations, social conditions, judicial relations, etc., have been regulated by international custom or treaty. The League Covenant had added to this the matter of peace and war itself, the Permanent Court of International Justice had begun to establish the beginnings of an international juridical order, and the International Labour Office had started to regulate the social conditions of working people by international agreement. The challenge, coming from a large and consciously organized section of mankind, is bound to affect every one of these matters in the law, as it affects them in politics, economics, etc.; it is therefore bound to have a much profounder effect and significance.

Quite apart from the present war, which has completely severed legal relations between the belligerent parties, this vertical split between conflicting sections of mankind has arrested the further development of a general International Law, while it has destroyed many existing international legal relations. Broadly speaking, legal relations continue between the contending parties only in matters which concern comparatively superficial relations, such as questions of transport, postal communications, etc., while they had become impossible in matters demanding a more far-reaching community of social values. If we attempt to classify international legal relations in the light of this problem, we might say that legal relations are affected in the following order :—

(*a*) Treaties regarding technical co-operation (transport, navigation, etc.) demand a very small community of social standards and are possible between States which, however divergent in their political and social purposes, have attained a comparable degree of technical efficiency.

(*b*) Commercial legal relations can continue on a limited scale, but to the extent that the increasing State control over all spheres of life made international commerce a matter of State policy, commercial legal relations were bound to be affected. Accordingly we have been able to watch an intensification of commercial relations within the conflicting groups, but a decisive weakening in commercial relations between the different groups.

(*c*) International agreement on social conditions is, of course, deeply affected by the split. The organization of labour and industry is an integral part of the principles on which a State is based, and the early withdrawal of Germany, Italy, and Japan from the International Labour Office proves the impossibility of co-operation once a minimum community of purposes has disappeared.

(*d*) Educational and cultural co-operation, as expressed by international Press or Broadcasting Conventions, is quite obviously affected, and had practically broken down between the conflicting groups for a considerable period before the actual outbreak of war.

(*e*) It follows, as a matter of course, that, as between such conflicting groups, any treaty which substitutes a peaceful method

> of settlement for force is bound to break down, whether this breakdown takes the form of a repudiation of existing treaties (League Covenant, Locarno Treaties, etc.), of a tacit breach, or merely of a refusal to conclude further agreements.

In conclusion it can be said that, quite apart from war, the international political social revolution, in steady process for the last twenty-five years and sharpened beyond compromise by the emergence of the Fascist group of Powers, has left nothing but a skeleton of more or less formal international relations intact in reality, however imposing the edifice might still have been on paper.

This "vertical" split, however, would not have prevented such States as continued to agree on certain fundamental principles and ways of life from maintaining the existing rules of International Law, for what they were worth, in their mutual relations, no longer as a universal but as a partial International Law. It must be admitted that not even this conclusion was drawn by the majority of international lawyers, who continued to teach the old principles of International Law as being of universal application. But the possibility of adhering to the existing principles of International Law has largely disappeared through what was characterized above as a "horizontal" split—namely, through a profound change in the social structure and technique of all States.

The dominant factor here is the universal increase of State control which manifests itself in all walks of life. While this change is bound to be apparent in many spheres of International Law—for example, in the international rules regarding the immunity of foreign State property from seizure and jurisdiction, or the international responsibility of States for expressions of opinion, by Press, speech, radio, etc.—we will confine ourselves here to an examination of the effects of this fundamental change upon that part of International Law which is particularly important in the present war—that is, the Laws of Warfare and the Laws of Neutrality.

Before entering into a discussion of these particular aspects, it should be observed that the very distinction between peace and war has become questionable through the now prevalent practice of starting invasion or other acts of war without declaration, through the unofficial international intervention in civil conflicts, such as the Spanish Civil War, and through the attitude of non-belligerency—that is, an attitude half-way between participation in the war and neutrality, which to-day characterizes the attitude of several major Powers, notably the United States and Japan. Yet the clear distinction between peace and war is an elementary foundation of the existing science of International Law.

I. Laws of Warfare

(1) The embodiment of a large number of rules regarding the conduct of war on land and sea, in the Hague Conventions of 1907, used to be regarded by many as evidence of the progress of humanitarian conduct in international relations. Even as a matter of principle, this was at any time a rather doubtful assertion for those who think that war is essentially the negation of humanitarian principles, and the attempt to confine it within certain limits, even if practicable, means a legalization and thus an encouragement of evil. Quite apart from this point of principle, a detailed study of the conventions made it easy to see that numerous exceptions and reservations, such as necessity clauses and similar subterfuges, made the evasion of these rules a comparatively easy matter for any State which wished to evade them. Be that as it may, any measure of comfort which international lawyers may have derived from the existence of a large body of rules regarding the conduct of war, must completely disappear as a result of a development of a social technique of life which has made these rules almost completely

inapplicable. The basic idea and principle behind all rules of warfare, whether they concern land, sea, or air, is the distinction between military and non-military objectives. This distinction has become meaningless through the increasingly totalitarian character of war, and three factors in particular have undermined the basis of the existing rules of warfare :

(*a*) The growing importance of economic warfare for a military decision;

(*b*) The development of air warfare with a largely new technique of attack;

(*c*) The extension of the number of those who, without being directly members of the military forces, are as essential a part of the war machinery as the forces. In fact it might well be said that not a single person within the State, except perhaps lunatics and completely incapacitated people, does not of necessity play a part in the prosecution of the war, be he a member of the serving forces, of civilian defence, an industrial worker, an agricultural labourer, the owner of assets which can be realized for the State, or just a member of the public in general.

It is not that the objects of war have much altered. Land war still has the object of defeating the armed forces on land and securing control of enemy territory; sea war still has the auxiliary function of securing control of the sea for one side, while depriving the other side of its use; of air warfare one might say that it combines certain aspects of land and sea war, but adds some new possibilities—viz., that of defeating the enemy on land by its own power. It is not the objects of war, but the methods which have changed. Modern warfare must be seen in the light of these methods, which are a reflection of modern social conditions. War is now a struggle of entire, thoroughly organized nations, a struggle of which military warfare is but one of many aspects, a struggle comprising working capacity, raw material, industrial capacity, food production, propaganda, onslaught on mind as much as on matter; it is this reflection of the transformation of modern society which has knocked the bottom out of the former rules of warfare. The definition of a military objective which is usually quoted as authoritative is that it must be "an object of which the destruction or injury would constitute a distinct military advantage to the belligerent." How difficult it has become to apply this distinction may be illustrated by some examples.

(1) Article 25, Hague Regulations, enacts that "the attack by bombardment, by any means whatever, of towns, villages, habitations, and buildings, which are not defended, is prohibited."

(2) The Hague Air Warfare Rules of 1922, which are not law, but a draft code of air warfare, set up by an authoritative body of

experts from different countries and therefore widely quoted as a standard of reference, say that aerial bombardment is legitimate only when directed at a military objective. Minute distinctions are elaborated to show what may and may not legitimately be bombarded; the principle is that military formations and concentrations, arms manufacture, and transport used for military purposes are legitimate objects, but everything else in principle is illegitimate, as an attack upon the civilian population.

(3) The London Naval Treaty of 1930 says that submarines must conform to the established rules of International Law to which surface vessels are subject, and that in particular, except in cases of persistent refusal to stop on being duly warned and in face of resistance to positive search, a warship, whether a surface vessel or submarine, may not render incapable of navigation a merchant vessel without first taking steps to put the passengers, crew, and ship's papers in a place of safety.

All these rules were reasonable and practicable as long as there was a fairly clear distinction between military and non-military objectives. This is no longer the case.

In regard to the bombardment of civilian populations in the course of land warfare, the bombardment, cruel and barbarous as it may be, is now often part of a strategic plan. It played a decisive part in the German operations in the Low Countries and in France, where populations were bombed out of towns in order to block roads, vital for the supplies and troops of the enemy. These operations undoubtedly formed part of a strategic plan, and are one of the results of systematic co-operation between land army and air force. A new weapon will always, sooner or later, modify the law in accordance with its needs.

Again, the rule about the bombardment of open towns from the air presupposes that such distinctions as made, for example, in the Hague rules, are practicable. But in an industrialized country it is extremely difficult to find any place which is not either a military objective or in the immediate neighbourhood of military objectives, in which case even the Hague rules make bombing legitimate. And if they further suggest that where military objectives are so placed that they cannot be bombarded without indiscriminate bombardment of the civil population, the aircraft must abstain from bombardment, developments have brushed these suggestions aside. To-day we know that the weakening of the morale, the undermining of the power of resistance of the civilian population, sleeplessness, nervousness, etc., are as much part of the objects of war as any attack upon troop concentrations or warships. The novelty of the weapon does not alter the fact that it serves the object of overcoming enemy resistance. We can, of course, still recognize and condemn sheer cruelty; this is a matter of sentiment and ethical judgment to be applied to the merits of the case, but a legal rule demands clear-cut distinctions capable of general application.

The rule about the sinking of enemy ships presupposes that the attacking ship, whether surface ship or submarine, lingers on the spot for a while in order to carry out the various necessary measures. In regard to aircraft it has been suggested that it must comply with the same rules, and therefore act only in an auxiliary capacity in regard to the capture of enemy merchantmen. It is not by accident, not even by wanton cruelty, but merely as a result of the cruelty which is the attribute of war backed by modern weapons that these rules have never been applied. A submarine, by coming to the surface, exposes itself to attack from enemy warships or 'planes, and a 'plane which goes away to call in the aid of a warship, the nearest of which may be hundreds of miles away, may not only lose the prize, but find itself confronted by superior enemy forces when it does return. The rules of sea warfare are very much rules based on the existence of a surface navy. No wonder, therefore, that

Great Britain not only acted legitimately but also in her interests when she condemned German methods of sea warfare, as long as Great Britain had undisputed command of the seas. The events from April to June, 1940, have changed this position. With Germany disposing of many surface communications along a prolonged coast-line, it has become as necessary for British submarines to sink German ships as it has been the practice from the very beginning of the German submarines to sink British ships.

The paramount factor which is bound to defeat all attempts at regulating this type of warfare is the overwhelming importance of economic warfare, the object of isolating the enemy from all supplies, whether arms, raw materials, food, or anything else. No belligerent will be deterred from this object by rules of warfare if they jeopardize it. It is this fact which makes it necessary for every belligerent to cut off the enemy from all trade—imports and exports alike—yet on paper International Law still operates with the notion of contraband—which means that such neutral goods as are of direct military use to the enemy may be seized by the other belligerent, but only on their way into the enemy country. On exports International Law says nothing; but it goes without saying to-day that the stopping of enemy exports is as vital as that of enemy imports. Yet so far only rather few international lawyers have fully recognized this development. Needless to say, the practice of belligerents has taken very little notice of these and other rules of law.

Humanity can always be shown, even among the stark cruelty of modern war. But the dubious attempt to make the conduct of modern war respectable and "Christian" by legal rules has faded out.

II. Laws of Neutrality

The Law of Neutrality presupposes first and foremost impartiality on the side of the neutral State. From that a large number of neutral rights and duties have been derived. Three factors above all make the Law of Neutrality possible:—

(1) Wars which are not universal, but conducted between a limited number of States, with powerful States remaining outside;

(2) A type of war where the distinction between neutral supplies for military purposes and for non-military purposes is possible and practicable;

(3) Social conditions, where the State can wash its hands of the economic activities of its citizens.

All these foundations of Neutrality have disappeared.

(1) The present war, as previously the last one, especially after the United States had entered the war, is universal in the sense that no State can remain disinterested. Every one must sooner or later choose its position and take sides. The only alternative is to become a mere passive victim;

(2) The impossibility of a practicable distinction between military and non-military objectives has already been discussed;

(3) The increase of State control over the economic life of the nation makes the question of supplies to belligerents a political one. At the time when these rules were framed trade and industry were entirely private. Wars were a source of profit to business in neutral countries. The Government could sit back and see some of its citizens, and perhaps its industry and commerce, become prosperous with the wars of others. To-day this is entirely different, since the supply question, both from the angle of the neutral and that of the belligerent, is so strongly political that the neutral government must take control. It has two alternatives: It can either cut off all trade links with the belligerents, and thus isolate the neutral country, at the expense of trade, in order to prevent it from being drawn into the war, or, alternatively, the neutral government will use the direction of supplies to one or the other side

as a political weapon of the first magnitude. The first course was attempted by the U.S.A. in the Neutrality Act of 1937, which, however, left some loopholes. One of those is the fact that where the President declines to declare a state of war, as in the case of the Japanese War against China, the Neutrality Act does not come into operation. But on the whole the Act of 1937 was action of the first type, and the United States is now veering round to the opposite course. Consequently Neutrality becomes Non-belligerency—that is to say, owing to the government control of economic policy towards the belligerents, there can be little pretence of impartiality; in other words, the so-called neutral takes part, although a limited part, in the struggle.

We might sum up by saying that the traditional Law of Neutrality is principally affected by four factors; first, the disappearance of the balance of power in the relations between belligerents and non-belligerents; second, the predominantly economic character of modern war which has made the maintenance of neutrality, and of neutral trade with belligerents in particular, untenable; third, the elimination of the division of political activities as public and economic activities as private; fourth, the ideological character of war which, like the present one, goes to the roots of existence, is a struggle between rival ideologies more than between any particular nations and does not tolerate neutrality.

Conclusions and Prospects

The demolition of much of the existing International Law may at first sight appear a somewhat negative and destructive performance, and it may be that not only legal conservatism but this consideration as well has prevented the majority of international lawyers from drawing what may appear to be such obvious conclusions. Even if it were an entirely negative achievement, it would nevertheless be a necessary task to perform. For a law does not become any more real by the failure of its professional exponents to recognize that it has ceased to be valid. In fact, however, the analysis of International Law in the sense attempted here is far from being purely destructive. The lawyer must take note of social and political changes, and where the municipal lawyer may be pardoned for being a little less apprehensive, owing to the existence of an articulate constitutional machinery, the international lawyer has no such excuse. He must have his ear on the ground. He must have a clear insight into the political and social changes in international society. No legislator will tell him when to abandon the law and substitute a new one. In times of greater social stability the elaboration of existing notions and rules may be the lawyer's paramount task. But in days of profound crisis, such as ours, the lawyer's paramount task is to co-operate with politicians, economists, sociologists, and scientists, in preparing the ground for the "shape of things to come."

A few indications of the tasks which await the international lawyer at the present day might be briefly outlined.

Firstly, the realization of the need of some measure of common values in the field of ethics, social and economic life, etc., must lead to a re-examination of the different types of international legal relations with regard to the degree of community which they require. A hierarchy such as that outlined above on pages 30–32 will be the result.

Secondly, the realization of the increasingly active function of the State, through its control of a growing number of activities in all countries, is bound to lead to the transformation of a loose, but universal, international society, to certain more closely-knit blocks of States. Within these groups political, as well as economic, social, cultural, and consequently legal relations, will be very close, and tend to produce eventual merger. On the other hand, relations between one group and another will be much more restricted than in past days.

Several such international blocks are in process of formation: on the one hand, there is Hitler's "New Order" for the European Continent, and its counterpart, the Far Eastern New Order under Japanese leadership; on the other hand, there are the revived and enlarged British Commonwealth of Nations, and the makings of a Pan-American Union.

This leads us to one of the most constructive tasks to be faced at the present moment: an appraisal of the different alternatives of future international legal developments.

One fact stands out clearly: that the Nation-State in the old sense has ceased to be a reality, let alone to have a future. In this respect at least there is no difference between the warring factions.

On the one side, the idea of the "New Order" built up round the Axis idea envisages an international unity far beyond any military or diplomatic alliance. It envisages a unity under the domination of one nation which intends to weld a multitude of others into a complete political, economic, social, and cultural unity. A Continent united under Nazi domination might live under a law of terror and a peace of the grave. But it will be a supernational development of a sort. All the more clearly there must be on the other side the vision of a different international legal order, which also overcomes the Nation-State. It appears that there are essentially three main ideas of such a new international order, but there seems as yet little clarity as to the relation in which they stand to one another.

First there emerges the conception of a new, better, and stronger League of Nations—a League of independent states which will outlaw aggression, and will avoid the deficiencies of the old League by stronger, more comprehensive, and more strictly regulated obligations, backed by executive power and international military force.

Second there emerges the idea of an International Commonwealth, based on the model of the British Commonwealth of Nations. Its essential feature is a strong community of ideas, traditions, habits of life, but a minimum of legal organization. For the particularity of the British Commonwealth of Nations consists in the looseness of legal and constitutional ties, which would lead to complete disintegration except for the strong sense of cohesion backed by the common racial stock, common history and tradition, common forms of government, habits of life, etc.

Third there emerges the idea of a Federal Union as a closer association of nations, the dominant feature of which is the abandonment of absolute national sovereignty in favour of a federal authority which will have control over the essential matters of common concern to the States united in it, but leave liberty and independence to the States in all other matters.

The first of these conceptions, therefore, emphasizes the machinery by which to fight aggression, the second the community of outlook and ideas necessary to achieve international collaboration, the third the constitutional form necessary to achieve international development above and beyond the national State.

It would appear that each of these conceptions emphasizes one side of the truth, and that, as this pamphlet has attempted to demonstrate, all three are essential to a development beyond the international chaos of to-day. Law requires authority; a law between sovereigns is impossible. Law demands the power to impose sanctions in case of breach. Finally Law requires a basic community of ideas, otherwise there can be no will to live and work together, between nations any more than between individuals.

THE THINKER'S LIBRARY *(continued from p. 2 of cover)*

45. **Men of the Dawn** (Illus.) — Dorothy Davison
46. **The Mind in the Making** — James Harvey Robinson
47. **The Expression of the Emotions in Man and Animals** (Illus.) — Charles Darwin
    Revised and Abridged by Surg. Rear-Admiral Beadnell
48. **Psychology for Everyman** (and Woman) — A. E. Mander
49. **The Religion of the Open Mind** — A. Gowans Whyte
50. **Letters on Reasoning** — J. M. Robertson
51. **The Social Record of Christianity** — Joseph McCabe
52. **Five Stages of Greek Religion** — Prof. Gilbert Murray
53. **The Life of Jesus** — Ernest Renan
54. **Selected Works of Voltaire** — Trans. by Joseph McCabe
55. **What Are We to Do With Our Lives?** — H. G. Wells
56. **Do What You Will** — Aldous Huxley
57. **Clearer Thinking: Logic for Everyman** — A. E. Mander
58. **History of Ancient Philosophy** — A. W. Benn
59. **Your Body: How it is Built and How it Works** (Illus.) — Dr. D. Stark Murray
60. **What is Man?** — Mark Twain
61. **Man and His Universe** — J. Langdon-Davies
62. **First Principles** (2s. 6d. net) — Herbert Spencer
63. **Rights of Man** With Foreword by G. D. H. Cole. — Thomas Paine
64. **This Human Nature** — Charles Duff
65. **Dictionary of Scientific Terms** — C. M. Beadnell, C.B., F.Z.S.
66. **A Book of Good Faith.** Selections from the Works of Montaigne; arranged, with an Introduction, by Gerald Bullett
67. **The Universe of Science** (Revised edition) — Prof. H. Levy
68. **Liberty To-day** (Revised edition) — C. E. M. Joad
69. **The Age of Reason** — Thomas Paine
70. **The Fair Haven** — Samuel Butler
71. **A Candidate for Truth.** Passages from Ralph Waldo Emerson; chosen and arranged by Gerald Bullett
72. **A Short History of Women** — John Langdon-Davies
73. **Natural Causes and Supernatural Seemings** — Henry Maudsley, M.D.
74. **Morals, Manners, and Men** — Havelock Ellis
75. **Pages from a Lawyer's Notebooks** — E. S. P. Haynes
76. **An Architect of Nature** — Luther Burbank
77. **Act of God** — F. Tennyson Jesse
78. **The Man *versus* the State** — Herbert Spencer
    With an Introduction by Lord Snell, C.B.E., LL.D.
79. **The World as I See It** — Albert Einstein
80. **Jocasta's Crime** — Lord Raglan
81. **The Twilight of the Gods** — Richard Garnett
82. **Kingship** — A. M. Hocart
83. **Religion Without Revelation** — Julian Huxley
84. **Let the People Think** — Bertrand Russell
85. **The Myth of the Mind** — Frank Kenyon

London: WATTS & CO., 5 & 6 Johnson's Court, Fleet Street, E.C.4.

THE NEW COMMONWEALTH INSTITUTE MONOGRAPHS

THE LEGAL PROCESS AND INTERNATIONAL ORDER

BY

PROFESSOR HANS KELSEN

LONDON
CONSTABLE & CO LTD
1935

PUBLISHED BY

Constable and Company Ltd.
LONDON

·

Oxford University Press
BOMBAY CALCUTTA MADRAS

·

The Macmillan Company
of Canada, Limited
TORONTO

·

Printed by
LOXLEY BROTHERS LIMITED
50, *Southwark Bridge Road*
London, S.E.1

SERIES A. No. 1

THE LEGAL PROCESS AND INTERNATIONAL ORDER

FOREWORD

Professor Hans Kelsen, the author of the first of the New Commonwealth *Research Monographs, is so well known as an international authority in all scientific circles that a formal introduction is not necessary. For the interest of the general reader we append the following brief biographical notes.*

Professor Hans Kelsen at present holds the Chair of International Law at the Institut Universitaire de Hautes Etudes Internationales in Geneva. Born in Prague, he became Professor at Vienna University (1911-1930), *and afterwards at the University of Cologne* (1930-1933). *In addition to his academic work in Austria, Professor Hans Kelsen was entrusted by the Austrian Government with the task of working out a draft of the Federal Constitution. Throughout the period* 1919-1929 *he was a member and permanent* rapporteur *of the Austrian Constitutional Court.*

Chief among the honours that have been awarded to this distinguished authority in recognition of his work are: Associate Membership of the Académie Royale de Sciences, des Lettres et des Beaux-Arts de Belgique; a Membership of the American Academy of Political and Social Science, Philadelphia; a Foreign Membership of the Utrechtsch Genootschap van Kunsten en Wetenschappen; a Foreign Honorary Membership of the American Academy of Arts and Sciences, Boston; a Corresponding Membership of the Royal Italian Academy of Sciences of the Institute of Bologna.

Among his publications we may mention the following:

Hauptprobleme der Staatsrechtslehre, 1911, 2. *Aufl.* 1923.

Das Problem der Souveränität und die Theorie des Völkerrechts, 1920, 2. *Aufl.* 1929.

Der soziologische und juristische Staatsbegriff, 1922, 2. *Aufl.* 1929.

Allgemeine Staatslehre, 1925.

Sozialismus und Staat, 1920, 2. *Aufl.* 1923.

Vom Wesen und Wert der Demokratie, 1920, 2. *Aufl.* 1929.

Les rapports de système entre le droit interne et le droit international public, 1927.

Die philosophischen Grundlagen der Naturrechtslehre und des Rechtspositivismus, 1928.

Théorie générale du droit international public, 1933.

Unrecht und Unrechtsfolge im Völkerrecht, 1933.

Staatsform und Weltanschauung, 1933.

Reine Rechtslehre, 1934.

March, 1935

THE NEW COMMONWEALTH INSTITUTE

I.

IN the great battle which human ingenuity has been waging against its most terrible enemy, war, every victory nearly always seems to be followed by a defeat. In spite of the advent of the League of Nations and notwithstanding the conclusion of the Briand-Kellogg Pact, which was greeted with so much enthusiasm by all friends of peace—that pact whereby war as an instrument of national policy is solemnly outlawed—we are faced to-day with the deplorable fact that the world's efforts to achieve an all-round disarmament, if they have not actually utterly failed, at any rate seem to have very little prospect of attaining any kind of really satisfactory result.

Anyone who is concerned to follow and to further the trend towards the pacification of the world, and who seeks to understand the factors that prevent any real and permanent success in this direction, must come to the conclusion that, in this great enterprise of reform, the trouble is not so much any lack of good intentions on the part of those concerned as a failure to achieve a clear insight into the problem. It is not really a question of a moral or political purpose—for as to the absolute necessity for peace there are no two opinions. There is scarcely a single State or a single statesman to-day that would have the courage to refuse publicly allegiance to this ideal. The only question, the only point at issue, is how this ideal can be translated into reality. On this matter opinions are divergent, and that is where all the difficulties arise. We have, therefore, simply and solely to reach a decision as to the appropriate means to attain an end on which there need be no further debate. In short, the problem is primarily a problem of social technology.

II.

When the Disarmament Conference is considered in this light, we have first of all to be quite clear in our minds about its juridical basis. That basis is Article 8 of the League Covenant, which states in its first paragraph the principle—

> that the maintenance of peace requires the reduction of national armaments to the lowest point consistent with national safety and the enforcement by common action of international obligations.

This principle, the general line of the League's peace policy, is, in more than one respect, questionable. Can a course of action aiming at disarmament seriously hope to be successful if, at the outset, it is impeded by a barrier like "national security," which has hitherto been the watchword justifying the most intensive armament building. How are we going to get a reduction of national armaments if every State is going to be able to claim that its war preparations are such as not only are required for its own defence, but may also be required by its duty to take part in the "common action" of the League? Can the "maintenance of peace," *i.e.*, the elimination of war, be really attained by a process of gradual reduction of the means of war? Might not war be made just as well with smaller armies and navies, indeed, perhaps more easily with the smaller than with the larger instruments of warfare? One thinks particularly of the possibilities in the way of aero-chemical warfare.

Reduction of armaments manifestly has to be the preliminary step to a total disarmament, since only the latter can make war an impossibility.

But *in the present condition of international organisation* can we seriously proceed to remove war from the scheme of things? That is, indeed, frankly the aim of the efforts for world peace embodied in the League of Nations Covenant. Can it really only be a question of *war*, when the experience of recent years has shown us that *reprisals* can well take on forms akin to those of war? If we want to eliminate war and other more or less similar acts of coercion, as expedients of self-help, from international relationships, we have to appreciate the nature of our international order, and especially to recognise the function performed in the whole system by that element which it is desired to extrude as being injurious : just as a surgeon must know exactly the function of an organ if he proposes to remove it from the human body in order to maintain and to stimulate life in that body.

III.

The international organism whose reform is to be sought through the elimination of war and similar acts of coercion is what is called international law, the *jus gentium*. As such it is a *juridical order*. This conception must be firmly grasped and upheld, and it is particularly necessary for people with a pacifist approach to the question. There is nothing so dangerous for the idea of peace as the view—a view which has no foundation in the facts—that the existing system of inter-State relationships is not a system of law in the real and strict sense of the term. There is no greater delusion than to imagine that the value and significance of international organisation is enhanced by attributing to it a moral and not a legal character. In the interests of peace it is better to speak of international *right* than—as only too often happens—to hold forth about a nebulous justice, and then to neglect the development of an international law which is still in its infancy. If the League of Nations Covenant had said a little less about justice and had paid a little more attention to the technical side of the formation of law, it would have better performed its task.

But if it is accepted that the system now governing the mutual relations of States is a positive system of law, then as an inevitable consequence one obtains straightaway a significant insight into the technical legal function which war and other acts of coercion grouped under the name of " reprisals " have to exercise within the existing international system.

IV.

All law is in essence a system of compulsion. It is to be distinguished from all other social machinery and particularly from ethical postulates in that it seeks to bring about the socially desired condition by establishing as a pre-requisite an act of coercion, the consequence no less than condition of any untoward conduct on the part of the subjects to be governed by such and such rules. Thus, in domestic law you have civil enforcements and penal enforcements. Law is a system connoting compulsion, and as such an instrument of social technology of a quite specific character. It is a means and not an end. For the ends that may be pursued by law, as a means, are of the most divergent character. We make use of law when we think we must have recourse to acts of compulsion in order to bring about or to maintain a specific social condition.

If international law is authentic law, law in the same sense as the juridical systems of individual States, then it must, just like these systems, be a system instituting compulsion; it must obligate the States which are subject to this law to a specific rule of conduct, and lay down a definite sanction to meet the case that a State may not proceed in that fashion, an act of coercion to be directed against that State. If in the international system which exists already in a positive form there were no such act of coercion in evidence, if it were not demonstrable that the obligations of States as stipulated by international law exhibit the same characteristics as the legal obligations of individuals within the State, that the technical process of regulation and restraint in international law is identical with that of domestic law, then indeed there could be no question of an *international law* in the real sense of the term. It would mean that the development of international organisation had not reached the first step which—on the pattern of the development of the State—is necessary in order to attain a state of peace. As it is, however, positive international law does in fact provide for such a compulsion. It is not a civil execution exactly, still less a penal measure, yet the specific sanctions of international law reveal a complete analogy to that of municipal law. Those sanctions in international law are war and reprisals.

V.

Now it is generally recognised that reprisals, within the meaning of positive international law, can be applied only as a retaliatory measure against a wrong that has been inflicted, that is to say, as the consequence of a violation of international law. That international law in the general sense admits war, too, but only on this condition, as the theory of the so-called "just war" requires, is still disputed by many teachers of international law. There are still jurists who take the view that every State has the prerogative—only restricted by particular treaties—to make war whenever and against whatever State it likes, without thereby violating international law. But this notion is incompatible with the validity of an international juridical system. One cannot assume that every State, by law, indeed in duty bound by international *common* law, is required to respect a certain sphere of interests of other States, *i.e.*, to eschew intervention in that sphere, a sphere which, precisely for that reason and only for that reason, is described as a legal sphere, and at the same time maintain that any State may in war-time not only indulge in arbitrary invasion on that sphere, but even, if it has the power, may destroy that sphere, and, as a result, bring about the destruction of that State itself, without any violation of the law being discerned in such a proceeding. It is frankly meaningless to contend that a reprisal limited to the injury of particular interests is bound up in international law with specific conditions while proclaiming war, on the other hand—which by definition is a violation of *all* the interests of the other State—as an action, so to speak, authorised to the various States by international law.

Anyone who rejects the theory of the just war denies, indeed, the legal nature of international law, and takes up a position whence international law can scarcely claim any validity as a system of rules. The doctrine that international law permits war and reprisals only as retributive measures for a wrong that has been perpetrated, that any other war represents a violation of international law, derives, as a matter of fact, not merely as the natural consequence of the idea of international law as a system of law, but it also corresponds to the facts that constitute international law.

Certainly one cannot maintain that wars have always been waged only as retributive measures against wrongs that have been perpetrated ; there have been any number of illicit wars. But the States have always deemed is necessary to try and justify the war as being a retribution for a wrong. It is precisely in that fact, in the assumption that such a *justification* is necessary, that the significance of objective international law is made plain ; and in the present state of international law there is no other way of affording that indication.

VI.

The present state of international law is characterised by the fact that international common law—considered from a technical standpoint—is still in the stage of a *primitive system of law*, that is to say, it is at a stage from which the legal system of the individual States originally developed. This is a condition of extensive decentralisation. There are not—as in a technically developed system of law—central organisms dividing among themselves the function of making and executing law. The general rules valid for the whole community have not been consciously laid down by a legislator in an exact and regulated procedure, but —as in the beginnings of the development of law within the individual State—they have been evolved by custom, that is to say, by the practice of the persons concerned with that law, the members of the community.

Within the framework of international common law there are no central tribunals whose business it is to apply general rules of law to particular cases. What happens is—just as when the vendetta system obtained and when the creditor was entitled to get his due himself from a debtor failing to pay—that the application of the law is entrusted to the members of the community themselves who are affected or interested. A State injured by another State is the one to decide whether a violation of international law has taken place, and if the other State denies the breach which is imputed to it, there is, under international common law, no objective procedure by which the dispute can be determined. Thus the State whose rights are impugned itself retaliates at its own discretion for the wrong perpetrated, in its own opinion, with the measures of coercion peculiar to international law, war or reprisal.

VII.

Here you have the elementary legal technique of self-help, whence originated the law of the modern State. Similarly international law may be expected eventually to proceed beyond this first phase. Inside of a particular legal community, as for example the collection of States forming the League, or the other collection bound by the Briand-Kellogg Pact, remarkable progress has already been made ; and it is to be noted that progress is to be made only within the framework of such specific legal communities. All the efforts that have been made in this direction, and particularly the manifold attempts to eliminate war from international relations, aim consciously or unconsciously at transcending the legal technique of self-help. If they are to be crowned with lasting success, we must never lose sight of the legal structure of the community whose organisation it is our purpose to reform. We must bear in mind, above all, that it is a question of progress in legal technique, and that this progress is bound up with a development step by step that proceeds from the very nature of law, one which law has already gone through at an earlier period—within the framework of the legal system of the individual State.

If we may be allowed to draw analogies in the sphere of law from that of nature, to establish a parallel between the development of the legal community of mankind with the development of man himself, subject as he is to the so-called fundamental law of biogenesis, we may, perhaps, postulate that this law, in a certain sense, finds its application no less in the development of public right. That law as formulated by the famous biologist, Ernst Heckel, says, as we know : the individual human being, as an embryo, passes through all the stages of evolution that the whole human race has up to now passed through. In the sphere of law it is the other way round : here, as is appropriate to the species, the entire community bound by international law has to pass through all the stages of the evolution which the individual State-community has passed through, to reach the embryonic condition in which it still is to-day. Certainly the evolution of legal technique with regard to the law governing the community of States may be very much more rapid than the process extending over thousands of years, whereby the evolution of the legal system of the individual State came to reach the condition in which it is to-day. But, similarly, the human embryo covers in a few months a distance which mankind has needed several thousands of years to cover. Along this road, however—so it appears—no essential stage can be missed.

It is true that one must not overlook the difference between a development which is natural and fully independent of the arbitrary will of man and the technical progress of social institutions, owing their existence to the spirit and the active impulsion of man. But this difference is not so considerable as to invalidate our view of a social progress governed by an immanent law which originates in the nature of man and the social arrangements befitting the nature of man. Considered from the point of view of its evolution, human society is, after all, a piece of nature. Man in his active understanding and deliberate will to progress is the more certain of success the more carefully he heeds nature in its social representations, *i.e.*, the primordial nature of the social representations, their inner structure.

VIII.

Faced with the task of consciously developing the technique of international law, we are in the happy position, as it were, of having a pattern in the evolution of the legal system of the individual State.

This model shows the following typical stages (I am not here taking into consideration the law-functions in the narrower sense of the term, nor the military and religious functions of the community). First of all, complete decentralisation. Out of that State, depicted above, there are formed, as the first central organisms, not, as one might think, organisms for legislation, but organisms for the purpose of law-promulgation enunciating what shall be the law. For a long time law is developed by custom, and in particular communities, in contractual forms, while central courts are already in operation. Not otherwise is it in international law. And when we see that the erection of a central legislature, indeed, mere codification of the prevailing customary law (which to a certain extent is always a central act of law-creation, in other words legislation) ensues only in a technically very advanced stage of the legal system of the individual State, then we shall understand why the efforts to establish a world parliament or any kind of international legislature, even though its efficacy be confined to a particular collectivity in international law, are at present to be regarded as sheer chasing after illusions. We must, indeed, regard attempts to codify international law (for codification is never merely a declaratory process, but to a considerable degree a creative one), taking into account the present state of international law, as definitely premature.

IX.

Precisely in this matter of the creation of general rules, the evolution of municipal law reveals a phenomenon which is particularly to be noted for our discussion on the technique of international law. It is the State courts themselves which, at the beginning, develop the legal system by the fact that they not only carry out the prevailing customary law, but also change that law. They do this by applying new rules of law corresponding to a changed legal consciousness, although indeed it is under the guise of a mere interpretation of the existing law. In the primitive legal community law, in its general connotation, is regarded as unalterable. Changes in the law, such as are required by changing circumstances, take place only by devious means. And the instrument for these changes in the law is the court, which, by virtue of its authority, contrives essentially to modify even laws established by contract.

That is the way which—at first, at any rate—is marked out for the development of international law. Every day the need is felt more strongly for some means of modifying and developing existing international law, not merely the common law, but specifically the law created by collective treaties, and for some means other than the cumbersome method of obtaining the agreement of all those persons deriving duties or rights from the rule which it is desired to change—a method which impedes any real progress. Particularly is the need being appreciated for some way of escape from the *status quo* laid down by the Peace Treaties, regarded by many people as unjust and, indeed, intolerable. Of this need almost everyone is persuaded to-day, but in this direction there is no other hope except in the construction of a strong, really obligatory arbitration system, a jurisdiction permitting of no exception. The authority of such a judicial system will be the more considerable the more complete its scope is, and the greater its authority the easier it will be to give the tribunals power not only to apply the existing law, but also to pronounce judgment in equity, which means creating new law. Indeed, the greater the authority of an international court having jurisdiction over all disputes, the less necessary it is to empower it expressly to apply any other than the positive law that already exists. A sovereign court does that by itself—as our experience of the judicial process in the individual State shows us. The creation of a real, that is to say, technically perfect, judicature, even though it be only within a specific collectivity of States, must precede any strivings after the establishment of international legislative organisms as also any attempt to codify international law. That is the organic process of development. It will make very much easier achievement of those other two purposes which to-day seem impossible. Indeed, it will alone make such achievement possible.

X.

Our appreciation of the evolution of law within the individual State furnishes also very valuable lessons as to the course likely to be taken by a developing international jurisdiction, the course that logically it should take, and consequently the direction in which we have consciously to proceed in the matter of international judicial organisation if we are to achieve our object.

We must distinguish two phases of activity on the part of a tribunal. First of all, the actual determination as to whether or not the alleged violation of rights imputed to the conduct of one party by the other does in fact constitute such a violation. The second issue will vary according to the decision on that first point. If it is established that there has been no breach of rights, the claim instituted by the first party is dismissed. If, on the other hand, the verdict is that there has been a breach of rights, the court lays down the consequent procedure—in the first place, the obligation to compensate for damage done, and then, should the law-breaker refuse redress, decline to submit to the ruling of the court, thereby adding yet another breach of the law to the original violation, the executory measure to be applied to the law-breaker.

The actual legal pronouncement has to be separated therefore from the material application of sanctions; and especially so, inasmuch as it has to be admitted that, historically, a centralisation of the law-declaring process long preceded any centralisation of sanctions. Originally the courts, after establishing the fact that a breach of the law had been committed, empowered the person whose right had been impugned to proceed to measures of self-help. It was only the question of whether he had suffered a wrong, at first, which was withdrawn from his private judgment. And, from the point of view of the evolution of legal technique, there is in this surrender of the right of private judgment by the injured party a far greater advance than in the much later developing abandonment of self-help, *i.e.*, when the individual was no longer entitled to take his own measures of coercion against the law-breaker, when self-help duly authorised by an objective legal pronouncement is replaced by the executory act prescribed by central organs of the State. It is that stage to which, in the development of international law, corresponds the disarmament of the individual States and the arming of the international legal community embracing them (to use the current jargon).

XI.

And in this connection I should like to point out that if the international collectivity of States is to be understood as a legal community and is to be upheld as such, it is a short-sighted and illusory conception to imagine that disarmament of the individual States, or even any substantial reduction of their armaments, is possible without at the same time, or previously, a central executive power being created, qualified to take over that legal function exercised up till then by the armed power of the individual States, namely, retribution for breach of the law and execution of the penalty prescribed by international common law. To the extent that it is desired to preserve a specific state of affairs as a state of law, we have to will the requisite guarantee that makes it a state of law, to face up to the possibility of the appropriate sanctions.

It is, therefore, futile to aim at doing away with war by an international treaty unless there is an international act of coercion prescribed in place of war as a means of redress for any hypothetical violation of the law, and unless the necessary preliminary organisation has been created for the performance of such an executory measure. It would be absurd to suggest to a person bent on securing his rights, and only his rights, that he must refrain from self-help so long as he cannot count on effective aid from the legal community.

To hope to prevent war before an international executive power has been instituted to carry out the judgments of an International Court, and one which is strong enough to ensure obedience to those judgments, is tantamount to bestowing an advantage upon such as are determined to enforce their own interests, if necessary, in violation of international law; in other words, actually to place a premium upon violation of international law. That would be not a step forward, but a dangerous step backward in the development of international organisation. For it would mean no more, but also no less, than taking away again from that system the character or legality which it has with so much difficulty acquired. What would a law-breaker have to bother about if he had not even to reckon at the very least on proceedings being taken against him by the injured party, the latter being indeed legally entitled so to proceed?

The belief that the international order cannot be based on anything else except the goodwill of the States and the public opinion of the peoples is one of the most dangerous illusions—no less dangerous and no less illusory than the notion of *anarchism* as applied to the system of restraints of the individual State. It is, indeed, nothing else but inter-State anarchy. Nor is international executive force superfluous if we cherish the distinctly vague conception of an international boycott of the law-breaker, since, after all, any such boycott measures have to be organised and in some way or another guaranteed.

It were folly, too, to think that in the present state of international organisation it could be possible to keep in a completely disarmed or virtually disarmed condition any one *particular State, i.e.*, an organism which, from every other point of view, counts as a State, has the duties and the rights of a State—especially if it be a State of considerable importance from the point of view of population and territory—while all the other neighbouring States remain armed, indeed must remain armed for the purpose of defending and maintaining their rights, and therewith international law. In the present stage of international juridical development to be without weapons is—in a certain sense—to be without rights.

XII.

All efforts aiming at total or partial disarmament, whether it be all round or unilateral, are doomed to failure, not only because now and for a long time ahead they cannot be linked up with the establishment of a centralised executive power, a centralised force possessed of armaments, but above all because the necessary pre-requisites from the point of view of the development of international legal technique are absent. Law, no more than nature, can miss a stage in its evolutionary path. And, after all, it is useless to proceed with the construction of a majestic façade before the foundations of the building have been laid.

The foundation of all legal organisation as of any legal community is the *judicial process*. Before you can seriously think of establishing a central police force or armed force for the purposes of any particular collection of States, as for instance, the League of Nations, and even though it be only for the purpose of executing the judgments of a central court, you must endeavour to realise that condition of affairs in which, though self-help as a matter of principle still obtains, it is a restricted self-help: that is, at least, if you are going to keep in line with the progress observed by the evolution of legal processes within the individual State community. Every State may take retaliatory action by the use of its own weapons against a wrong inflicted upon it, but it is only entitled to take such action when specifically empowered to do so by a judgment delivered in an impartial court establishing after impartial examination of the facts that the wrongful act has been perpetrated.

These three phases of every proper legal procedure—establishment of the fact that a wrong has been done, delivery of judgment as to the consequences deriving from the wrong, and fulfilment of those consequences—not only represent a logical sequence, but they are equally decisive for the course to be taken by any conceivable reform of that procedure. One cannot bring to perfection the process of implementing the sanction of the law through its centralisation while leaving the first phase, *i.e.*, determination of the fact of wrong, in a condition of utter primitiveness. Self-help cannot be eliminated, nor can it be curtailed until the much more serious question of auto-decision on the question of right or wrong has been disposed of. The States desirous of living together in a more intimate legal community than is warranted by international common law must, first of all and before anything else, be brought to a state of agreement wherein they undertake the obligation *to refrain from any war, any act of reprisal similar to war, any coercive action of any kind, indeed any interference in the guise of a sanction in the sphere of interests of another State that are protected by international law, except by virtue of judicial decision empowering them so to proceed.* That means, however, that the States in question submit all disputes, without any exception, to a central tribunal, that you must not be content with outlawing war while leaving the States free to take much more disagreeable measures by way of reprisals. It means, in particular, that the hypocritical and fateful distinction between justiciable and political disputes goes by the board and, not least, that by the side of a central tribunal with jurisdiction over all disputes, no special tribunals set up by specific arbitration treaties can be allowed.

That both the League of Nations Covenant and the Briand-Kellogg Pact are still a long way from this goal, although both of them—or rather *because* of them—have set up still more ambitious goals, indeed, too ambitious, I need not explain in any greater detail. They would have been more useful to the progress of international organisation and to peace if the former had contented itself with establishing an authentic international juridical community, and the latter had refrained from trying to eliminate war altogether and, instead, had linked it up wlth a previous judicial decision—which thereby admitted of no exception; in other words, had stipulated that it ought to be only an instrument for the execution of that judgment.

XIII.

The constitution of a system of legal obligations among States should not be limited to laying down the rule that no kind of coercive action is to be levied against another State of the community, save by the authority of the judgment of a court. Provision must also be made for the contingency that a State may infringe this rule and, without waiting to be empowered by a judicial decree, without indeed making any attempt to obtain any such authority, proceed to take steps against another member State amounting to war, reprisals of the nature of war or some form of interference in the sphere of rights protected by international law. In this direction, as a rule, it is sufficient to prescribe measures similar to those in domestic law coming under the heading " Emergency." When once the individual States of a legal community are authorised to take coercive action against another member of that community, only on the authorisation of a central organism is it possible to make provision for the expedient of emergency action. Of such a character is the self-help resorted to on his own responsibility by a person under threat, as an exception to the rule that acts of coercion shall only be undertaken at the instigation of the judicial authority.

The idea of emergency action finds no application in the framework of international common law, because self-help is here the rule. A State the victim of aggression must be duly authorised to take emergency action, *i.e.*, action consisting in warding off such aggression by the appropriate means, against that State which is responsible for an act of coercion, whether war or war-like reprisals or any other action involving the application of armed force (in the fullest sense of the term) in violation of the system of rules on which the community in question is based, and without being empowered by decree of the central court. The most recently concluded treaties that have sought to define the aggressor have done valuable preliminary work in this field, although it is at least open to question whether a casuistical enumeration of cases of aggression is of any real value from the technical legal standpoint. Within the *cadre* of a duly constituted juridical community, such as I have depicted above, some formula of general application like "no coercion without authorisation" will, perhaps, be more useful, as it is more flexible. It should be noted, moreover, that the emphasis does not lie on the concept of "aggression." The decisive thing is not that the State commits aggression, but that it does so contrary to the law. Why, a State authorised by the tribunal to proceed by some act of coercion, say, a war-like reprisal, against another State that, perhaps, by mere negligence, has violated its obligations, is an "aggressor," inasmuch as it initiates the hostile action. But then it is an aggression which is legally admissible. What matters is *illicit* application of coercion. Only against such an act, not against any other breach of the law, should emergency action be authorised. And it should only come into operation as a result of a simultaneous invocation of the court which has to determine whether the situation is such that emergency action is legitimate, as also to ascertain whether or not the emergency action taken was excessive. For the means specified as legitimate redress for an illicit act of coercion must be proportionate to the actual act of aggression. Such action should not go beyond the scope of defence against illicit intervention.

XIV.

One serious drawback to the legal process of self-help consists in the fact it can only be successful when it is not directed against a law-breaker possessing more formidable instruments of power than the injured party. But, by international common law, not only is that war deemed to be just which the victim of an injustice wages, but also any such war waged by that State's allies against the law-breaker. A war waged by a State whose rights have not been *directly* infringed, in fulfilment of its obligations to an alliance, for the defence of its ally in respect of some violation of the law affecting that ally, is *legal relief.* Its object is to vindicate the violated law. Every infringement of a subjective right is, in the first place, an infringement of objective law, and it is the concern not only of the person directly affected, but of all members of the legal community. Whether or to what extent they are incited to obtain redress for the wrong that has been done depends on the technical processes of the legal system.

Every juridical community is by implication a community based on legal relief. The right to self-help is ever bound up with the right to make an alliance with other subjects bound by the same law for the successful performance of self-help. And that is the state of affairs which normally precedes the institution of a central executive power accompanied by the disarming of the several members of the community. Whenever a number of States bind themselves to have all disputes that may arise between them settled by a common tribunal, there will be a judicial pronouncement affirming the violation of the law which will make it possible to proceed against the violator of the law who may be unwilling to defer to that judgment. That legal possibility is available not only to the State directly injured in its rights, but also to all other States of that juridical community; and this is so even though there may be no express agreement on such legal succour. This faculty indeed proceeds from international common law. Only, when the States are formally bound to afford such legal succour and not merely authorised so to do, the treaty that establishes the tribunal must contain a clause expressly making this stipulation. That means from the point of view of legal technique a substantial advance.

At that stage—but only at that stage—it becomes comparatively easy, or I should say no longer quite so impossible as at present, to compass the establishment of a central executive power, the process going hand in hand with a gradual disarming of the individual States.

XV.

Only at this stage, or at the very earliest when the International Court has acquired an exclusive jurisdiction over all disputes without exception between States of the international juridical community, can we hope to give the tribunal any substantial measure of jurisdiction over disputes between individuals and States, in other words, afford individuals the opportunity of obtaining redress by invocation of the tribunal. For let us be quite clear as to the extraordinary scope of a measure of this kind. It is the first effective step to the *super-State*, as it may be called in a strictly legal sense and not merely in the jargon of demagogic politics.

For if and when between the individual and the international legal community the individual State is no longer the indispensable mediator, when the legal community of the nations with its specific organisms is directly at the disposal of the individual, even should he claim redress against his own State, when this individual State will in certain cases be able to proceed against its own subjects only after authorisation from an international tribunal—then, indeed, from the point of view of legal technique, there will be no longer any essential distinction between the international legal system, *i.e.*, the system of international law on which that particular legal community is based, and the legal system of the individual State. The moment this specific system of international law applies directly to the individual human being, it must abandon those primitive forms of hue and cry and the *posse comitatus* which are characteristic of the regulation of inter-State relations by international common law and must give place to those forms of individual treatment and apportionment of culpability which correspond to the advanced technique of the legal system of the individual State. It is only the simple-minded enthusiast who can imagine such a far-reaching abdication on the part of the State authority *vis-à-vis* its subjects before the highest grade of inter-State judicial process has been reached.

XVI.

Like the national courts, the International Court requires certain auxiliary organisms in order to be able to fulfil its functions along these lines. Where the court specially needs a certain amount of support by other organisms is in the determination of the *casus fœderis*, the so-called question of fact. In the criminal justice of the State, which international justice in its present form resembles far more closely than it does the civil process, it is above all the task of the police to procure all the factual material likely to be important for the question of fact, such material being placed at the disposal of the public prosecutor or of the examining magistrate. It would be entirely conceivable that in the ultimate and complete structure of international justice particular organisms should be created for the purpose of determining the actual facts either of all or specified breaches of the law for which the contracting States would be responsible, and particularly where these violations of the law were perpetrated upon the territory of the responsible State, prior to handing over the material thus acquired to the court. Let there be no illusion about this being an attempt to create an international policing instrument likely to wound the susceptibilities of the governments that are anxiously intent on maintaining the appearance of sovereignty. For that very reason it would be highly desirable that any such commissions or commissioners of investigation should from the outset be defined as auxiliary organisms of the International Court and made subordinate to it, while being appointed also by it. It must be the International Court in whose name and by whose authority such organisms function, a tribunal to which the States at length have agreed to defer their submission to a certain extent, following as a matter of course from consciousness of international legality.

It must be no fresh " tribunal " interfering in the " domestic " affairs of States. Such a tribunal, failing an immediate dependence on the International Court, must necessarily take on a political character which will hardly be compatible with the prestige of the States. When we look at the matter specifically from this point of view, we must see that it would be of the utmost importance to bind up the work of these organisms as closely as possible with the judicial process; by that I mean that it should come into operation from case to case, a concrete violation of the law having been alleged and proceedings having been instituted at the International Court against any particular State, but then it should be backed up with every available means and the strongest guarantees for the success of its examination of the case.

XVII.

It goes without saying that, within an international legal community whose centre of gravity is in the administration of international justice, there must be a place for an organism whose special function it is to prevent disputes between States, or, in the event of them having arisen, to endeavour to get them settled out of court, in short, by bringing the parties together to make an amicable settlement. Such an organism is exemplified in the League of Nations Council. But an institution of this kind devoted to mediation should not in any way be in competition with the central judicial body—as is the case with the League of Nations Council and the Permanent Court of Justice. The members of the community ought not to have the option of pleading their case before one or the other tribunal. The authority of the judicial organism should only be set aside when the Council has successfully intervened and when the dispute has been removed by amicable arrangement.

Out of this examination of the structure of international law, out of our recognition of the intimate connection that prevails between its technical evolution and the progress of international organisation, there emerges the following lesson : that the forces working for world peace should not be directed to aims which to-day, in view of the present state of international organisation, are not yet attainable, that no attempts at reform should be undertaken such as are doomed to fail—however good may be the intentions of all the governments—since their failure must further envenom the international atmosphere and compromise the idea of peace, the only single hope we have of a better future for the world. Let us rather concentrate and mobilise the energies of those who are wedded to the idea of peace for the construction of an international judicial system, thus establishing the indispensable basic condition for the achievement of any further progress.

The Foreign Policy of a Free Democracy

by Ambassador Philip C. Jessup [1]

You Veterans of Foreign Wars are on record as an organization deeply concerned with promoting the welfare of our country. No group of citizens has a greater right to be heard on matters of national interest than those who have served in our armed forces during war. No group has a greater responsibility for rendering public service through an intelligent watchful interest in the future of the United States. As a veteran of World War I, I claim a share in that right and acknowledge a share in that responsibility. Discharge from active service did not discharge us from our duties as citizens. Obviously the kind of service required in peace is different from that required in war. It is not generally recognized that it is nevertheless a vital and an arduous service.

I should be very happy if I could report to you that peace is safe and secure, but it is not. Peace is being maintained by the United States and a large group of like-minded nations. We are fighting for a just and permanent peace on the Atlantic and Pacific fronts today just as much as we were between Pearl Harbor and V–E and V–J days. We cannot relax our efforts for a day, for an hour.

Those efforts must be on an all-out national basis. You veterans who bore the brunt of World War II were backed by every resource of your government and by men and women working in a thousand different ways throughout this country and abroad. It was impossible for civilians during the war to sit back and say, "Let's leave it to the armed

[1] Address made at the Golden Jubilee National Convention of Veterans of Foreign Wars, Miami, Fla., on Aug. 24, 1949, and released to the press on the same date.

forces." It is equally impossible for you now to leave the job of maintaining the peace—which is the prevention of another war—to those working full time on the problem in the diplomatic or military or other government service. You won't be drafted, and you aren't asked to enlist in active service. But your help—the help of your great organization—is essential.

We know that the job of winning the war included not only military effort but also scientific, economic, and financial effort. Keeping the peace also requires a multiple effort. If the United States weakens its military strength, the peace is not secure. The same is true if we weaken our foreign policy. It is also true if we do not remain strong economically, financially, and morally.

It is not bombast to say the United States is the most powerful country in the world. Some people in some nations may state that fact with envy; most people in most nations say it with hope. Only those who do not want peace say it with fear. Our national program has been clearly stated. It is based on national strength to be used in cooperation with other nations through the United Nations in the interest and for the well-being of all the world. That is the program laid down in the inaugural address of the President of the United States. Every Department and agency of the government has a part to play in carrying out that program. Every citizen has a vital stake in its success.

I am not going to talk about the elements of our economic, financial, and military strength. I do want to speak of our moral strength and our foreign policy.

It is not an American habit to talk much about moral strength, or those things which are called spiritual values. I make no apology for raising that theme. We know that the Communists are fighting all over the world to capture the mind and the spirit of men so that they can then enslave them by the ruthless totalitarian methods which kill the spirit, darken the mind, and torture the body. They begin with beautiful promises. They have cunning and skillful agents trained in corrupting the mind. They have the greatest success where there is ignorance or despair. Our job is to dispel the ignorance and to replace despair with hope.

On the Atlantic front our chief problem was the weary despair which the war and its ruin inevitably brought. The Marshall Plan, the Atlantic pact, and the Military Aid Program are bringing back hope.

On the Pacific front they need hope also, but the great problem is the vast ignorance of hundreds of millions of people on which Communism feeds. These people do not know that in countries ruled by Communists there is no freedom. They do not know that the prophets of Communism have publicly proclaimed that they will encourage national independence merely as a stepping stone to a new and terrible slavery. They do not know what our civilization and political principles have produced in the way of a free and prosperous life for the people of a great country.

Our idea of freedom and the good life is something we have for export. If we don't export it, the people who do not know it exists will buy the cheap shoddy promises of Communism. To back our export we need to have the fire of conviction which established this country and which in this generation has brought us to victory in two world wars. That same fire of conviction can keep us at peace.

Our peace strategy is global. The Atlantic and Pacific fronts are only illustrative. As in the war we have our allies, and our strategy must be a joint strategy. With our allies we have preponderant peace forces. We must be constantly alert that no trickery on the part of those who do not seek peace and that no error on our own part, brings us to the loss, or to the abuse, of that great power.

It is true today as it was when spoken 40 years ago by a great Secretary of War and Secretary of State—Elihu Root—that "We wish for no victories but those of peace; for no territory except our own; for no sovereignty except the sovereignty over ourselves."

That is our fundamental strength. Unlike the Soviet Union, we do not want more territory or subject peoples. We want all peoples to be free and prosperous because we believe that progress means a united move upward rather than climbing on the backs of others who are pushed down. We have acted on that belief, and we are putting it into practice through the United Nations, the symbol of international cooperation.

The broad outlines of a positive and forward-looking postwar foreign policy based on that conviction began to take form, and the framework within which it would operate began to emerge, before the war ended. The guiding principles and the general methods by which we hoped to build a better world were developed and enunciated in a series of United Nations conferences beginning in 1943 and culminating with the establishment of the United Nations Organization in 1945. We foresaw the basic needs of the world for food and set up the Food and Agriculture Organization. We knew postwar relief was necessary and established United Nations Relief and Rehabilitation Administration. We anticipated the requirements for economic and financial help, and created the World Bank and the International Monetary Fund. These and other specialized international agencies have all been brought into the general framework of the United Nations.

In all these remarkable efforts looking toward world reconstruction, recovery, and development in an environment of peace and harmony, there was no animosity or antagonism toward any of the participating nations. All the plans laid in that period assumed the continued cooperation of all the Allied powers in a common endeavor to create a better world. That assumption has been proved wrong. The Soviet Union refuses to cooperate in improving the welfare of mankind and in insuring international peace and security. This opposition does not invalidate the strategy of international cooperation. It merely increases the need for united effort on the basis of clear and unimpeachable principles.

This opposition is not only obstructive, but aggressively so. It not only is a challenge to the beliefs and aspirations of the free peoples, but also a threat to their security and welfare. It is a challenge that must be taken up, a threat that must be countered. There is no reason for hysteria. There is need for calm determination.

Let us frankly acknowledge that many of the actions and much of the effort of the United States in international affairs in recent months have been directed toward countering the clear threat to ourselves and other free peoples. We could not have done otherwise without betraying all that we stand for. Let us also frankly admit that self-interest, if we had taken that as the sole guide, would have dictated the same course.

The realities of the situation have required us to develop new methods and measures to meet them successfully, but they have not diverted us from our long-range, primary objectives. We still seek a just and enduring peace, in which all peoples will be free to achieve better living conditions and a wider enjoyment of human rights. We still firmly support the United Nations as the most feasible and effective means by which the nations of the world can work together to keep the peace and promote the welfare of their peoples.

The United Nations should not be judged by utopian standards, but by the world as it is. As long as deep-seated differences among its members persist, the United Nations is bound to be affected by that division. Nevertheless, the fact of primary importance is that the United Nations continues to function in spite of the East-West conflict, even though its effectiveness is diminished. It provides a common meeting ground for all the nations which genuinely seek the solution of problems by consultation and collaboration. By the continuity of its operations, the United Nations strengthens the habit of working together. Above all, it contains the contending forces within a recognized forum and requires them to justify their actions to the world in terms of the purposes and provisions of the Charter. The United Nations looms larger and larger as the manifest conscience of mankind.

Within the limits of the matters with which the United Nations was expected to deal, it has gradually and painstakingly achieved a record of real accomplishment. A look at that record should caution us against taking an unduly pessimistic view of the ability of the United Nations to deal with particular cases. If the representatives of the United Nations had been as easily discouraged as some observers, they would not have manifested the patience and perseverance that eventually brings success.

Last December, for example, when the Dutch took military action against the Republicans in Indonesia, headlines and comments in this country took the following line:

> Once again the world is afforded an excellent illustration of United Nations impotence in such situations.
>
> Revival of the Indonesian war is another challenge to United Nations authority and world peace.
>
> The United Nations will be holding a post-mortem on a *fait accompli*. Its history in Palestine does not suggest that it will be any more effective in Indonesia in urging withdrawal to the old lines while arbitration and mediation is talked.

Yet the United Nations continued its efforts and was able a few months later to bring about a cessation of armed conflict and an agreement of the parties to resume negotiations. The headlines and comments following this development reflected a great change in sentiment, as indicated by these samples:

> The agreement . . . is another victory for the United Nations.
>
> The United Nations Commission provided the machinery for arriving at the truce.
>
> The United Nations Commission on Indonesia has been active and successful.

The parties are now meeting in a round-table conference at The Hague with the United Nations Commission participating.

Similarly, the ups and down of the Palestine case have been accompanied by corresponding variations in the public evaluation of the United Nations efforts to obtain a peaceful settlement. Last fall, such statements as these appeared in the press of this country:

> The best thing for the United Nations to do, in the matter of Palestine, is to withdraw as gracefully as possible.
>
> Both the prestige and authority of the United Nations appear to be seriously endangered by the situation in Palestine.
>
> It has involved the United Nations' greatest admission of defeat of the purposes of its own existence.
>
> Why doesn't the United Nations admit its inability to function and pull out of the whole mess?

But Ralph Bunche and his fellow mediators would not give up so easily. They persisted through weary weeks of negotiation and finally, only a month ago, succeeded in obtaining an armistice between Israel and the last of the neighboring states with which it had been in conflict. This time the tone of the comments were quite different, as shown by the following:

> To the scoffers . . . who say that the United Nations is helpless or useless or worse, the story of this phase of the Palestine problem should give pause, and food for thought.
>
> The achievement of the United Nations in Palestine is a great gain for the world and for the prestige and future effectiveness of the United Nations.
>
> Dr. Bunche succeeded in his task partly because of his personality, partly because of the framework in which he operated.

The parties are now discussing final settlements at Geneva with a United Nations Commission participating.

When the decision was made to submit the question of the Berlin blockade to the United Nations during the session of the General Assembly last fall, some feared that the consequences might be fatal to the United Nations. Much of the reaction in this country was along the following lines:

> Reference to the United Nations will not bring a solution.
>
> Do we want to dramatize the fact that we are not succeeding in using the United Nations as a mechanism for arriving at agreements?

Reference of the Berlin question to the United Nations did not bring an immediate solution. Yet it is generally conceded that the United Nations contributed significantly to the solution that was subsequently achieved. This appraisal is reflected in such press comments as the following:

> The agreement concerning Berlin is an accomplishment of the United Nations of the greatest importance.
>
> Despite the profound differences of principle between East and West, despite the veto, it remains a great and useful thing that the United Nations exists to provide a forum where all these efforts at finding a meeting ground can take place.

These experiences demonstrate that there is no justification for discouragement if progress toward the solution of the problems that remain, and new ones which arise, is slower and less spectacular than we would like. We have had no days as black as some of those which preceded victory in the war. If the majority of the members of the United Nations persevere in their patient efforts to achieve an effective system of collective security, they will win because they are right. This truth cannot forever be concealed from other peoples because iron curtains will eventually rust away when exposed to truth.

The United States has never been afraid to face the future. Times of peace and prosperity as well as those of danger and distress need forethought. If we did not plan ahead for peace, we would be less likely to reach the goal and less likely to retain the gains when they are made. It is Communist, and not American doctrine, that enmity and war are inevitable.

Consistent with our faith and with our word pledged through the ratification of the United Nations Charter, we have cooperated in the efforts of the United Nations to work toward disarmament. Little progress has yet been made because the Soviet Union has refused to accept the conclusions of the majority in the Commission for Conventional Armaments regarding the essential features of an effective plan of regulation. The Soviet Union tried to shift the blame for this lack of progress, but the other members recognized their proposals as a mere propaganda maneuver and rejected them.

The General Assembly requested the Commission to give highest priority to the development of a plan for a census of armaments and armed forces, with a control organization for verifying the information to be submitted to the states subscribing to the plan. This request reflected the belief, shared by the United States, that disarmament cannot be based on promises alone but only on duly certified knowledge of the facts: This means that the whole international community must have full information about armaments and armed forces, checked and double-checked by neutral observers, as a necessary prerequisite to any actual reduction and regulation of conventional arms.

It must be emphasized that the plan for an arms census and verification of the figures will not go into effect even for those countries which have supported it unless and until it has been approved in the Security Council and the General Assembly and has been subscribed to by the United States and other governments. In other words, the plan will become a reality only after each member of the United Nations has had an opportunity to review it and decide whether it wishes to accept the plan. We are not going to exchange arms for empty promises.

We have gone forward also in the search for safe control of the most dangerous weapon. The majority of the United Nations Atomic Energy Commission has developed a plan for international control of atomic energy, based largely on proposals made by the United States. We offered to give up atomic weapons and to transfer to an international authority atomic activities dangerous to international security, but only upon the absolutely essential condition that a system of effective and enforceable safeguards has first been established and is in actual operation.

The plan of the majority of the Commission, incorporating this condition, has been approved by the General Assembly as providing "the necessary basis" for a system which would safeguard international security. The Commission, however, is unable to proceed further because the Soviet Union has refused to accept the plan approved by the majority of the Commission and by the General Assembly. In accordance with the provisions of the General Assembly resolution and our standard policy, we have begun talks among the six sponsoring powers. We have never closed the door to the Soviet Union for a discussion of any international problem.

One of the plain facts in the present situation is that the Soviet Union is contemptuous of weakness but respects strength. It was the strength of the West which led the Soviet Union to abandon the Berlin blockade and to make at least some moves toward agreement in the recent meeting of the Council of Foreign Ministers in Paris. Our strength is made up of unity with the free peoples of the world; of industrial power; of military power; and of calm confidence in the soundness of our domestic system and our peaceful foreign policy.

We had revealed that strength in several ways. There was the Berlin airlift. That great operation saved the people of Berlin from the starvation with which the Berlin blockade threatened them. I want to pay tribute to the men who organized it and operated it.

Then there was the steady progress toward the organization of a Western German Government. Here the basic unity of purpose and of policy between France, the United Kingdom, and the United States was a most potent factor. That is a unity we must preserve, strengthen, and extend.

We have other friends and allies for peace in all parts of the world. We are closely bound to our good neighbors south of the Rio Grande and have formalized that unity in the defensive pact of Rio de Janeiro, which was concluded within the framework of the United Nations Charter. We have similarly concluded the North Atlantic Treaty with eleven nations who form the North Atlantic community, again acting in conformity with the Charter. We are working closely with other members of the United Nations for our mutual benefit and strength to promote the common purpose of maintaining peace and the good life.

These close associations are not and cannot be the result of domination and dictation. The Soviet Union believes in that method as did Hitler. We do not believe in it. There are always differences of opinion between the closest of friends. Those differences can be resolved by mutual understanding and accommodation because the common purpose is basic. When the Soviet Union comes to realize the soundness of that common purpose and the method of achieving it we stand ready to work equally with them. It must not be forgotten that we are as friendly to the Russian people as to other people. We are not trying to conquer Russia. We are not rivals for the domination of the world because we do not want to dominate the world. If their government will abandon the dream of world domination which throughout history has destroyed such blind dreamers, a full share in international cooperation will be theirs.

At this moment in history we must continue the process of helping Western Europe to rebuild itself in economic stability and in the sense of safety which comes from a well-planned common defense if any state should again be misled into contemplating the fatal step of committing aggression against the democratic forces of the world.

The only way the Western European members of the pact can rapidly acquire an effective defense is for the United States to supplement what they are doing for themselves and each other by supplying arms and equipment from this country, as proposed in the Military Assistance Program. This aid will enable the pact members in Europe to turn their shadow armies into effective forces that will become the nucleus of the integrated defense essential to the maintenance of peace in the North Atlantic area. The development of an actual defense-in-being in Western Europe will give the people of those countries the reassurance that they require for further economic and social progress, and will prove to be a stabilizing influence in Europe and the world.

No one regrets more than do the government and people of the United States that we must devote to arms and other defense measures part of our substance and energy, which we would prefer to use for more productive purposes.

The menace of aggressive Communism to the liberties and rights of free peoples is the immediate and pressing problem that must be overcome. We are confident that the concerted effort of the free nations will succeed in overcoming it. But we are well aware that this is not the only problem, nor in the long perspective of history perhaps, the most significant. We will not hesitate to do what is necessary to help the free nations preserve their independence and integrity. Neither will we lose sight of the constructive and humane tasks which we set ourselves while the war was being fought.

The Secretary of State under the President is charged with the mighty responsibility of waging peace so that this country will not need to wage war. He is supported by all the resources of our government. He acts in consultation with other officers of the government and within the framework of decisions by the Congress. Like all other officers of the United States of America he is responsible, and responsive, to the people. Do not ever get the idea that the men and women carrying on our foreign relations are the actors on the stage and that you, the citizens of the United States, are just the audience. We are all in this great world problem together. You have the privilege of the free citizen to criticize foreign policy. You have the responsibility of the free citizen to participate in its formation and execution.

The Fallacy of a "Preventive War"

by Ambassador Philip C. Jessup [1]

THE CURRENT DEBATES on American foreign policy are a good sign of the awakened popular interest in our international relations. It is no longer necessary, as it was 30 years ago, to try to persuade people that they should have an intense personal interest in such questions. In 1922, Elihu Root, who in addition to his many other distinctions was an Honorary Chancellor of Union College, wrote the inaugural article in *Foreign Affairs*. In that article he said:

"The control of foreign relations by modern democracies creates a new and pressing demand for popular education in international affairs. . . . A self-respecting democracy which undertakes to control the action of its government as a member of this community of nations, and wishes to respond fairly and fully, not only to the demands of its own interests, but to the moral obligations of a member of the community, is bound to try to understand this great and complicated subject so that it may act, not upon prejudice and error, but upon knowledge and understanding."

It would be fortunate if one could say that foreign policy is really very simple, but that would not be true. Foreign policy has to cover the whole world, which is full of complications. If we commonly used the expression "domestic policy" to describe everything our Government does in regard to agriculture, taxation, conservation, crime, interstate commerce, defense, veterans' affairs, finance, the mails, and the dozens of other governmental functions, we would find that domestic policy covered a less complicated bundle of problems than those which have to be met by our foreign policy. This is true because almost every subject which the Government deals with internally has its duplicate in the international field. As the President said in his State of the Union message on January 8, "the state of our Nation is in great part the state of our friends and allies throughout the world." Foreign policy actually also must cover relations with our enemies as well.

In the same article to which I have referred, Mr. Root, who had been Secretary of War, Secretary of State, and United States Senator from New York, and who therefore had a remarkably broad familiarity with public affairs, made some further wise comments which are pertinent today:

"There is one specially important result which should follow from such a popular understanding of foreign affairs. That is, a sense of public responsibility in speech and writing, or perhaps it would be better stated as a public sense of private responsibility for words used in discussing international affairs. . . . It cannot, however, be expected that every individual in a great democracy will naturally practice restraint. Political demagogues will seek popularity by public speeches, full of insult to foreign countries, and yellow journals will seek to increase their circulation by appeals to prejudice against foreigners. Hitherto these have been passed over because the speakers and writers were regarded as irresponsible, but if the democracy of which the speakers and publishers are a part is to control international intercourse that irresponsibility ends, and it is the business of the democracy to see to it that practices by its members which lead directly towards war are discouraged and condemned."

In the course of the current debates on foreign policy, there has appeared a line of argument which is no less dangerous because its authors have been unwilling to be perfectly frank. One development of this theme has received wide circulation through its publication in a weekly magazine. The comment to which I refer is based on the following passage from the President's message on the State of the Union:

"If we build our strength—and we are building it—the Soviet rulers may face the facts and lay aside their plans to take over the world. That is what we hope will happen, and that is what we are trying to bring about. That is the only realistic road to peace."

[1] Address made at Union College at Schenectady, N. Y. on Feb 23 and released to the press on the same date.

This statement by the President was part of a general exposition of the aggressive policies of the Soviet Union and of the contrasting peaceful policies of the United States. He outlined three points in our foreign policy.

The first covered the economic assistance program which we are carrying out in various countries. The President showed that this was one of the most effective ways to counter the typical Soviet Communist propaganda and their subversive techniques. He reminded us of the tremendous effect of the Marshall Plan on the stabilization of the European countries. He pointed out the way in which our programs of economic development will help to meet the basic causes of human distress upon which Communist propaganda attempts to feed.

Secondly, he mentioned our military assistance to countries which want to defend themselves. Here he referred to the North Atlantic Treaty Organization. He referred to the courage and confidence inspired by the appointment of General Eisenhower. He pointed to the record of U. N. armed resistance to aggression in Korea and our general support for independent governments of Asia. In a later part of his speech he dwelt at length upon the essential need of our own great rearmament effort.

Thirdly, the President pointed out that our foreign policy program includes our determination to continue to work for peaceful settlements of international disputes. He repeated our willingness to engage in negotiations with the Soviet Union as well as with any one else. He repeated our fixed determination to avoid appeasement.

The attack upon this program is based upon a very different idea. This other idea is that the United States can save itself only by resorting to preventive war. This is the inescapable logic of the position even though the conclusion is hedged by saying that maybe war is inevitable and maybe it is not. This line of thinking is obviously based on the cowardly and defeatist attitude which thinks that the United States and the other countries of the free world have no strength whatever except the atomic bomb. It assumes that we are incapable of determination, that we cannot stand a prolonged effort, that there is no strength or value in the basic traditions and principles of our democracy and our way of life. To put it crudely, this line of argument is based on the theory that the American people have no guts. It argues that when we are faced by a brutal enemy we cannot hold out either in the struggle for men's minds or in the struggle to save their bodies from destruction.

The American people have not accepted these propositions. They have not given their government any mandate to go to war. On the contrary, the American people clearly believe in the policy of peace through strength which the President outlined.

Let us summarize again the essential points in that program and then look at the alternative.

The first point in the program is building defensive strength.

The second point is at least to keep open the possibility of negotiation. In the latest note sent by the United States, France, and the United Kingdom to the Soviet Union regarding a meeting of the Foreign Ministers we have again said that we are perfectly willing to sit down and talk with them and have urged them to agree really to explore the basic causes of tensions.

The third point is that these steps are designed to deter the Soviet Union from launching an attack on the rest of the world.

The fourth point is that if the Soviet Union insists upon forcing war upon the world, the steps we are taking will put us in the best possible position to defend ourselves and to gain the victory.

The fifth point is that if the Soviets are deterred from starting the war, we may find ourselves in a rather long period of armed truce. In such a period the program we are following will enable the United States at least to hold its own. Both reason and history tell us that the corrosive elements of self-destruction are potent in a totalitarian police state and not in our democracy.

The sixth point is that there may or may not be a change in Soviet policy, but if such a change does occur we will be in a position to take advantage of it.

The seventh point is that if there is no change in Soviet policy, we have not left undone anything which we ought to have done and we will have lost none of the essential strength of our position.

The only alternative course to follow would be to start a war against the Soviet Union now. That is the policy to which the irresponsibles would inevitably drive us even though they are afraid to admit the logical conclusion of their arguments and seek to conceal it.

The task of our foreign policy is to guide the United States along a road which will preserve peace so long as peace can be maintained with justice and freedom. The United States will fight, if necessary, to preserve freedom and justice, but it will not make war merely because the road to peace is inevitably long and hard and tiresome.

Many of those who attack the foreign policy of the United States seem to be quite indifferent to the fact that they are constantly supporting the propaganda of the Soviet Union. They seem bent on convincing the other peoples of the world—just as the Communist propaganda tries to convince them—that we are a country bankrupt in ideas, resources, and courage. The result of their propaganda, like the result of Communist propaganda, is to persuade some people that we are constantly losing and that Soviet imperialism is the "wave of the future." These people know in their hearts that this line is just as false when they utter it as when the Soviet Union utters it. For whatever motive or reason, however, they ignore the injury which they are doing to their country and to the whole cause of the free world. As Mr. Root said: "Such public expressions by our own citizens bring discredit upon our country and injure its business and imperil its peace. . . . They will practically cease whenever the American public really condemns and resents them so that neither public office nor newspaper advertising or circulation can be obtained by them."

Actually, if one reviews the results of American foreign policy one finds a situation very different from that which is pictured by the irresponsibles. As a result of the Marshall Plan, Europe has been rescued from its terrible postwar difficulties and the Communist attempt to capture Western European governments has been defeated all along the line. As a result of the North Atlantic Treaty, the countries of Western Europe, together with Canada and the United States, under the military leadership of General Eisenhower are creating a strong defensive force. As a result of the Truman Doctrine, Greece has been saved from the Communists and is now contributing strength to the general position of the free world. With assistance from our military aid program, Turkey is strong and resolute.

As a result of the President's courageous decision on June 25 and of the overwhelming support of the members of the United Nations, the flagrant aggression in Korea has been met by force and is in check. The Communist aggression in Korea has been branded as such by the General Assembly of the United Nations.

Not all of our problems have been solved. There always have been, and there always will be, unresolved problems in the international scene. Progress toward the solution of many of these problems is being made. In spite of the opposition of the Soviet Government, we are advancing in our effort to reestablish Germany and Japan as democratic members of the community of nations stripped of any possibility or desire for a return to the aggressive regimes which brought about their countries' downfall. In the Western Hemisphere a solid basis of collaboration with the American republics has grown steadily firmer. Next month the Foreign Ministers of all the American republics will meet in Washington to consolidate their efforts in meeting our common problems.

There have been long periods in the history of American foreign policy when we were at peace and without anxiety that our disagreements with other governments might sharpen into war. For decades we devoted our energies to the perfection of plans and procedures for the pacific settlement of international disputes. Today we are confronted by the active hostility of a government which, despite its signature of the United Nations Charter, has consistently refused to resort to the traditional processes of pacific settlement—conciliation, mediation, arbitration, judicial settlement. The Soviet Union does not recognize any abstract concept of the rule of law or the impartial administration of justice. For them law and the administration of justice are merely the instruments of the all-powerful state. In actuality this means the Party and its controlling oligarchy. This attitude in international affairs reflects the barbaric crudity of its internal system which respects only force as personified in the police state. No philosophic verbiage can conceal this fact, which inevitably colors the whole face of international relations today. Fortunately, the United Nations remains as a focus for the efforts of the law-abiding community to maintain decent standards of international conduct. We have normal differences and disagreements from time to time with governments other than those of the Soviet bloc, but these issues do not poison our relationships. Nor does it deflect us from the great democratic principle of the equality of states. In spite of Communist provocations and domestic vilification it will remain the object and the obligation of American foreign policy to seek peaceful adjustments of all issues without surrender or appeasement. We must be strong and resourceful. Above all we must have the moral strength which comes from conviction in the rightness of our cause.

Execution of Certain German War Criminals Stayed

[*Released to the press February 15*]

Each of the German war criminals whose death sentence was sustained in the recent decisions of United States High Commissioner John J. McCloy and Gen. Thomas T. Handy filed petitions for habeas corpus in the United States District Court for the District of Columbia. These petitions were all denied by the court on the ground that there was no jurisdiction.

An appeal was taken in each of the cases and was docketed in the United States Circuit Court of Appeals today. In the light of this development, the Solicitor General of the United States has advised the Department of State and the Department of the Army that the executions should be stayed. Accordingly, instructions have been issued staying the executions until further action by the United States Circuit Court of Appeals.